THE FIFTH THUNDERBOLT

ROY M. BURGESS

This edition published by Mill Tower Books 2023

ISBN: 978-1-7394807-2-1

Acknowledgements

There is a theory that the first draft of a novel should be dreadful. I'm pleased to say that I nailed that. In common with a lot of writers I need regular reassurance, encouragement and wine. I now shudder when I think of that first draft but I'm grateful for all the people who pointed me in the right direction. Thanks to Mary, Jessica (with the magic red pen), Keith, Martin, Sue, Emma and Linda. Thanks also to Pulp Studio for a great cover.

1

Everybody should have a mate like Rupert, if only to boost their ego. Whatever problems I had, I was flying compared to the sorry mess in front of me. He hadn't always been like this. I suspect we wouldn't be friends if he had. Right now, the body odour-o-meter was at six, nudging up. Should I mention it? Bollocks to that. That's not how we cowards roll.

We'd first met a couple of years ago when he arrived in our office as an intern. When my girlfriend left with my best mate, who was also my business partner, I looked very much like Rupert did now. My thinking, my actions, every which way, I was a mess, maybe even an eight on the scale.

"You want me to do what?"

Rupert looked like I'd asked him to organise a clown convention. All I'd done was suggest he try the Five Tweet Challenge, the thing that got me over my personal slump and onto the crest of a wave. Okay, it crashed back down again. It also involved Rupert ending up in prison, so I could understand his reluctance. A bit. At least we'd given him his old job back with the software company. He even got paid these days.

"Try the stupid challenge. You act on one tweet per night. Five nights, five tweets. That's all I'm asking."

Rupert scratched his unshaven chin before replying. "It's not gonna work again, is it, Frankie?"

"How do you know if you don't try? Come on, once you pick one, I'll get a round in."

That seemed to do the trick. Rupert unlocked his phone, all the time muttering about how it would go wrong.

The Twitter Challenge, dreamt up by Ambrose, the barman here at The Crown had earned him a promotion to new best mate status. It worked, turning my life around, despite my initial opposition. I met a gorgeous woman, started a publishing phenomenon and became mega-successful. All was peachy until Robbie (my then-fiancée) and her dad (an investor in my business) buggered off with all my money, and the police arrested me for being a suspected master criminal. Funny how things turn out. Oh, and it emerged that Rupert was Robbie's brother and up to his neck in the scheme to defraud me and ruin my life. You couldn't make it up. I shrugged my shoulders and snapped back to the present. I leaned forward, keen to get started. Rupert put his phone on the table so we could both see it.

"Right. It's 6.59. When it gets to 7 o'clock, you refresh the screen, and you have to act on one of the first five tweets. Agreed?"

"Suppose so," said Rupert.

Ambrose issued the same challenge in January of last year. I was just as sceptical and miserable as Rupert was now, but it worked. There've been obstacles, I admit, but the rewards are stacking up. My career is going well and I own a tidy little house. I've come a long way. Apart from the house, it's opposite the pub.

"Right. Refresh the screen."

We both stared at the first tweet. It was from the Royal Mint.

"How come you're following them?" I asked.

"Numismatist."

"Didn't realise you had an old one." I cheered and crashed my imaginary cymbal. Not even a flicker from Rupert.

"Ha-ha, hilarious. I've collected coins since I was a kid."

"You got it from your dad. He collected thousands of mine, the robbin' bastard."

I grinned, marvelling at my rapier wit. We looked again at the tweet.

Last week to spend your round £1 coins before they cease to be legal tender.

Rupert considered this. "Have you got any left?" he asked.

I searched through the change in my pocket. "Yep. Two of 'em, look."

"Good. It's about time you spent them at the bar." Rupert sat back, pleased with himself.

"Nice try. You need to pick a tweet first," I said.

"I suppose I could spend the last of my coins at the shop. That would get me out and about."

"You got any?"

Rupert reached into his pocket and emptied the contents onto the table. There were three pound coins, all the new shape, 46p in change, a new ten-pound note, and a dodgy-looking hanky.

"Let's have a look at that."

Rupert proffered the hanky.

I backed away. "Not that, you clown. The tenner. I haven't seen one of the new ones yet."

"Horrible things. It keeps jumping out of my pocket. It's like it's making a run for it."

"Again, I know the feeling, thanks to your dad."

Rupert sighed and drank the last of his pint.

"Did you get your money back?"

"Not yet. My solicitor reckons it could take years before I see anything," I said.

3

"I'm so sorry, mate."

"You've no need to apologise for what your dad and sister did. They punished you for the software stuff. But yeah, harvesting bank details from our customers was a pretty shitty thing to do. However, you did your time."

"Three months hardly seems enough," said Rupert.

"Don't forget the two years suspended bit. Best of all, you dropped your dad right in the shit by agreeing to give evidence. Just don't pull that sort of stunt again. Things are okay now that the mess is behind us."

"Yeah?"

"Writing with Jen is so easy. Our reputation is exploding. Anyway, stop trying to distract me. You don't have any old pound coins. Next tweet."

Pure indulgence in Belize - The Toucan Palace for your next vacation.

"Oops." Rupert sat upright and looked embarrassed—as he should. "It's a nice place to stay if you get to visit. Very exclusive."

"It's expensive. Cost me about half a million quid altogether for you and your family to bugger off on a nice little jolly."

"Sorry. Dad reckoned we needed somewhere safe until the police tired of looking for us," said Rupert.

"How did that work out?"

"We were fine while we stayed there. It was the move to Spain that gave us away."

"It was your dodgy software and my detecting skills that gave you away. I take it we are safe to move on to the next tweet?"

"Unless you fancy subsidising a trip for old time's sake. A staff treat. A couple of weeks away. Joke! Violence solves nothing."

"Bollocks, it would solve one or two things just now. Next

tweet."

Ilkley Cinema. The week ahead - Monday's film club has a 60s music theme - Thunderbolts And Lightning and A Hard Day's Night double bill.

I perked up.

"What about that one?" I asked.

"How does sitting in a cinema by myself differ from sitting in the pub? "

"You won't be by yourself. I'll come with you."

"Okay, after all those months working with you, I know the second one is The Beatles. Never heard of the other one."

"Thunderbolts And Lightning?"

"Nope, never heard of it," said Rupert.

"But it's a classic, brilliant."

"Still never heard of it. Who's in it?"

"Roddy Lightning."

"Who the buggery bollocks is Roddy Lightning?"

"Roddy Lightning And The Thunderbolts!" I said this as if that explained everything.

"At the risk of repeating myself, who the chuff are Roddy Lightning And The Thunderbolts?"

"You've never heard of Roddy Lightning And The Thunderbolts?"

"At least you appear to have got the gist of what I was saying. Never heard of 'em."

"You've never heard of Roddy Lightning And The Thunderbolts?"

"Are you stuck on a loop?"

"You've never seen *Thunderbolts And Lightning*? I blame your dad for such a poor education."

"What, the dad that's banged-up for eighteen years for his little misdemeanours, including stealing all your money? That dad?"

"Okay, not the ideal role model, but, at the very least, he

should've introduced you to *Thunderbolts And Lightning*."
Rupert took a drink before realising his glass was empty.

"So, it's good, is it?"

"Good? It's the best film ever made," I said.

"Why have I never heard of it?"

"Because you're a peasant."

"Is this meant to be helping me?"

"Is it working?"

"No. But anything for a peaceful life. I pick this one. We'll go to see Rod And The Lightbulbs at the cinema."

Rupert was grinning at me, a breakthrough of sorts. I picked up the empty glasses and set off for the bar. Brenda had expected my move, and two pints were already waiting. She was holding a book of raffle tickets.

"Can I interest you in supporting our charity raffle? We're raising funds for the local care home."

"What could I win?" This seemed a reasonable question before I parted with two quid.

"First prize is a pamper day at a spa. Second is a meat hamper."

"Don't suppose third prize is a tent?"

Brenda looked puzzled for a second.

"Oh, pamper, hamper, and camper. Hilarious. You should write for a living. Two quid, please."

"No thanks. I think I'll stick with the beer."

I paid for the beer and returned to the table. Maybe I was being tight, but the exchange with Rupert had reminded me how much money I lost in the whole mess.

"So, how are things going with Jen?" Rupert asked as I put the beers down.

"Everything's great. We work well together."

"I didn't mean in a professional sense. I assumed you two would get together, seeing as my sister is unavailable for several years."

"Me and Jen? No. Platonic and professional at all times. We work together, and we're close friends."

"You're saying you're not tempted? Jen's a good-looking woman."

"She is, but we agreed we were both getting over losing people and needed a friend more than anything," I said.

"In your case, by losing, you mean going to prison."

"I was trying to be delicate."

"Don't worry about being delicate. My sister knew what she was doing. We both knew the risks and got caught. Has she been in touch?"

"She wrote to me last month, saying how sorry she was," I said.

"Will you get back together?"

"I wouldn't have thought so. Difficult to come back from all that."

"Anyway, you'll have shacked up with Jen by the time she gets out."

"Not going to happen. Told you, good friends."

"Yeah, right? I've seen the way she looks at you."

Rupert paused and picked at the beer mat on the table. He was about to speak, then stopped.

"Go on. What were you going to say?"

Rupert seemed to pluck up courage.

"It's just this thing of the writing partnership. I know you work well together, but you can write by yourself. You may just have to risk it and stand on your own two feet one day. It's called growing up."

I thought about getting annoyed, but decided Rupert had a point. Did I rely on Jen to prop me up? Enjoying a long drink, I hoped we could change the subject. Jen was great. I'd like nothing more than to take things further, but it was so risky.

Jen's partner, Sean, had died of cancer almost four years ago. I never knew him, but it hit Jen very hard and she still struggles with grief. I'd had the stuffing kicked out of me when Robbie disappeared with all our cash just before our wedding. Jen's friendship and the writing partnership were the only things that kept me going for months. I couldn't risk all that, could I?

I'd spent a lot of time trying to work out how Jen felt about me. How would she react if I suggested a change in our relationship? As a newcomer to probationary adult status, I suppose I should talk to her about it. Maybe once we've got the script finished. Then we'd have more time. I was thinking of Jen's smile when I realised Rupert was looking at me, brow furrowed.

"What are you doing, sitting there with a big, soppy grin?" he asked.

"Nothing. What were you saying?"

"I was saying if I were you, I wouldn't hang about. Jen won't be happy being single forever. Face it, the chances of somebody better looking than you coming along are pretty good."

"Fuck off."

He had a point, though.

2

Although a partner in the software business, my involvement was almost silent these days. I still had a desk in our old office above the community centre, but Spud was running things full time. Jen and I had a new office, with a brass plaque on the door. 'Vince Taylor Productions'. We had formalised our writing partnership and started attracting attention as Vince Taylor. Neither of us liked the idea of fame. Writing under a pseudonym was our way of staying under the radar.

The office was a converted cottage. I'd invested in it after I sold the barn that was to be my marital home before things went tits up with Robbie.

Our desks faced each other; a kitchen at the back. We'd nicknamed upstairs 'the boardroom'. I switched on the music when I arrived. A lovely, gentle start to the day, thanks to Sam Cooke. Jen put up with the music as long as it wasn't too loud, but insisted it was off for brainstorming sessions. I heard the front door open, and Jen appeared with coffees and bacon sandwiches.

"You'll make somebody very happy one day," I laughed as I accepted the cup.

"How do you mean, one day? Thought I already did?"

"You do, especially if you got brown sauce."

"Of course." Jen handed over two sachets.

I'd been thinking about the chat I'd had with Rupert in the pub. I'd tried to keep a lid on my feelings for Jen, but I had to admit she was bright, funny, beautiful, and caring. What would she see in me? There was also the thing about not upsetting what we had from a professional perspective. We worked well together. The new script was coming along.

"I had a drink with Rupert last night," I said.

"How's he coping now he's out?" Jen settled into her seat and opened the brown paper bag.

"He's been miserable, to be honest. I persuaded him to do the five tweet challenge."

"Good idea," said Jen. "It worked for you, right up to the point it didn't."

"True. Then again, without it, we wouldn't even have met. No way would we have all this." I spread my arms to point out our empire.

"Fair point. So, when does Rupert start?"

"Started last night. In fact, his first choice is a trip to the cinema tonight. There's a double bill—The Beatles and Roddy Lightning. I said I'd go with him. Why don't you come along? I'll buy the popcorn."

"You know how to impress a girl."

Was Jen flirting?

"I'll throw in a bag of Maltesers if you play your cards right." I'd always been a big spender.

"It all sounds lovely, but you've forgotten our meeting with Jason."

"Shit. Is that tonight?"

"Sure is. He's due here at 7 o'clock. I rearranged the writer's workshop and everything. It was the only time he was free."

I took a bite of my sandwich and pondered. It impressed

me that Jen still ran the workshop, even with everything else that was going on. It had been where we met, and where I started writing.

"Remind me, what's the meeting for?"

"We're meeting the Hollywood money man."

"Sounds like the child catcher. Is he over from Hollywood?"

"Don't think so, but whatever the English equivalent is."

"Cricklewood?" I offered.

"Not the same ring to it. Anyway, wherever he's from, this guy decides if we get the investment to make our little film. Jason's been working hard at this over the last few weeks. The deal is almost there. They just want to make sure we aren't a bunch of psychos and they can trust us."

"So it's as much a social thing as a formal meeting?"

"I suppose so. I think Jason was planning a brief presentation, then we run through the synopsis for the script, ideas for locations, that sort of thing."

"Why don't we take them to the cinema? Where better to meet to discuss films?"

"Makes a kind of sense. We could eat first."

"Why not go the whole hog - hot dogs at the cinema? Fizzy pop and sweets. Show 'em the fun side of the script."

"Give Jason a call, see what he thinks," said Jen. "I'm in if he is."

He was. He'll meet us there at 6.

Jen was just pulling into the car park in Ilkley when my phone rang.

"What do you mean, something came up?"

It was Rupert.

"Sorry. I know I'm crap, but I can't help it. It's not like you'll be by yourself."

"That's not the point. What about the challenge, change

your life - all that shit?"

"No need to worry on that front. This is changing my life in a good way."

"What the hell are you up to?"

"Not now, okay? I'll tell you tomorrow. Meet me for a pint, 6-ish?"

"Okay, but why can't you tell me now?"

"Because I'd rather do it face to face."

"You in trouble?"

"No, nothing like that. I'll explain tomorrow."

The line went dead. What was going on? He'd sounded cheerful enough. Not despondent, like he did the other night. Why the big mystery? Jen switched off the engine and turned to me.

"I gather Rupert's not coming after all?"

"No. The man is being very mysterious. I think the devious git is standing us up because he's met a woman."

"That would be good, wouldn't it?"

"Suppose so, but he's going to miss the film."

"He may just cope. I think that's Jason's car just pulling in. Come on."

Jen was right. The Porsche Cayenne belonged to our producer. It turned out that the money man was, in fact, a money woman. Flic, short for Felicity, apparently. We all shook hands and headed for the pub, and Jason volunteered to get drinks. Jason worked for the production company that had approached us about adapting *The Woman In The Yellow Raincoat* for TV. He'd handed over the project to a team in the US and, after many revisions, it became *The Girl In The Red Tee-shirt*.

Flic grinned across the table.

"You look surprised, Frankie."

"Sorry, you've thrown me. I was expecting—"

"A man?"

"No. Well, yes, but also some Californian vegetarian with a Bluetooth earpiece."

"Instead, you got a gobby Mancunian bird with a love of pork scratchings. Disappointed?"

"No, far from it." I suspect I blushed a bit as a pair of piercing blue eyes cut through me. Jen came to the rescue.

"So, Flic, what drew you to film production?"

"I needed to eat," she laughed. "I was the typical starving wannabe actress. After a bit, I noticed that decisions about my career or lack of it were all made by men. I waved goodbye to being the next big soap star, sat down, made a plan and worked my way up the ladder."

"Sounds great."

"It is. I love it, and I get to work with good people like yourselves."

"So, you *are* interested in helping us make the film?" I'd recovered myself now.

"Let's say it intrigued me enough for me to spend a pleasant evening with good company, a glass of wine and my favourite film."

"You mean *Hard Day's Night*?"

"No, I mean *Thunderbolts and Lightning*. I admit, I love The Beatles, but give me Thunderbolts any day."

It was Jen's turn to laugh.

"Wow. Were you two separated at birth? I've met nobody else who's even heard of the film, and you two think it's the best thing since cheesy wotsits."

Flic became very animated.

"I've loved it since I was a kid. It's like concentrating everything good about the English summer into an hour and a half, and the music is superb."

I think I loved this woman already.

"Exactly. It's that sort of feeling that I wanted to make sure we captured with our film," I said.

"So, who's giving me the elevator pitch?"

I was a bit thrown by this. Hadn't Jason been working on the deal for ages? The man himself arrived just in time with the drinks and stepped in.

"Jen does it better than me," he said, all charming smile and serene confidence. He distributed the drinks. All four of us clinked glasses, and Jen took a deep breath.

"Okay," she said. "What if we kidnapped the young hero from Thunderbolts and Lightning, only nicely? The kidnappers are hopeless but loveable. They only want the ransom money to keep an orphanage open. The hero helps—sort of Stockholm syndrome. All set against the beautiful countryside, odd characters and wall to wall sunshine."

"Right." The word stretched out for far too long, not a good sign. I suspect my attempt at effortless charm came out more like panic.

"You don't like it?"

"I do, apart from the orphanage thing. It's a bit shit, and it's been done. Blues Brothers?"

"So we come up with another reason. Saving a music venue, building a donkey sanctuary?"

"Something like that. Look, I love the idea of the atmosphere of Thunderbolts. I also know that you two can write and develop a brilliant script. In principle, we're interested. Start working on the new ideas. Jason, start putting out tentative feelers for a director and locations. We'll get together tomorrow and work out some numbers. We may need to raise more money, but I've got a partner in mind. I'm interested, but you have a lot of work to do. It's all theoretical at the moment. There's no way I could commit to investing yet, but I'm intrigued by you two. Get the story straightened out. Once you have that, we can talk again. Oh, and you might want to finish the script as well."

I looked at Jen, who nodded and raised her glass to Flic.

Challenge accepted. We had work to do.

"Come on, you lot." Jason looked at his watch. "We need to get inside if we want to see this film."

As we entered the cinema, I held back, trying not to be too barefaced that I wanted to sit next to Jen. My phone vibrated in my pocket. I couldn't resist looking at the text. It was from Joe. He was back in the UK and did I fancy a drink? That was a bit of a surprise.

I'd met Joe because of the Twitter challenge. He'd owned the best record shop in the entire world, or at least my part of it. Out of the blue, he'd sold the shop to Ambrose and bought a club in Ibiza. As mid-life crises go, it was a spectacular one. It would be good to see him. I texted my suggestion of 6 o'clock tomorrow in the Crown. By the time I finished, the others had sat down. I'd lost out on the spot next to Jen. I could hardly tap Jason on the shoulder and ask him to budge up, so I slid in beside Flic.

The seating was all armchairs and two-seater sofas. Very comfy. It's a good job that I loved the films. It would be too easy to fall asleep here. As soon as we sat down, the lights dimmed, and the ads started. I let my mind wander. I was curious about Joe. He'd only just upped sticks and settled in Ibiza. Was he back for good? I had to admit I'd missed him. He had an infectious love of life, a real party animal. I realised I had no idea how old the guy was. Fifty-ish? He was one of those people who could be anywhere between thirty and sixty. It would be good to catch up. Shit. I'd arranged to see Rupert tomorrow. Should I rearrange? Rupert and Joe had met before. Assuming Rupert didn't have devastating news to impart, he shouldn't object to Joe joining us.

I felt a nudge in my ribs. It was Flic offering the Maltesers. I reached in and managed to sneak three without looking greedy. Watching the box go back down the line, I felt a stab of jealousy as Jen laughed at something Jason said. Flic leaned in closer.

"I assumed you and Jen were an item."

"No, just good friends, writing partners."

"It's how you look at her. Are you sure that's how you feel?"

"Jen's great, everything anybody could want. I just worry that I'll screw things up, and we'd lose what we have now."

"So you *do* fancy her. I knew it." Flic grinned at me. "My radar seldom lets me down. Tell her how you feel. You might just regret it otherwise."

I was about to answer, but the volume level ramped up. The film was underway. I sneaked a look along the line and saw Jen giggling like a schoolgirl. Nothing I could do now. I had a movie to watch.

After ten minutes, I realised I had a big, dopey grin on my face. Flic was the same. I loved this film and could sing along to every song, but I spared us all from unnecessary suffering. Come to think of it, I knew every line of dialogue. It didn't matter. It was magical. I admit to a tear in my eye at the end as Roddy embraced the girl in the last scene. The house lights came on too soon as the credits rolled. Flic was still grinning.

"That was fantastic. Brilliant suggestion, Frankie. What did you two think?" asked Flic.

"Loved it," said Jen, as she pushed a stray lock of red hair away from her face.

"I can see why we'd want to recreate the atmosphere," said Jason. "But we're not suggesting a musical, are we?"

"God, no. I'm not up to songwriting, not yet anyway. How about you, Jen?"

"I think not. We've got enough to do. Tell you what, though, I'm hungry."

"Yes," said Flic. "I just thought I could murder a pizza."

I could eat pizza twenty hours a day, given a chance. "Well, we could skip the second film and discuss the project over a bottle of wine."

Three heads nodded, and we were soon on the street.

3

"Did you just sniff me?"

"No, cos that would be weird," I said, blushing.

"You did. As I walked into the office just now, you sniffed me."

Jen's grin made me relax a little.

"It's not as if I got right in close or anything. I just like how you smell," I said.

"Terrific. Now I smell."

This was a weird start to Tuesday morning. I continued to squirm.

"Look, it's not that I like how you smell, as such."

"So you don't like how I smell, charming."

Jen appeared to be enjoying this. I just wanted to stop coming across as a pervert. "Don't look so worried. I'm just pulling your plonker." Say nothing, just don't, I chanted to myself. "It's my shampoo. You can try some if you like," said Jen.

"That's okay, thanks. Better on you."

I watched as Jen dropped her backpack on the floor and flopped into her seat.

"Now you're giving me a look," she said.

"No, but you look different."

"Different good or different bad?"

For once, I saw a potential trap and sidestepped it.

"Just different. Haircut?"

"What, since you last saw me at ten o'clock yesterday?"

"I had a great time last night," I said.

"So did I, to be honest. Flic seemed nice."

I agreed.

"Yeah. Nice that she might want to back the film."

"Suppose we ought to crack on and get the script finished."

"I was just working on the dialogue for the opening scene."

Jen pressed the remote, and the big screen on the wall now showed the document I was working on.

"Go on, admit it, the big screen was an excellent investment," I said.

"Yeah, okay. It's still one of your boy's toys, but it makes working together easier." Jen read the script for a minute before saying, "I'm wearing glasses."

"Sorry?"

"I'm wearing glasses. You wanted to know what was different. I'm wearing specs."

"But you always wear glasses."

"No, I don't."

"Are you sure?"

"I think I would've noticed when I was putting my eyeliner on."

"Fair point."

My phone rang. I glanced down and sent it to voicemail.

"Was that your mum again?"

"Yes. Don't look at me like that. We're busy. She only wants to gossip and tell me the list of things my dad's done wrong."

"We're never too busy for you to talk to your mum. It might just be gossip to you, but it means a lot to her."

"But it's the same conversation every time."

"Doesn't matter. It's not for your benefit. You'd be doing something for somebody else for a change. You're a great bloke, but you can be selfish."

"I'll call her later."

"Promise?"

"I promise I'll call her later."

Was I selfish? I admit I'd been a bit focused on myself. I'd been through a lot and wanted to protect what I had. Protecting yourself wasn't the same as being selfish. I'd just been putting myself first. I wondered how the dictionary defined selfish. Now wasn't the time to look it up.

We both stared at the screen. Jen sighed and pushed her chair back.

"I'm not sure that bit works." Apparently, we were back at work. Jen pointed at the screen. "Would he say that?"

"You're right. I've changed it five times already this morning. In fact, I may have a radical suggestion."

"Go on."

"Our hero is mid-thirties and gets kidnapped by local kids, then uses his charm and wit to win his captors round and get released," I said.

"Do you want him to carry a gun and shoot his way out?"

"No, nothing like that. Why don't we make him older?"

"Interesting." I realised the act of chewing a pen could be attractive. "Go on, I'm listening."

"Make him mid-seventies, a loveable grandad that somehow bridges the generation gap and shows the gang the error of their ways."

"Then he shoots them all?"

"No. No shooting."

"Shame."

I knew Jen was taking the piss. She sat for a bit, thinking things through.

"You know what? I like it. Do you have a cunning plan up your sleeve?"

"Might have," I said. I'd been rumbled. "You said yourself how much you enjoyed the film last night. Roddy's a star."

"He was a star. Fifty years ago."

"You never lose it."

"Is he even still alive?" I was just about to answer when Jen laughed again. "Of course, he's still alive. You've googled him already, haven't you?"

"What do you think?" I said. "From what I can see, Roddy Lightning is in his late seventies and living in a big house on the south coast."

"What's he been in recently?"

"Nothing for a while, I admit. But wouldn't it be great to work with such a big star? What do you say?"

"How do we even approach him?"

"That's Jason's problem. I'm sure he can sort it. But, even if he can't, I've convinced myself that the story would work better with an older character."

"I think you may be right. Why don't I mull it over while you put the coffee on?"

"I see what you did there. Back in a minute."

As I busied myself with the new coffee machine, Jen popped her head round the kitchen door.

"Flic seemed nice."

"Yeah, you said."

"You seemed to get on very well."

"I appear to be honing my schmoozing technique."

"Is that all it was, schmoozing?"

"Yes, course. Why?"

"Oh, you just looked very cosy."

Was it Jen's turn to be jealous? Could that be a good sign?

"No, nothing like that. In fact, Flic assumed we were a couple."

"Us? What made her think that?"

"Just the way we talked to each other."

"Arguing?" Jen grinned at me.

I filled both mugs with strong, black coffee.

"No, just comfortable. I told her we were writing partners, good friends, and that you were concentrating on making sure Charley was okay. Besides, I have to devote myself to my art!"

"Penguin?"

"What?"

"Penguin or KitKat?" Jen was peering into the *Shaun The Sheep* biscuit barrel.

"Go mad and have both," I said.

"Good call. Now let's go and re-write this script and get to know Grandad Lightning."

We moved back into the office. Was this my chance to tell Jen how I felt? What if she rejected me? I decided it was best to approach it with a glass of wine inside us.

Anyway, Jen's phone rang.

"Jason, hi."

I waved my arms and pointed at the phone.

"Tell him about the new idea," I said in a strange half-whisper.

"Hang on, Frankie's telling me something." Jen let out what I can only describe as a giggle. "Yeah, he is."

He is what? Jen looked at me, so I tried again.

"Bring Jason up to speed with the new plan."

Jen nodded and leaned back in her seat. After listening to one end of the conversation, I got bored after a minute or two. I created a new document. The new version. This was going to be good! Not that long ago, I would've fought tooth and nail against scrapping anything I'd already written. There were weeks of work on that version of the script. I used to see it as effort down the drain, but Jen had taught me that trying to fix something that was so wrong would just drive you mad. Better to start again. To remind us, we had a picture drawn by Charley, Jen's five-year-old daughter, with the acronym FUBAR across it in big, spidery letters. We didn't explain that it stood for Fucked Up Beyond All Recognition, but she was happy to draw anything.

In a fit of enthusiasm, I deleted the old script. Two seconds later, the cold sweat hit me. Shit. There was some great stuff in that document that we could use. Jen had wandered into the kitchen and hadn't seen what I'd done. I restored the file, and my heart rate returned to normal. I unwrapped the KitKat and got to work.

This time, everything flowed. I had a vivid mental picture of the story and the dialogue poured onto the page. Sometimes, I dipped into the old script to extract part of a scene that still worked for the new version. If only every writing session was like this. The adrenaline flow matched the outpouring of words. Even the disappointment when I saw the untouched, cold coffee had no effect. Then my stomach rumbled. This was my body's way of telling me to take a break.

"Wow. You've been busy," said Jen as she plonked another coffee in front of me. "Thought I'd make myself useful. Sorry I was so long."

I hadn't noticed that she'd been gone for over an hour.

"What were you up to?"

"Uh, nothing much. Just chatting."

"What did Jason think?"

"About what?"

"You know, the new idea - totally re-working the film we want to pitch. That sort of thing."

"He's fine, sort of. He wants to see a new synopsis and an idea of how long the new script will take. Other than that, we just crack on."

We spent the next few hours writing a very detailed synopsis. The large whiteboard that covered the whole of one wall gradually filled with post-it notes. I loved this bit, seeing the ideas pour out of us and onto the wall. Jen even bought into my multi-coloured system. Yellow for scenes, blue for characters and pink for questions we still had to answer.

"Your fanatical devotion to post-its is impressive."

Did Jen mean this was some sort of putdown?

"I'll take that as a compliment. I love these little beauties. So useful. Easy to move around, keeping thoughts clear - unbeatable."

"But they curl up and fall off the wall," said Jen, picking one offender from the floor and attempting to stick it back up.

"Actually, I've been meaning to mention that. Have you noticed that not all of them curl?"

"Yeah, that'll be the wall doing some magic trick and rejecting the ideas. If it falls off, we have to replace it with something better."

It was not always clear to me when Jen was joking. I took a deep breath and prepared to impart the wisdom of the post-it king.

"It's all in how you pull it," I said.

Jen sniggered. That's the only way to describe her reaction; she sniggered. I pressed on.

"I thought we'd agreed that being smutty and childish was my department?"

"Most days it is. You're quite good at it, but sometimes I like to join in," said Jen, sniggering again.

"Allow me to show the wrong way." I took the yellow pad from the desk and peeled a note from left to right before sticking it on the wall.

"Ever thought about getting a job on one of those shopping

channels?"

"Actually, I think I'd be good at it."

"You're smug enough." The sniggering was progressing towards outright mockery.

"Right, watch this. Pull the post-it straight down from the pad like so." I demonstrated in full shopping channel mode and stuck the note beside the previous one.

"Okay, oh-great-one. They look identical."

I had to admit; they did.

"Give it a few minutes, then you'll see the magic."

"Strange how you're still single," said Jen.

"You may mock."

"Thank you very much; I will."

"You carry on. I'll make us a cup of tea."

"In that case, feel free to break into the chocolate-covered ginger biscuits."

I set off for the kitchen, glancing at the board to see if curling had started. It hadn't. As I waited for the kettle to boil, I reflected on how I enjoyed days like this. We were in our own cosy world, being creative, producing stuff. It had to beat any other job out there. Why would I want to change anything?

Last year had been such a whirlwind. Meeting Jen at the writer's workshop and how she encouraged me to create *The Woman In The Yellow Raincoat*. It didn't take long to realise that Jen was a better writer than I could ever be, and, because of some weird miracle, she wanted to team up—hence the partnership. She'd also warned me about Robbie and her dad being dodgy. Being stupid, I ignored her and fell in love with Robbie.

The kettle clicked and jolted me from my memories. We'd agreed to drink tea in the afternoons to counter the massive coffee intake in the morning. I filled the smiley-faced teapot and immediately poured myself a cup. I drank my tea weak and uncontaminated by milk or sugar. Just wave a tea bag somewhere near a cup, and I was happy. Jen must've been a builder in a previous life. Her only concession was three sweeteners rather than sugar.

With the packet of biscuits between my teeth, I reversed through the door into the office. Placing a mug in front of Jen, I flopped into my seat. Jen held out a hand as I struggled with the seal on the biscuits. I passed the pack over, and she opened it within seconds. She took one and slid the packet across the desk.

"I'm sorry, by the way," said Jen.

"Sorry? What for?"

"The quip about being single. I know it still hurts how Robbie took off. Things could've been very different by now."

"No need to apologise. Besides, had I listened to you in the first place, I wouldn't have trusted Robbie to be anywhere near the finances."

"Even I didn't think that she could use the business to launder money from her dad's drug deals. Then she steals everything and jilts you just before the wedding. Anyway, I'm sorry I brought it up."

"Don't be daft. There's nothing to apologise for. Besides, without you, there wouldn't have been any business to defraud. Being with Robbie was like being strapped to one of those fireworks that jump around all over the place. Half the time, I was just clinging on. I went from having nothing to having a lot, then back to nothing again. You kept a cool head throughout it and did more than anybody to rebuild things. To rebuild me. You even let me make up stories to tell your daughter that turned into a series of books that bought my house."

"I still think you should've published those under your own name."

"No. We agreed we write and publish together as Vince

Taylor. I tried being famous and didn't like it. No real-life dramas that mirror the fiction we write. I like what I have and intend to keep it."

"Good for you. That reminds me, did you see your old mate DI Cagney on the news the other night?"

"Hardly a mate of mine, accusing me of being a master criminal, then taking the acclaim when I solved the case for him. What's the big-headed glory hunter been doing now?"

"He was appealing to witnesses to something or other. Didn't seem to have a clue what had happened."

"Sounds about right. Couldn't find his own arse in a phone box, that bloke. Frankie Dale, however, is the king of the post-its. Look at that."

The demonstration note had curled from the bottom and was about to fall to the floor. Its partner was flat and intact.

"Okay. You are, without doubt, a superior being. You get to be in charge of the whiteboard. Let's get the outline finished, then you can write it up while I go to collect Charley from school."

"Deal."

Being right about peeling post-its was enough for me.

4

It was weird that Ambrose wasn't behind the bar when I arrived. He still did the odd shift to help, but his work life was now the record shop. His devotion to his wife Stella and newly adopted daughter, Issy, was touching too.

Rupert was already in the corner, and drinks were on the table. Sarcasm was in order since he'd ducked out of the cinema trip.

"Glad you could fit me into your busy schedule."

Rupert fidgeted.

"Sorry about that. How was the cinema?"

"The film was brilliant. Just as good as I remember it."

"Thought there were two films?"

"Yeah, we sort of swerved The Beatles one. Went for pizza instead, so you missed out." I took a long drink, then followed Rupert's eyes as he scanned the pub nervously. "What are you looking for?"

"How do you mean?"

"You've looked at the door twice. You expecting somebody?"

"Just looking."

He picked up his glass. As he drank, I asked him again why he hadn't come to the cinema. He downed half of the pint in one go.

"Like I said, something came up."

"Something life-changing, you said."

"Yeah, it could be. Well, it is, for sure." His eyes flicked around the pub again.

"I wish you'd stop looking at the door. My company isn't exciting enough for you?"

"No. I mean, yes. Well, no, it's not that. Do you want another drink?"

"Once you tell me what's going on." Just then, the door opened. It was Joe. "Hello, stranger. Come here." I stood up and actually gave him a hug.

"Blimey! I've not been away that long. Can I get you a drink?"

"No. You sit down. I'll get them. What do you want?"

"G&T, please, very large."

Brenda was already on it, and three drinks quickly appeared. As she busied herself with the till, I glanced in the mirror behind the bar and could have sworn I saw Joe and Rupert having an affectionate moment.

I abandoned the change and grabbed the drinks.

"So, this life-changing event." I looked at Rupert and then at Joe. Joe grinned and took Rupert's hand. "You mean…"

"Absolutely. Rupert and I are one."

"Fuck me! I mean, congratulations. I had no idea. Well, Joe - I had an inkling, but Rupert? You sly devil. Look, I'm very pleased for you."

So much for Rupert having found a woman. I'd never considered for one moment that he was gay. Even if I had, Joe would have been a long way down the list of guesses. He was old enough to be Rupert's dad.

Rupert went from looking terrified to beaming.

"You don't know what a relief it is to tell someone."

"So you've never come out to your family?"

"I believe you've met my dad."

"Fair point." The relief flooding through my mate was visible.

"My mum knows. I think she always has, but she found it difficult. Until she met this wonderful bloke." He squeezed Joe's hand.

"Charmed the pants off her," said Joe, and his infectious laugh boomed out across the pub.

I raised my glass, "To changing lives." They joined in the toast before Joe spoke.

"Actually, that's not our only news."

"You're not pregnant, are you? Rupert, I thought you'd be more careful."

"No, dickhead. Now, that would be life-changing. Might sting a bit as well."

We all considered that for a moment.

"Go on then. What else is changing?"

"Well, you may have noticed I'm back from Ibiza," said Joe. "Let's just say I missed certain things about home." The two of them grinned at each other. "Anyway, the sale of the club completes this weekend. I even made a small profit on it, so all is good. Now we can start the next adventure."

"Which is?"

"Well. I own the building where the record shop is, and Ambrose rents half of the cellar."

"Only half? But it's huge."

"Exactly. The other half is housing junk at the moment. However, it will become the number one supper club and entertainment venue in the district within four months. In fact, it would still be the best, even if it wasn't the only one."

"Four months? For a full conversion?"

"It'll be tight but doable. The trouble is, Rupert here is going to be busy, busy, busy and doesn't have time to fanny about with you doing Twitter challenges. Sorry, and all that."

"Hey, don't worry. It was a way of getting him out of the doldrums. I think you've managed that. Anyway, Rupert, why were you so fucking miserable at the weekend when we met up?"

Rupert held his hands up.

"I was tragic. Joe was living a thousand miles away, tarting it up in his own club every night."

"Why didn't you fly out to join him?"

"Not allowed. Part of my release. Every week, I need to see a parole officer to make sure I stay out of trouble. I can't believe Joe sold up so we could be together."

"It's fine, tarting it up every night in Ibiza when you're single, but when you meet somebody you want to be with…" They were so happy it was a bit sickening. "Besides, I can tart it up as much as I like in the new club in four months," added Joe with a wink.

Rupert excused himself and went off to the loo. Joe's eyes followed him all the way. It was nice to see the pair of them so happy. Maybe it was time to come clean with Jen about how I felt.

"So, any plans to make an honest woman of Jen?"

I'd forgotten that Joe had the unerring knack of knowing what I was thinking.

"We're friends, and we work together," I said.

"And?"

"And nowt."

"You're not telling me there isn't a spark there?"

"Have you lot been gossiping about us?"

"Of course we have. It was obvious last summer you fancied Jen something shocking, and I'd say she feels the same. Ambrose thinks so too."

"So you're all in on it?"

"Absolutely."

"But what if I make a pass at her and she rejects me?"

"Make a pass? Are we back in the fifties? Besides, that proves I'm right, and there is something there. Carpe diem and all that. You're just too chicken to try."

Joe could have a point there. The trouble was, everything was tied together. It was a mess. Any romance in my head was complicated by the work partnership. She gave me confidence, and I knew I could do anything with her beside me. I'd barely admitted it to myself, but I still felt like an imposter, even with all our success. One day, somebody would work it out and unmask me as a fake. I was only a proper writer alongside Jen.

Rupert returned to his seat.

"Speaking of chicken, I could murder a curry." Nice subject change, if I said so myself. The others nodded, and we all finished our drinks in one.

My life seemed to have become a straight line along this road. My local, The Crown, with my new house directly opposite. Out of my front door, turn left, up the hill a hundred yards to the office, another two hundred yards to the best Indian restaurant in the world. My life was pretty self-contained and relatively happy.

I'd waved goodnight to my mates and tottered off towards home, full of chicken tikka masala and Indian beer. Within seconds, I realised my mistake. I was a little too full of lager and urgently needed the loo. I could go back to the restaurant but decided to just quicken my pace. It was only a couple of minutes from home. A sheen of sweat appeared on my forehead. My legs were now moving at the rate of the coyote as he chases the road runner over a cliff. Things were suddenly desperate. The office! I could call in there and use the loo. Just yards from our little sanctuary, I fumbled for my keys and crashed through the front door at break-neck speed, taking the stairs two at a time.

Relief. You'd think I would learn the lesson that I was approaching the age where, if you saw a toilet, you use it, just in case.

I was used to the rhythmic tapping of Jen typing or the music that I insisted on most of the day, but now it was eerily silent and creepy. It didn't help that I hadn't switched the lights on - they hadn't been a priority. I found the switch and made my way downstairs. With the lights on, our friendly, comfortable office was back. I looked at my watch. It was only nine o'clock. Rather than going straight home to sit in front of the telly, I started the music and settled in for an hour, reviewing the script.

Changing the main character to an older man was working well. The words were soon flowing (just like the Indian lager). After another trip upstairs, I remembered the six-pack of beers in the fridge and helped myself. Probably not my most sensible decision, but the adrenaline was pumping, and I wanted to keep working. On my way back to my seat, I noticed the framed photo on Jen's desk. She and Charley were on the beach at Bridlington when we visited my parents. Mum and Dad had really taken to them, another sign that Jen could just be the one.

I looked again at the synopsis we'd created. It was pleasing to see how much we'd achieved today. The tricky task was convincing Flic to sign a large cheque to finance the project. She must see so many scripts and story ideas in her job. How could we make ours stand out and clinch the deal? Leaning back in my seat, I swigged my beer. There must be something I could do. One of the post-its decided it was time to give up. Retrieving it from the floor, I straightened the edges and stuck it to the wall. It was the note about our hero being kidnapped. My mind flicked to Liam Neeson in *Taken*, and I tried my best impersonation.

"Flic, I don't have money. But what I do have are a very

particular set of skills, skills I have acquired over a very long career, skills that make me a bit of a geek with computers. I can do clever stuff."

I'd finished my bad impersonation but was well impressed with where my mind had gone. Why not put together a presentation for Flic and make it into a mini version of our film? The animation software from my work on *The Woman In The Yellow Raincoat* website was still on my Mac. I set about my task. Within an hour, I'd created a cartoon version of myself and scoured the internet for clips from *Thunderbolts And Lightning*. Using the clips was dodgy as far as copyright law was concerned, but I wasn't planning to publish this. If I could get it right, I'd pitch it to Flic, then we move on to making the actual film.

It took longer than I'd initially thought. Still, eventually, I had a cartoon of me standing in a clip from the film, pointing out the sunshine and beautiful countryside in the long sweeping shot. I wanted the cartoon of me to run through the entire synopsis using clips from *Thunderbolts* and various animations to bring the ideas to life. It was clunky but, with more work, it was possible. As Liam had said, I had special skills. Also, I had friends in the IT business who had even more skills and I could conscript them to help. Another beer was required.

Yawning, I flopped back into the chair. It was getting late. After this beer, go home and sleep. I had plenty to do to get the pitch into a fit state to share. I needed to create a cartoon of Jen to share storytelling duties. My mind drifted back to Jen. I really needed to get my act together and talk to her. Then again, should I complicate things just as the film was looking like a possibility?

I shuffled forward in my seat and opened a new document. I would make a list for and against telling Jen how I felt. Lists are like old friends. I was comfortable with them, and they usually helped me sort things out. Two pages, each with headings in bold type—*Jen Good* and *Jen Bad*. Devising a scoring system could come later. Let's just get something down. I opened another can and burped loudly. Before long, the *Jen Good* page was coming together.

1. She smells nice
2. She makes me laugh
3. She's beautiful and sexy. (Should this be two points? Come back to it.)
4. We can talk for hours without getting bored
5. She made sure I didn't fall apart when the business with Robbie blew up
6. She's kind
7. She looks gorgeous (too close to 3?)
8. She's a great mum to Charley
9. She improves my writing
10. She gives me the confidence to try anything
11. She makes me laugh (think I've said that - check later)
12. I'm often sad when I'm not with her
13. She smells nice
14. She knows all the words to *Think* by Aretha
15. The little black dress
16. She understands how to put salt in the dishwasher

I pushed my seat back, pleased with my work. The *Jen Bad* page was more difficult. It seemed to take ages, but I was determined to be thorough. This was important.

1. Can be bossy (just a bit)
2. Makes that snorting noise when she laughs
3. Might dump me, and I lose my writing partner
4. Been known to fart and blame Charley (makes me laugh, so could go on other list)

* * *

That was it. It took ages, but that was the sum of arguments against asking Jen on a proper date. I was, as usual, being an arsehole. I looked at my watch. It was almost four o'clock.

Bugger.

Throwing the empty cans in the bin, I switched off the lights and locked the door behind me. I told myself that was a good night's work, as I set off down the hill. I could see my little house in the distance, and it all felt very nice. Maybe I should've gone to the loo before I left. For the second time tonight, I picked up the pace before bursting through the front door and launching myself upstairs. I really must learn from my mistakes.

5

I woke up at eight the following day. By some miracle, I felt full of energy. I'd slept really well, something I put down to sorting out my thoughts about Jen. Now to hatch the plan. We'd got into a cosy habit of spending Saturday evenings together at her place. While Jen was conjuring up something magical in the kitchen, I took on the role of chief storyteller for Charley. She was a fantastic cook. That should've gone on my list last night. Even better, she enjoys it, which was lucky, as I enjoy eating. Once Charley had settled, we'd eat and talk about work, then watch a film with a second bottle of wine. This week, I planned to open my heart and explain what I felt about her and determine if she felt the same. After that, the plan was shrouded in too many ifs and maybes. Still, you can imagine.

As I arrived at the office, I could see Jen walking back from dropping Charley off at school. I left the door open for her and busied myself with making coffee.

"I brought croissants." This woman just gets better. The coffee machine was doing its magic, so I grabbed a couple of plates and went through to the office. Jen had already flopped in her seat, coat still buttoned.

"You okay? You look, erm, frazzled," I said.

"Nothing that two coffees and my weight in French pastries won't cure. Charley just had a full-on strop on the way to school."

"But she's always good as gold."

"She's been acting up over the last few weeks. I thought this sort of behaviour started in their teens, not at five. Maybe single parenting is more complex than I thought. What if not having a dad while growing up is damaging her?"

Should I volunteer for the job? No, stick with the plan.

"Why don't you take your coat off while I get the coffees? You can make a start on the croissant mountain."

"You're a good man, Frankie Dale or Vince Taylor, whatever your name is." She laughed; she was as much Vince as I was. We used it as our professional name for any writing projects. "I have an idea about the opening scene. Maybe we could start there?"

"Of course," I said, two coffees in hand. The big screen came to life. The next bit happened in slow motion. I saw the document from last night spread across the screen. Oh shit, the *Bad Jen* page was 56 inches across.

"There you go," as I almost dropped one cup on Jen's desk.

"What the f—"

"Nothing." I quickly toggled to the script document, but I suspect the actual Jen had seen *Bad Jen*.

Bollocks.

I braced myself for her following comment, but my phone rang. I made a grab for it.

"Hi, Jason. Good to hear from you." Jen had turned away and was busily typing on her laptop. Maybe she hadn't seen the list or hadn't registered what it said. Why had I left the document open? Idiot. "Sorry, Jason, say that again. Really? That's excellent news. Yes, she's here. I'll pass you over. You can tell her the good news yourself."

Jason's news was that Flic had identified a probable

partner to finance the film. I passed the phone to Jen. She sat back with coffee in one hand and phone in the other, her feet on the desk.

Jason wanted to meet up with a potential director. This was getting a lot closer to actually happening. As Jen and Jason continued to chat, I busied myself with the opening scene. Almost fifteen minutes later, they were still talking. Well, Jason seemed to be. Jen was just giggling like a schoolgirl. At least she appeared to be in a good mood. Maybe I'd got away with it, and she hadn't seen the list.

"Look, I'd better go. I need to get back to bossing Frankie about."

Bollocks.

Without another word, Jen walked over and placed my phone on the desk. She'd seen it.

"Look, I'm sorry if you, you know."

"I thought you were maturing these days."

"I can explain, I promise. How about I bring a bottle of wine over this evening? I'll order pizza, and we can talk."

"Sorry, can't tonight. Jason just asked me out to dinner."

"But he can't."

"Yes, he can. He asked last week, but I said no. He just asked again, and today, I felt like having some adult company. So, I'm going to take the rest of the day off, buy myself something nice to wear, and transform myself into a creature of great beauty. I've emailed you the suggested changes to the opening scene. At the risk of being bossy, I suggest you crack on with that. See you tomorrow."

Then she was gone. I stared at the wall. What the hell had just happened? I'd been here half an hour, and everything had just turned to shit. We should be about to celebrate that we had progress with the film, not split up before getting together. Why did I have to make that list? I restored it to the screen so I could delete it. Instead, I added a line.

5 Gets a proper strop on when I act like an arsehole.
That'll show her.

By eleven, I'd had enough of the office. I wasn't getting anything worthwhile done and was just fretting about Jen. Locking the office door, I could see the bus sitting in traffic. I sauntered across to the stop and still had to wait. Ten minutes later, I was walking into Ambrose's record shop.

The man himself was serving a customer, so I made my way through the racks of albums to the soundtracks. It was pleasing to see the tidy shelves in alphabetical order, and I targeted S-Z. Reminding myself not to get tempted by shiny things, I flicked past *Saturday Night Fever*, *Showgirls* and *The Sound Of Music*. Being obsessive, I moved a rebel copy of *Rent* to the L-R section. I'd gone through more than half of the rack before reaching *Titanic*, then *Trainspotting*. My heart sank as I got to the end of the section.

"Is this what you're after?" It was Ambrose.

"Joe used to do that. Sneak up on people with what they're looking for."

"He taught me well. Actually, he called in this morning and suggested I put it aside for you."

I took the treasured piece of vinyl in my hands and opened the gatefold sleeve. I'd spent hours looking at the pictures and memorising the lyrics as a kid. Then there was the fire, and the copy suffered death by fireman's hose. Perhaps the fixation was entering a new phase. Fingers crossed, we could get the older version of the smiling face on the cover to star in our film.

"So what's the fascination with *Thunderbolts And Lightning*? I'd never heard of it until Rupert mentioned it."

I was about to launch into my tirade about how could he

never have heard of it but decided action was better.

"Play it. Now. Stick the kettle on, and let's listen to the soundtrack. It's been too long since we caught up."

"Good idea. Come through." Ambrose led the way to his office, pausing only to replace the Steve Earle album playing on the impressive sound system.

"So what's so special about Roddy Lightning And The Thunderbolts?"

"Where do I start? The thing to remember is that when they made it, the competition was The Beatles or The Monkees running around, being whacky and wonderful music. Roddy had glorious music, but the film had a good, engaging story. It even looks like a classic French art movie but is totally absorbing. Then there's Roddy himself. He was one charming bastard. The sort of bloke you knew was going to cop off with your girlfriend at the end of the night, but you wouldn't mind because it's Roddy. You'd even take him for a pint afterwards, have a laugh and let some of the cool rub off on you."

"So how come I still sell shitloads of Beatles albums but only one Roddy album? Assuming you buy it."

"I've often wondered that. I suspect somebody made some poor decisions. Certainly, the hits dried up, but he was big in the States at one time. Actually, this is one of my favourites."

We settled back and listened in silence for a minute. It instantly transported me back to those Sunday afternoons watching the film with my dad. It almost seemed like every week was football highlights followed by this film. Logically, I knew it was probably only two or three times in my entire childhood, but the memory was so vivid.

The song ended, and we were back in real life.

"So, how're things?"

The enormous sigh let Ambrose know that all was not well, and I unloaded. I told him about the good stuff — the film and everything professional. Thanks to that morning's phone call, he knew about Rupert and Joe. Then I got to Jen and the mess I made of everything. Now Jason was complicating things even further.

"So you fucked up. Again."

"What do you mean—again?"

"Cheryl? Robbie?"

"Robbie was hardly my fault. That she robbed me blind and fled the country had a lot to do with that one."

"But you take my point. You do have form."

"Maybe I'm not cut out for having proper relationships. Should I just give in and become a sad single bloke?"

"What do you mean become? You're smashing it from where I'm sitting." I was about to protest when Ambrose glanced at the CCTV. A customer was looking around for somebody to pay.

"Back in a minute. Then I want to hear how you plan to win Jen over."

Win her over? I'd be lucky to get her to speak to me again. I'd never seen her as angry as she was this morning. Anyway, she was bound to have a great time with Jason. He was flashy, but I saw how chatty they were at the cinema. My phone burst into life. It was Jason. Shit. I panicked and hit the red button. I couldn't talk to him now.

"You look shifty. What are you up to?" Ambrose was back.

"Just had a call from Jason."

"How did that go?"

"It didn't. I sent it to voicemail."

"Very grown-up. Isn't Jason the producer of the film you're busy writing? The one that's a joint effort with the woman you've just pissed off?"

"Sounds about right."

"You're going to have to speak to both of them. Pretty sharpish, unless you really want to blow things up."

"But…"

"Fuck, but. Have you forgotten how pathetic you were before you met Jen?"

"Bit strong."

"But true."

He had a point. Things were pretty bad before we got together to write. I took a sip of the tea.

"Can I at least hide here for a bit?"

"No. Get your arse in gear and sort this mess out."

I needed a fix of new music before I left.

"Can I have the new Liam Gallagher album, then?"

"No."

"Why not? This is a record shop."

"It's not out until Friday. Come back then, and you can have it, assuming you've sorted things. Now, take your *Thunderbolts And Lightning* and bugger off."

"Your customer service needs some polishing." If Ambrose wore glasses, he would have looked over them. I took the hint and my carrier bag and left the shop.

6

I acted like a grown-up and decided I would call Jason back. Straight after I'd been to the pub. It was lunchtime, and I was hungry. For once, I didn't fancy The Crown. Somewhere that nobody knew my name would be better, so I could sit in a corner and assess my situation. Some would call it sulking. The Rat and Fiddle was just around the corner, one of the few pubs in my area that I'd never been to. I considered calling Ambrose to see if he fancied closing the shop for an hour. He would tell me to go back to the office and get some work done. Instead, I pushed the heavy door open. First impressions were mixed. A lovely, Victorian tiled floor, ornate brass light fittings, and dark polished wood, but a disturbing air of menace prevailed. It was quiet, like walking into a saloon in the wild west, and the piano player stopped. I considered reversing straight out until a voice cut through the gloom.

"Pint?"

"Please, Brenda." Brenda? From The Crown? "What are you doing here?"

"I could ask you the same question. Never seen you outside your normal habitat."

"I just fancied a quiet drink and something to eat."

"Picked the right place. We're good at quiet. Wrong place if you want anything fancy to eat. Could do you a pork pie and a bag of crisps if you like."

"Perfect. So, what are you doing here?"

"Just helping while the landlady's away. I do afternoons here, then jump on the bus to the Crown for the evening session. One long, glamorous adventure is my life. Any sauce?"

"Brown, please."

"Have a seat and I'll bring it over."

I turned to choose my table, and the lights flickered into action. It came as a surprise to see that two tables housed drinkers already. Two men, in raincoats, sitting in opposite corners. They seemed unaffected by the sudden lights and just stared ahead. My mind flashed back to last year, just after Cheryl had left me. If not for Ambrose, I would have become the third man in a raincoat sitting in the dark. I nodded to them, then took my seat in the third corner and stared straight ahead.

Was I making a mess of things all over again? A list would be my standard plan now, but that had caused most of my current problems.

The old man to my left prised himself from his seat. He steadied his legs with both hands on the table, the half-full glass swaying even more than he was. The three strides to the jukebox seemed to take an age, but he was on a mission. Without looking at the labels, one coin and three presses later, he was done and began the long journey back to his seat. Big Country's *Fields Of Fire* blasted at ear-shattering levels. Brenda screamed something about 'bloody noise' before the volume dropped to just 'very loud'. This pub was full of surprises.

Okay, so where was I? I'd pissed off Jen by listing her bad points in my spreadsheet. It felt unfair that I'd also recorded four times as many good points, but she wasn't interested in that. She wouldn't end our writing partnership over something like that, would she? Then again, she was a better writer than I could ever be. What was to stop her teaming up with Jason to write other scripts and ditch me? More to the point, I loved her.

Wow!

I'd not admitted that to myself before. The writing is excellent, but the relationship with Jen meant so much more to me. Had I pushed her away and into Jason's arms?

I had a nemesis. I'd never had one of those before. A rival. Of course, it was a complication that Jason was the producer who was pulling together our first film project. I'd just rejected his call and was hiding in a back street pub when he was trying to arrange for me to meet one of my heroes.

What a mess. The music had finished, and silence resumed. Brenda plonked the pork pie and crisps in front of me.

"Cheer up, you miserable bugger. You're depressing those two miserable buggers."

I laughed despite feeling grumpy and cut the pie in half. There are few things in life better than a good pork pie, and this was a good pork pie. Brenda could tell from my face that it was good.

"That's more like it. Enjoy."

Brenda wandered off back to the bar. This was an exceptional pie. The world looked better. Yes, Jen was angry at me, but she was much more mature than I was. We'd be able to talk once she didn't want to kill me. Yes, she was going on a date with Jason, but it's not like they're picking out curtains. He also had a vested interest in making the film a success. There was no reason three mature grown-ups couldn't work together in this situation. Especially if I could nobble the budding romance before it started.

Things were looking up. Maybe a second pie was in order.

* * *

"Jason, hi. Sorry I missed you earlier." I was back at the office, being all professional. "How are things?"

"It's all good here, mate. I'm having a couple of days in the Leeds office. I would come across to see you, but today I'm tied up in meetings for another project." Was he avoiding me? What an immature prick. Stop it. Keep it professional. "The good news is, I've tracked down Roddy's agent. She seemed a bit surprised to hear from me, but here's the good news: he is up for talking to us about the role. The downside is that he wants us to go to him rather than meet in London."

"That's not a problem, is it?"

"No, not if you and Jen are up for a road trip. He lives on the south coast, some manor house on a vast estate. I'll text you the address so you can check it out. It's imposing, very impressive. Could you do it next week?"

"Of course, whatever it takes."

"Okay. I'll speak to Jen, check her availability, and set something up. Got to dash. See you soon."

He hung up. It occurred to me he knew Jen wasn't in the office with me, but I let it go. I'd also forgotten to tell him about my great idea for pitching to Flic. Next time. Then the horror hit me. A long trip with the two of them. That could be awkward. Of course, it could be worse. Jen was unlikely to leave Charley as it would mean an overnight stay. I could end up making the trip with just Jason.

Bugger.

The text came through with Roddy's address. I couldn't resist looking it up online. Whoa. It looked like a place a couple of dodgy billionaires would club together to buy. Ornate gardens, sweeping lawns, sports cars in the drive. Roddy had done well for himself. I wondered what he'd been up to over the last forty years. More to the point, I was going to meet Roddy Lightning! I called Dad to let him know. It was my mum that answered.

"Oh, hello, love. You've just missed him. He's just nipped out to the shop, but he shouldn't be too long. The second time he's been this morning. Went for a paper and came back with all sorts but no paper. I told him not to bother, but he's collecting tokens for a cheap holiday. Why do we need a cheap holiday? We live at the seaside already. Anyway, how's Charley getting on?"

Typical. Not how are you? What's happening in your life? Both Mum and Dad had bonded with Jen's daughter Charley on a couple of trips over to visit them.

"Charley's fine. She loves being at school."

"And what about her mum? Any sign of you doing the right thing?"

"How many times, Mum? We're friends and business partners. What's the big thing about making sure I get married?"

"Well, you're not getting any younger, are you? Besides, I bought a hat when you were supposed to get married to the last one. Still in the box." Her concern touched me.

"Never mind that. I rang to tell you I've got a meeting coming up with Roddy Lightning about him being in our film."

Mum was suddenly enthusiastic.

"Ooh, I had a right crush on him when I was younger."

"Is there anybody you didn't have a crush on?"

"Cheeky beggar. Ask him if he remembers meeting me at the ballroom in Blackpool Tower in 1979."

"Like he's going to remember meeting one fan forty years ago."

"He'll remember me all right. Remind him about the white dress. He said I looked like Debbie Harry on Top of the Pops."

"What happened?"

"Never you mind. Just say hello from me. Got to go. There's somebody at the door. Your dad'll have forgotten his keys again."

She hung up. I stared at the phone. I'm not sure I wanted to know about Debbie Harry lookalikes. My parents seem to have had this whole life before I was born that I knew nothing about.

7

The office was quiet and dark when I arrived on Thursday. Jen was usually in by now. Was she still mad at me? Worse, was she at Jason's hotel sleeping off last night? I removed the image from my mind. If I was working alone, I wanted music and created a playlist for the day. I picked a curious mix of Primal Scream, Happy Mondays and Leonard Cohen. Obviously, something strange going on in my brain. Caffeine soon joined the thoughts, and I settled to work on the script.

Just before noon, the front door opened, and Jen walked in. I smiled; Jen scowled. She was livid. My worst fears confirmed.

"Can I apologise again?"

"No need." Jen sat down and opened her laptop without looking at me.

"But there is. I'm sorry. In my defence, you only saw the negative side of the list."

"Oh, that's okay then. Silly me. Getting all upset because you turned me into a list. I should be grateful that you put in all that effort to categorise and classify me. What were the good bits? Brings chocolate biscuits to work?"

"Have you?" The cheeky grin didn't work.

"You can be a real immature prick sometimes, you know?"

"I thought we both knew that and accepted it as part of my charm?"

"It's just that I need something more than a prick at the moment." I tried not to smirk. Honestly, I did. Then the gods smiled and Jen laughed. "I give in. I suppose I'm destined to be a mother to two five-year-olds."

"Shall I put the coffee on?"

"It wouldn't harm things, I suppose. Especially if there's a KitKat left in the tin."

When I returned, Jen had hung her coat on the rack—a good sign? I placed the KitKat in front of her.

"You not having one?"

"Only one left."

"Good." Dare I hope we were getting back to normal? Should I ask about the date with Jason? Maybe not. In the end, it was Jen who brought up our producer's name.

"Aren't you going to ask how it went with Jason?"

"How what went?"

"You know what I mean. Dinner last night." Jen broke the KitKat into four pieces and seemed to make a point of not offering me one.

"Oh. Yeah. How did it go?"

"Very nice, thank you. His expenses came in very handy."

"And will there be a rematch?"

"Not decided yet. I mentioned it because Jason is sending through details of the meeting with Roddy and his agent. He wants us to handle the meeting and sell the idea to Roddy. Once it comes to a deal, he'll take over."

"Does that mean you're coming to see Roddy?" Hopes raised.

"Would you mind if I didn't?" Hopes crushed. "It means being away overnight, and I don't want to leave Charley at the moment."

"I understand. Look, if it means we're friends again, I'm

more than happy."

"We're still friends. Just promise—no being jealous of Jason or being a prick."

"You drive a hard deal."

"Take it or leave it, pal."

"Are we still on for spag bol on Saturday?"

"Of course, plonker. Bring pudding. Right, scene two."

It was as if someone had lifted an enormous weight off my chest. With a bit of luck, my plan for the weekend was back on course. Then the email from Jason arrived. I was meeting Roddy on Saturday at 5pm.

Bugger.

After Jen left the office for the night, I switched my attention to the presentation for Flic. We'd spent a large part of the afternoon putting together a standard PowerPoint, running through the synopsis, likely filming locations and why we wanted Roddy on board.

I'd felt self-conscious as we took turns to act as a presenter, filming both efforts on my iPad so we could iron out any issues. We were serious about this.

I was like a kid with a new school project. I reasoned we had the standard presentation to fall back on if I couldn't make this work. My plan was to integrate that with my animated film.

The first setback of the evening was discovering we'd run out of chocolate biscuits. I considered sprinting up the hill to buy snacks. How long could I work with a rumbling stomach? Then my phone rang.

"Hi Flic, how are you?"

I sensed the muffled voice at the other end was dealing with something else. I could hear what sounded like directions being given. Had she dialled my number without realising?

I was about to end the call when Flic's voice became clear.

"Frankie, sorry about that. Just getting into a cab. I'm with you now. Am I disturbing something important?"

"Not at all. I'm working on our presentation to you about the new synopsis."

"Great, that's why I'm calling. I spoke to Jason earlier, and he said the new story was just about there."

"It is. We're very excited about the new direction. We need to polish the presentation, but I was going to suggest to Jason that we try to get a slot with you towards the end of next week to run through it." Where had that come from? It would be a push it to have my project done within a week. I have to stop thinking on my feet.

"That would be nice, but maybe too late. We have a partner lined up, but they want to move straight away, something to do with their financial year-end. Why don't you send me what you've got so far? If you send it tonight, I can go into tomorrow's meeting armed and get a decision pronto."

I was now in a blind panic.

"But it's, you know, rough around the edges at the moment. Jason hasn't even seen the presentation yet."

"To be honest, it's your ideas I'm interested in, not whether you can put together a slick PowerPoint. I want to know that you have a story that people will pay to see on a big screen. We need to take a leap on this. Would you want to lose the chance by dicking around with background colours for a slide I'll see for two seconds?"

"When you put it like that, it makes sense."

"Right. I'll be in this cab for maybe an hour. Let's say you email me by nine o'clock, and I'll call you tomorrow."

"That sounds perfect."

"Cheers, Frankie. Speak tomorrow. Bye."

She was gone. My heart was pounding. I needed to speak to Jen, but my call went to voicemail. I looked at my watch.

Maybe she was putting Charley to bed. I left a garbled message and hung up. So much for polishing the presentation.

I looked again at what I had so far. There was a good bit of animation with the clips of Roddy from the sixties, coupled with some stock footage of the Yorkshire Dales in the summer. I also had the two versions of the practice sessions from this afternoon. I reckoned I could perhaps make a rough edit before nine o'clock. That would have to do.

By the time the pizza arrived, I had Jen's blessing and a ten-minute video for Flic. I crossed my fingers and emailed the link.

8

Sleep had been impossible. I'd spent all last night tossing and turning, fretting about how I could've improved the presentation. We'd taken so much care over dozens of script re-writes, yet the decision over whether we got to make the film came down to a slapped together, half thought-through piece of video. I needed Jen's calming influence and made my way to the office.

I went through the routine of coffee making, music selection and reading yesterday's script changes. At 8.45, a reminder popped up on my screen that Jen was not in the office today. She was at a funeral. It was the old guy who'd lived next door to her that had died. The couple had outlived their only son, and Jen was helping the old dear get through the day as best she could. Typical of Jen to be so caring. Also a bit inconvenient, if I was being honest. I was a nervous wreck and needed her here today.

Flic had texted last night to say she'd picked up the file I'd sent her but had then gone silent. I didn't know when her meeting was. Would she call Jason or me? I needed a distraction. Picking up my phone to recheck Facebook, I remembered the app Jen had recommended the last time I fretted like this. It was some kind of meditation thing. She swore it helped her, but I'd dismissed it as new-age bollocks. What she then called me was not at all Zen-like.

What harm could it do? I paused the music and clicked the app. I did as I was told and removed my shoes, noting the hole in my sock. Something else to worry about. A soothing woman's voice instructed me to stretch out on the floor. The loud crack from my neck was quite alarming, but I spotted a long-lost pen under the desk, so the morning was improving.

My new instructor was leading me through deep breathing exercises. I was to visualise a stream with crystal clear water as I breathed in and out from my diaphragm. I had no idea what my diaphragm was or if I even had one. Maybe I should've gone to the loo before I started. I tried not to fidget, but the water was proving a problem. What a load of old tosh.

I woke up two hours later. The soothing voice had got bored and buggered off.

Apart from an urgent need to use the facilities, I had to admit feeling refreshed. Maybe there was something in this meditation after all. I was just washing my hands when I heard the phone ring. Taking the stairs two at a time, I flung myself across the room and reached my desk just before the voicemail kicked in.

"Morning, Frankie. You sound out of breath. Not disturbing anything, I hope?"

"Hi, Flic. Just doing some weights and a few crunches. Breaks up the morning a bit."

"Pumping iron was not something I had you down for."

I knew I should take offence, but was too busy trying to get my breathing under control after running down the stairs. This was another reminder that I needed to do something about my fitness, though weights and crunches were a step too far. Flic was talking again, which was lucky.

"So, I just got out of the meeting to discuss funding your

project. I'll speak to Jason next, but I wanted to call you first."

Was this the big rejection? She wouldn't have bothered calling me to tell me we were rubbish—would she?

"To cut a long story short, I loved the new synopsis and how you presented it. I know I cut you short before you could polish it, but the idea was brilliant."

"Wow." Not the most professional response Flic would have heard, but it was all I could manage. "Does that mean we have a green light?"

"Let's say, more of an amber at the moment."

My heart sank. I had a flashback to my driving instructor many years ago, purple-faced and shouting that amber meant stop.

"Amber?"

"Nothing to worry about," said Flic. "I just feel so much of this project is your vision. It's your enthusiasm for Roddy and the Thunderbolts. The drive behind the script, even the quirky way of pitching the story."

"Don't forget about Jen. She's a co-writer. I couldn't do any of this without her."

"I'm very impressed with Jen. She brings out the best in you. You have complementary skills that work well together. However, that doesn't alter the fact that this project could fail without you."

"But I'm not going anywhere."

"Don't sound so worried. I'm saying that I'd like reassurance that you have skin in the game, as my American boss likes to say. I'd like you to invest as well."

"Invest? In the film? That would be a gigantic risk." Oops.

"So, it's okay for me to risk my company's money, but not for you to back yourself?"

"Sorry, that came out wrong. It just came as a bit of a shock. How much are you suggesting?"

"We thought fifty was about right."

I let out an involuntary squeak. I was pretty sure that was fifty thousand and not fifty quid. The silence that followed seemed to last forever. Flic was waiting for a more considered response.

"What about Jen?" I asked.

"Jen would be welcome to match your investment, but we're looking at you. We want to tie you in and make sure you're committed. This would do it for us."

"It's a lot of money."

"It is. Is it something you could come up with?"

"I'm not sure. I'd need to speak to Barney. He's my financial adviser. Can I be honest with you?"

"Of course."

"Until last year, I'd had no money to speak of. It was always a bit hand-to-mouth. Rubbish jobs, always skint. Then, almost without warning, the writing took off, and big money arrived. Losing most of it to fraud was devastating. Then, bit by bit, Jen helped me to rebuild. I'm not rich by any means, but I have a bit of a cushion. It feels safe. Risking everything is terrifying."

"I understand. I do. But sometimes, we must leap from the nest and prove that we can fly."

"Or hit the concrete face first and prove that we can't."

"I believe in you. I want you to do the same. Have a think. Speak to Barney and call me back. Please, don't leave it too long. Our partners are super keen to spend their money, but they have other projects in the pipeline. We'll speak soon."

With that, she was gone. What the hell did I do now?

9

The satnav was getting annoyed with me. I'd pulled off the A338 as instructed, but turned right, not left. I needed to pee and could see a pub in the distance. Taking this into account seemed beyond the satnav, so we had one of our frequent arguments. Just when I expected the voice to tell me I was on my own, I pulled into the car park and eased myself out of the seat. Stretching, everything cracked. My sulking friend in the car said we were about ten minutes away from the house. I looked at my watch. It would have to be a quick orange juice and back on the road.

I made the most of what remained of the sunshine and sat in the beer garden. Loud music had followed me all the way south, but now, in the quiet of a country pub garden, I had to confront my thoughts. The call from Flic had caused a sleepless night. Could I put that kind of money into the project? I'd got hold of Barney for five minutes before he hit the golf course. He confirmed that most of it could come from my "rainy day fund" (news to me I had one) and the rest from my OEIC (whatever that was). He advised caution, as it would leave me low on liquid funds. I now know that this has nothing to do with beer.

I had to decide. Did I risk the comparative financial

comfort I now enjoyed or stay in my safe world? Did I invest and make the film a reality, or did I tell Flic I didn't believe enough in my vision? Would she come up with the rest of the money if I said no? Would Jen be interested in putting the money in instead? Then again, how fair was that? This was too hard for now. I needed to push on.

Feeling refreshed, I pulled up by the enormous gates of the estate just fifteen minutes later. A large woman in a loud floral dress pinched the end of her cigarette and placed the remaining bit behind her ear. Leaning on her stick, she approached the open driver's window.

"Maggie?"

"Yes. You must be Frankie." I shook the outstretched hand. "It's good that you're on time. If we hurry, you'll get forty minutes with him."

My heart sank. A six hundred-mile round trip for just over half an hour. Were they playing mind games, or was he just so busy? Maggie saw the look on my face.

"It's almost ping o'clock. Every night at ten to six, the microwave goes on. When it goes ping, nothing gets between Roddy, his plate and Strictly if it's Saturday. Midweek it's antiques, quizzes and the soaps."

So much for the high-powered mind games.

"Follow me."

Maggie got back in her car, and the gates inched open. The drive was so long that I couldn't see the house or any signs of life. I pictured the slow, horse-drawn approach to the grand house. Maggie had other ideas and set off as if the pubs were about to close. The cattle grid rattled every filling, and I willed her to slow down as I lost sight of her altogether. I crested the brow of a small hill, almost losing the contents of my stomach before slamming on the anchors to avoid the sheep, staring as if to accuse me of something. I could see Maggie in the distance. Sweeping formal gardens stretched ahead. The house glinted in the late afternoon sunshine at the end of a long, broad avenue of mature trees. My sheep got bored and wandered off, and I was moving again. Rather than taking the route to the house, Maggie followed the more minor road to the right, heading to a small wooded area. She pulled up and got out of the car. I pulled in behind her as she took a carrier bag from the back seat.

"This way."

We took a small path through the trees and approached a somewhat grubby-looking caravan. Maggie knocked on the door before opening it.

"You decent? You have visitors," she called out.

A familiar voice called from inside.

"Just a minute, lover, havin' a piss."

Maggie sighed and shook her head. I grinned back. That was the voice I'd heard on film and record for most of my life. This was unreal. There was a flush, then the sound of water running. "Right, ready to receive visitors. Come in."

There he was. Older, smaller, but it was him. My hero. Roddy Lightning. Maggie went first.

"Hello, darling. This is Frankie. He's here to talk about the film, remember?"

"Which film? I ain't seen no film, not for ages."

"No, not one you've watched. A new one that Frankie wants you to be in."

"Bleedin' hell, I ain't been in a film for years. Have I?"

"It's like riding a bike. You'd be fine."

Maggie fussed over the contents of the carrier bag, and I shook hands with a legend. I was struck by how bony the hand was, but the blue eyes still penetrated.

"Have a seat, son. What was the name again?"

"Frankie. Frankie Dale."

"Any relation of Jim? I was in a Carry On film with him years ago."

"No. Not that I know."

"Well, it's good to meet you, Frankie. Any friend of Maggie's is a friend of mine. You never know; she might even make a cuppa if we wait long enough."

"The kettle's on, you old rogue. Now play nice."

Roddy winked at me and offered me the packet of chocolate hob-nobs from the shelf behind him. All this and chocolate biscuits too.

"First, thanks for seeing me, Mr–" Mr Lightning? I hadn't thought this through. Lightning wasn't his real name, was it? Roddy rescued me.

"Call me Roddy, son. Everybody else does."

"Roddy. Thanks for agreeing to see me."

"Any chance of a cuppa, Maggie? I'm parched here."

Right on cue, Maggie placed three mugs on the table. As she poured the tea, Roddy offered me the hob-nobs again. I added a second to the one already on the table in front of me.

"As Maggie said, I'm here to talk to you about a part in our film that I think you would be perfect for."

I launched into my synopsis and explained the mood we were looking to recreate, just like on *Thunderbolts And Lightning*.

Roddy didn't look enthusiastic. He glanced at Maggie. She pointed to her ear, signalling that the old guy should listen? Within seconds, he was staring over my shoulder and into the world beyond. Fighting nerves, I picked up my tea and paused. Roddy was now staring at me, and he didn't look altogether happy. Panic swept over me. This wasn't supposed to happen. Sweat trickled down my back and I stumbled over my words. It was all going wrong.

"Wait, I know you," said Roddy, pointing a bony finger at me.

"I, erm, I don't think we've ever met, Roddy."

This was excruciating now, and I wondered about making

a run for it. I could be back home by midnight and just pretend today hadn't happened.

"No. But I know you. You were on the telly. *The Woman In The Yellow Raincoat*. Fuck me, you wrote that, didn't you? Bloody loved it."

I couldn't help the grin that spread from my feet upwards. It was like somebody had flicked a switch. Enthusiasm gushed from every pore of Roddy's being. It was, in fact, as if lightning had struck the room.

For twenty minutes, Roddy asked questions and even suggested things for his character. My confidence grew; this might just work. The microwave ding broke the spell, and Roddy's sole focus moved to his evening meal. Maggie finished in the kitchen and took control of the meeting.

We agreed that, in principle, Roddy was interested, assuming we got the funding. We would send a script within a couple of weeks, and Jason would contact Maggie to discuss financial details. I fumbled for my copy of the Thunderbolts album in my shoulder bag, but Maggie shook her head.

"Next time," she whispered. Roddy had already switched on the TV and was tucking into his fish pie. She planted a light kiss on the top of his head and ushered me out of the caravan.

Outside, we walked back towards the parked cars. It was Maggie that spoke.

"You're desperate to ask about the caravan, aren't you?"

"Let's say I'm curious."

"It's been his home for the last ten years. Life has been hard for him. It's quite a story. All I'll say is that Roddy is a good man. Making some money from this film would be huge for him. Do you think you can make it happen?"

"I'll do everything I can. We've almost got finance lined

up. We should finish the next draft of the script this week. Jason's doing his bit as a producer. Obviously, when we get one, the director will influence casting, but I want to work with Roddy. He's one of my heroes. I want to help, and I want to make a brilliant film."

We reached the cars. The bulk of the house reflected the last of the day's sunshine as I looked across the fields.

"It's a beautiful house," I said.

"It is. Roddy bought it in the sixties for next to nothing."

"He owns it?" I was incredulous.

"He did, for a year. Lost it in the divorce settlement with his first wife. From what my dad told me, it was very messy. He was Roddy's manager from the early days. They were very close. I remember, as a kid, Roddy was always at our house. I worshipped him. Then, when dad died, he got a real criminal looking after him. Years later, I took over as manager, agent, mum - whatever. Life has been difficult for him, but I do what I can."

"How come he's in the caravan?"

"It was Penny's idea."

"Penny?"

"Thunderbolt 2. Penny Peal, the former Mrs Lightning. Fifty years on, and she's still making him pay. She lives in the big house and takes pleasure from knowing Roddy is living like that. Likes to keep him close so she can gloat. Maybe he'll tell you the full story one day."

I shook her hand and got back in the car. Maggie went from a standing start to sixty in the blink of an eye, and I set off in pursuit. She paused as the estate gates swung open, waved out of the window, and roared off into the countryside.

I took a more sedate course and soon pulled over into a lay-by. My mind was racing. I wanted to help Roddy. Making the film was the best way to achieve that. I'd struggled to get my head round it, risking all that money just to see my words acted out on a big screen. But now, it was different. Jen's comment about being selfish had hit home. This was no longer about me. By making the film, I could help Roddy get out of the caravan and back on his feet. Pulling out my phone, I sent three texts.

The first was to Flic.

I'm in. I'll even buy you a frock for the Oscars!

Then Barney.

Need to talk on Monday. I'm making the film.

Then Jason.

Meeting went well. Roddy is very keen. Will call on Monday.

Within seconds, he'd replied.

Great. Having dinner with Jen so will update her. Drive safe.

Hang on. Nobody said anything about dinner with Jen. Had he arranged my trip for today to get me out of the way? He lives in London. What the hell was he doing having dinner with Jen on a Saturday night? Tonight should be me having dinner with her. I had my plans all worked out. I'd only agreed to postpone the plan for a week, so we could meet with Roddy. Then the guy steams in and takes her to some swanky restaurant. That's no way to treat investors.

Bastard.

Now, the idea of spending the evening alone in some faceless hotel bar held no attraction. I looked at my watch. Almost ten to seven. I headed home. Far better to be miserable in my own bed, thank you very much. I called the hotel to let them know. Jason was picking up the bill, so I felt a little better. Pointing the car north, I turned up the music and put my foot down.

10

Seven o'clock on Monday morning saw me hard at work in the office. This was not normal. Somehow, the meeting with Roddy and deciding to invest energised me. Struck by lightning? Yesterday I'd put in a fourteen-hour shift, knowing Jen would spend the day with Charley. I'd broken the back of the script re-write. I spent this morning highlighting the passages of dialogue that needed polishing. Jen was a genius for getting the perfect phrase. It always worked best when we worked on that sort of thing together. She'd be in by ten. My second coffee of the morning was just biting.

I'd thought about Jen a lot since Saturday. Throwing myself into work seemed to be the only way to comprehend what was happening. It looked very much like she'd chosen Jason. I'd blown it without ever getting close. Maybe, if I worked hard and concentrated on not messing things up, she'd get bored with Jason and realise who matters most. I had to play the long game. Be patient and mature: not like me at all.

Needing a diversion to ensure I was ready to work on the dialogue when Jen arrived, I tinkered with some software I'd written for the website last year. It was a simple game I'd rigged up to keep Charley amused whenever she was in the office waiting for Jen to finish work. A series of characters walked across the screen. It depicted Charley as a cartoon hiding in the bushes and throwing custard pies at the unsuspecting targets. Each pie got bigger and messier until the last one got buried under an avalanche of custard. It knew it would have made Charley giggle, but I worried Jen would disapprove, so she never got to see it. Maybe one day. To cheer myself up, I created a version where the pies were being launched at Jason. I'd even password protected it and built in the functionality to end the program after the final round. There was no way I wanted certain people to see this version.

It was childish, but I was flying. A picture of Jason was required to make the character lifelike. Facebook. Jason was bound to be on, and I could steal a shot of him. Dismissing the word stalker from my mind, I started a new browser session. Fifteen fruitless minutes later, I concluded Jason was one of only ten people in the world that wasn't signed up. At least I couldn't find him. I trawled through every Jason Burden on the list, and none of them looked remotely like him. I tried Instagram next — nothing. Going into full stalker mode, I tried LinkedIn and Twitter. Nothing. It intrigued me. For a person to have no social media presence was unusual. When that person worked in the media industry, it beggared belief.

A rummage in the desk drawer produced a copy of our signed contract. I'd definitely spelt his name right. I went back to Google. Bingo! There were several hits, and it was him. There was the press release when the production company started two years ago and a few work-related stories after that. I paged down and noticed something odd. There was nothing older than three years. It was as if, before that, the guy didn't exist. Now I was in stalker mode. What was going on, and just who was Jason Burden?

The door handle clicked, snapping me out of my thoughts. Closing the browser, I flicked to the script and looked busy. Jen walked in with a drinks carrier and a paper bag.

"Morning. Celebratory bacon butties and coffee that'll make your hair stand up."

"Celebratory?" I asked.

"The meeting with Roddy. Sounds like it went well?"

"It did. Sticky at first, then he worked out that we'd written *The Woman In The Yellow Raincoat*. Turns out he's a big fan. We got on great after that. You should've been there. You'd love him."

"Looks like I'll get to meet him, assuming we'll be working together. By the way, Jason thinks he's got a director lined up. He wouldn't tell me who. Says he's superstitious and doesn't want to jinx it by telling me before he's approached him." Jen suddenly looked awkward. After a bit of thought, she spoke again. "Look, I know it would be strange for you if I were seeing Jason while we're all working together."

"So, you're seeing him then?"

"No. At least, not yet. We've had dinner together twice. He's based in London. I'm here. You know what it's like, and you know how I feel. Charley comes first. It's not like we're picking out curtains at IKEA."

"I suppose I just want to see you happy."

"You're a good friend, you know that? The best."

"Just be careful. How much do you really know about him?" Jen did a sort of double-take.

"How do you mean?"

I thought about telling her what I'd found. Then the word 'stalker' flashed before my eyes.

"Ignore me. I care about you, that's all."

"You're a sweetheart. Don't worry about me. I've got a sixth sense for when things aren't right. All is good so far. Brown or red?"

"What?"

"Sauce, for your butty."

"Surprise me. I like to live dangerously."

Jen went off to get plates. She was right; my personal feelings had to be reined in. We all had to work together if we were going to make a success of the film. We also needed a name for our masterpiece. When Jen returned, I went easy on the tomato sauce out of respect for my yellow tee shirt.

We sat at our desks and attacked breakfast. With a mouthful of butty, I spoke.

"We need a name," I said.

"Cedric."

"What?"

"Cedric. That's a name."

"It is, granted. Somehow I can't see Ricky Gervais announcing that the nominee for best picture is Cedric."

"Fair enough, but you weren't very specific." I knew I was being wound up.

"We're nearly finished with this draft of the script. At the end of the week we have to send it to Roddy, Jason and who knows who else but, so far, we just call it our film. We need a name—at the risk of getting a stupid answer."

"Well, you're not the only one who's been busy this weekend. I have a suggestion."

"I'm all ears."

"They're not that big. We can get them fixed after the film is a success." A screwed-up sheet of A4 bounced off Jen's head. She continued as if nothing had happened. "We want the film to capture a perfect, summery feeling. We set it in Yorkshire. My parents loved taking me up to the Dales when I was younger. I remember passing a sign for Hubberholme. We never actually went, but I loved the name."

"Viking, apparently."

"What?"

"The name. It comes from the old Norse for something or other."

Jen gave me a look.

"What's the Norse for shutting the fuck up?"

Rude. I was about to say as much, but let it go. I nodded, and Jen continued.

"We have a kidnapping where the victim strikes up an unexpected friendship with his captors." I nodded in agreement, and Jen looked very pleased with herself. She sat upright and wiped egg yolk from her chin.

"The Hubberholme Syndrome."

"You mean like Stockholm syndrome? Oh, my god. That's genius. I love it. *The Hubberholme Syndrome* it is." I immediately renamed the main script document and typed the title on the front page. We had a name and a location. Now, all we needed were the hundreds of other things to make a film, most of which were a complete mystery to me. That's where Jason came in handy, whoever he was.

It was just after lunchtime when we received identical texts from Jason. He wanted to know if we could attend a conference call at four o'clock. I knew this would be tricky for Jen, as she'd need to pick up Charley from school.

"It'll be fine. I'll bring Charley back here for an hour and bribe her with the promise of burgers on the way home."

A couple of minutes after we accepted the invitation, an email arrived with the call details. It had a formal agenda and everything. Imagine that: me following a formal agenda. We also hit a groove with the script and were pleased with ourselves. Jen grabbed her coat.

"Right, I'll get madame, so she is settled by the time we do the call."

"Hang on a minute, before you go. I have something to tell you."

Jen sat down again with one arm in her coat.

"Sounds serious. What's up?"

"Nothing's up. It's just something Flic asked for as part of the deal to fund the film."

"I knew she was after your body. Ah well, chin up. Take one for the team."

"She wants us to invest our money to ensure we're committed."

"How long have you known this?"

"A couple of days."

"And how much are we talking?"

"Fifty grand."

"What?"

"Between us."

"Oh, that's okay then. Where will I find cash like that? Most of my savings just got ploughed into a university fund for Charley. I can't raid it already. I assumed it would be a few years before I did that."

"That's why I'm putting in your share, if you'll let me."

"That's ridiculous. I can't let you do that."

"You can, and you must. I've cleared it with Barney. I can afford it, just. Without you, I'd still be in the pub every afternoon. The money I made resulted from our writing partnership. You've got Charley to take care of. What else am I going to spend it on?"

"I assumed records, dubious women, and drink."

"I could, but then our film doesn't get made. We've only just named it. We can't give up now. I put the cash up, and we both own a share of the film. The records, dubious women and drink can wait. Just say yes and go get your daughter from school."

"That's very generous. Thank you."

Jen stood up, pulled on her coat and gave me an exaggerated kiss on the cheek, and headed for the door.

I had a break and gave Rupert a call. He didn't answer. A few seconds later, I received a text.

"Sorry, in a meeting. Will call later."

Rupert was in his own meeting. They grow up so soon. It seemed like Rupert was working for me only last year and regularly cocking things up. Actually, it was only last year. Now he was working for Spud in the business that I was still a silent partner in. I noted I should call Spud to ensure everything was okay and went back to working on the script.

Fifteen minutes later, Charley burst through the front door, dumping her empty lunch box on my desk, high-fiving me and climbing into Jen's swivel chair. I'd planned to show Charley the game I'd been working on. Jen had other plans and quickly organised a colouring book, crayons, orange juice and a transfer to a seat on the rug by the coffee table. As ever, highly efficient and seemingly effortless. I had a quick chat with Charley about her day at school. Then, Jason's face had appeared on the big screen, and our meeting started.

Jason was very business-like and started running through the financial plan. He held up the contract that Flic had signed that morning.

I understood about half of what he said, but nodded wisely. I guessed Flic hadn't mentioned my investment, as all of this must have been prepared days ago. From what I could gather, Flic's company would release the money in chunks as we hit various milestones on the plan. They paid a fee to us for the script and a small percentage of the profits. The cost side of the slide was frightening. I decided that was for Jason and Flic to worry about.

I looked at Jen. She understood everything unless she was a better actress than I thought. Jason showed the next slide.

"Right. Item four on the agenda, appointing a director." I

sat up straight. "I've had a tentative discussion with somebody I think would be ideal for the project. He's showed that, in principle, he's interested. He wants to meet up with you guys and review the script. But he has a hectic schedule. It would mean filming the indoor scenes over the winter and then outside in the spring. Assuming all goes well, we begin before Christmas."

This was getting very real. It didn't feel like the time to ask, as a proper director was just about on board, but I wasn't sure how the timing would fit our idea of setting the film in the summer. I asked the obvious question.

"Jason, who is it?" The slide changed.

"Richard Tate, BAFTA award winner and one of the best British directors of his generation."

"Dick Tate?" said Jen. She was pretty animated.

"You seem quite excited," I said.

"Excited? Dick was my tutor for a year at university. I know him."

"But you did journalism?"

"I did, as part of a media studies degree. One year was filmmaking. We got to write a script and direct a short film as part of the final exam. The guy's a genius. He'd be perfect."

"He recognised the name on the script and remembers you fondly," said Jason. Jen blushed. "Look, if you two agree, I thought I'd set up a dinner next week so we can all meet up. Dick suggested inviting Roddy. He wants to make sure the old guy is up to the job."

"Sounds like a plan to me." Jen agreed.

"Okay. I'll set it up. Right, item five..."

I rapidly lost interest from that point, and my mind wandered. Jen was certainly enthusiastic when Dick Tate was mentioned. I knew his work, obviously. He'd made a couple of TV series in the nineties and the film about the church choir, but nothing to suggest that level of enthusiasm. Jen snapped me out of my reverie, saying goodbye to Jason. The meeting was over. I waved, and the screen went blank.

"So, dish the dirt. What's the story with Mr Tate?"

"No dirt. He's supportive and knows his stuff. He was brilliant."

"But?"

"No, but. Come on, Charley. Show uncle Frankie your picture, then it's time for tea."

There was something Jen wasn't telling me. Maybe that was just par for the course these days.

11

It wasn't my fault, okay? We'd been in a nice routine of spending Saturday evenings at Jen's, eating pizza and watching telly. When she cancelled on me again, I ended up in the pub. I remember Ambrose and his wife Stella being there until around ten. We had a good laugh. Then, after they left, Joe and Rupert called in 'for a swift one'. They took me to a club where I was the straightest bloke to have ever crossed the threshold. Once I got over the shock of the half-naked bar staff, I relaxed (helped by some weird cocktail that Joe came up with) and ended up dancing. Well, dancing as best I could on a podium, high above the dance floor. I still have no idea how I got up there. Or why! Even less about how I got down. There must've been a taxi. There always is. And, judging by the debris on my shirt, there'd been onions and something yellow. Oh, and there was an awful taste in my mouth and somebody had battered me over the head with a heavy thing. Maybe it was a hangover.

I tried to focus on my watch. Two-thirty. Not as late as I thought. Then I realised it was sunny outside. That would be half-past two in the afternoon then.

Bollocks.

It was cold, and I needed the toilet. Fighting my way out of the armchair, I was about to climb the stairs when I remembered I was the proud owner of a downstairs loo.

Result.

Being cold was a bit more complicated. I moved into my lovely new house early last summer. I was too excited to read any of the heating instructions. Now it was getting towards the end of October. I would have to be brave and work out how the thing operated. Not today, though. I needed coffee. My stomach complained, but I stayed upright long enough to battle the filter machine. As the magic liquid dripped through, I remembered my hoodie was hanging on the coat hook by the front door. Heating solved.

Next on my hierarchy of needs was food. Opening the fridge, expecting the worst, it didn't disappoint. My big plan for this morning had been a supermarket dash. I'd made a list and everything. Not a lot of use now as I stared at the empty fridge. Bread. There must be bread. I opened the bread bin, a housewarming present from Jen. Two crusts from a Hovis wholemeal loaf almost apologised as I inspected them for mould. I decided they were fine. A tomato sauce sandwich, it was.

I took my feast back to the armchair, flopped down, and sat on something hard. I realised it was my phone. The battery had given up at the end of a long night. I knew how it felt and fumbled at the side of my seat. Whoever had the idea of including a USB port in a chair was a genius, and within seconds, the phone was charging. It rang before I was halfway through my sandwich. It was a voicemail from my mum. She sounded odd and wanted me to call back. I decided I would call later and settled in with my coffee.

Flicking on the TV, I thought an afternoon of top-class football was in order. It was goalless at halftime between Brighton and Everton. The promise of Southampton against Newcastle later didn't excite. Even the telly was against me today, and I switched it off.

My phone flashed again. It suddenly dawned on me that something was wrong. I'd had seven missed calls, all from the same number. I called Mum back, and she answered on the first ring.

"Oh, hello, love. You needn't have rung me back. I know how busy you are."

"Sorry, it took a while. Bit of a late-night."

"I bet there was a woman involved, knowing you."

I decided against explaining where I'd actually been. That was far more complicated than I could cope with in my current state.

"You sounded like you needed to tell me something."

"Well, this week has been a bit of a performance."

"Why, what's up?"

"I don't want to worry you, but it's your dad." Now I was worried. "He's gone for a walk." Was that all? He'd done that before, I was pretty sure. She went on. "He's been forgetting things for a while. Well, I persuaded him to see the doctor, and he'd referred us to a consultant. The appointment was this week."

"Why didn't you say earlier? I could've taken him for you."

"We didn't want to bother you. You've a lot on. Anyway, we went on Friday. He asked your dad a lot of questions to test his memory."

"What sort of questions?"

"Well, silly bugger asked him what he'd had for breakfast. I said porridge, same as every morning for the last thirty years."

"Wasn't Dad supposed to answer?"

"That's what the doctor said. Got quite arsey with me. I told him it was too easy. I think after thirty years, anybody would remember that."

"Okay. What else did the doctor ask?"

"Asked him who the prime minister was. I was just about to say that idiot Cameron, but Dad got in first and said Theresa May. I was glad I said nothing, to be honest."

"Probably for the best. So Dad passed the test?"

"No, not really. The doctor asked him what year it was, and he said 1975."

"Dad said what?"

"He said it was 1975. The doctor asked him again later, and he said the same."

"What about the other questions?"

"He got most of them right, quite a few that I didn't know. I'd no idea that the clown on the zip wire wasn't mayor of London anymore. At least we won't see his ugly mug on telly again. It all seemed to go well. Then he said we had to get off because we had tickets to see Rod Hull at the Spa in Bridlington. Ridiculous. As if I'd go to see Rod Hull and that bloody emu. Never forgiven it for attacking Michael Parkinson. They should've shot the bloody thing years ago, if you ask me."

I didn't point out that Rod Hull died almost twenty years ago, and Emu was a puppet.

"So. What was the outcome?" I asked, but already feared the worst.

"He thinks it's dementia. He wants to do more tests but doesn't think it's Alzheimer's."

"So it could be worse. What happens now?"

"I'm not right sure. The consultant's introducing us to a support group, but he says there's no telling how things will develop. We just need to wait and see."

"Do you need me to do anything?"

"No. It's not that he's unwell. Just forgets stuff. Like I say, he has for a while."

"At least if it's 1975, the beer will be cheaper."

"I suppose so."

"I'll come over soon to see you both."

"That'd be nice. I'll tell your dad you called."

"Oh, and make sure he plays his music. I read somewhere that it can help with memories."

"No problem with that. Spends most of his life with those records you bought him. He's taken up drawing again as well."

"Well, that's good." Dad was always much better than me. He taught me to draw when I was a kid.

After I hung up, I sat staring into space. Is this what it's like getting older? I could sense the start of the move from them looking after me to be me looking after them. All that and Southampton against Newcastle with a hangover. What a crap day.

12

On Thursday of the following week, Jen left the office early to pick up Charley from school. She was to be dropped at her Gran's. We had a date. I wish. No, it was a meal with the Hubberholme team to kick off the film. We had a private dining room at a swanky hotel in Leeds. As well as Jen and me, Jason and Dick would be there. Maggie was driving Roddy up, and the two young actors cast as the kidnappers, Phil and Alice, were there too. The idea was to get to know each other. We were all staying over at the hotel. The following day, we'd booked a conference room to walk through the script. Dick was a real director, and the actors would speak our words for the first time. It was exciting and frightening.

Jen and I shared a taxi into Leeds. The driver had had a long day. I cracked the window open an inch. As we edged through the rush hour traffic, I saw my chance to question Jen about our director.

"Tell me more about Dick. How well did you know him?"

"As I say, we worked together for about six months. He was very supportive. He helped me to improve the film no end," said Jen.

"Are you blushing?"

"No. It's just hot in here." She opened her window too.

"Are you sure? I sensed there was something when Jason first announced his name."

"It's nothing. It was all a long time ago."

"So there was something. Come on. Spill."

"It was nothing. Dick… Well, he asked me out once or twice. It didn't come to anything."

"So he fancied you?"

"Don't sound so surprised. Yes, I suppose he did."

"And was it reciprocated? Did you fancy him?"

"He's very nice, but a lot older than me. I had a work placement thing for six months down in London. We sort of drifted apart."

"So you were together. You must have been so that you could drift apart."

"I suppose so. A bit."

"How can you be together a bit?"

"It was brief, okay? Can we talk about something else?"

So, I was up against Dick and Jason if I were to woo Jen. I smiled at the thought of using the word woo. We were passing a farm full of cows and I wondered if bulls would woo potential mates.

"What are you smirking at now?" asked Jen.

"I wasn't smirking. I was smiling whimsically."

"Looked like a smirk to me. Smirker." She dug her elbow into my ribs. "And no getting pissed tonight. Important day tomorrow."

"Yes, mum."

"Watch it. And tuck your shirt in."

The taxi pulled up outside the hotel. We could see Jason by the door. As the producer, he was our host for the evening. He greeted me with a firm handshake, Jen with a hug and kiss on both cheeks. Was that the greeting for a lover or a business associate?

"Come upstairs. Dick's in the bar with Phil and Alice. Maggie texted to say Roddy will be up in a few minutes."

The roof bar was busy. As we left the lift, Jason guided us to a group of seats in the corner. Dick hugged Jen, and there were three cheek kisses. Over the top? Handshakes all round, then Alice leaned in for the cheek kiss. Was it one or two? Dick had gone for three. In the end, I made a mess of it, and we sort of bumped noses. That would do. It broke the ice anyway, and Alice was as nervous as I was.

Two bottles of champagne arrived. I remembered Jen's warning and sipped. Then I noticed she soon accepted a second glass. Looked like all bets were off! Maggie came without Roddy. She explained the bar was too busy for him, and he'd meet us in the dining room when we were moving through.

It was like the first day at school. We were all nervous, looking at Jason as a kind of leader. I could see it was ridiculous. I plunged in to chat with Phil and Alice about their experience so far. It turned out that Alice was still at drama school, and this would be her first professional role. Phil was more experienced, having had a TV role last year when he'd been a corpse on Silent Witness—impressive. He told us both about how he'd prepared for the role. Out of the corner of my eye, I could see Jen in a huddle with Dick. As Jason spoke to a hotel staff member, Maggie was tapping on her phone. Jason nodded and gestured that we should follow him to the dining room.

I'd expected a long table for eight. Instead, the room had two tables of four. Jason explained we would shuffle the seating between each course. Everybody would sit with everybody else at some stage. At that point, the door opened, and a familiar face appeared. Roddy entered—all smiles and confidence. He danced as he moved towards us. I clapped. I just couldn't help it. Hesitantly at first, then with enthusiasm, the rest of the room joined in. Maggie introduced him to each of the team. He greeted all like long-lost friends. Kisses for Jen and Alice, handshake and hugs for the rest of us. He even did the catchphrase "Lightning might strike twice".

As the meal started, there was a polite hum of conversation. By dessert, raucous laughter from the other table as Roddy held court. Maggie looked on like a proud parent, even though she was twenty years younger than Roddy.

"He seems at home in this situation. He must do it a lot." Maggie shook her head.

"It must be ten years since he was out for a night like this. Somehow, he's always been able to flick a switch. I'm always amazed when the shy, private Roddy turns into showbiz Roddy," she said.

"He seems to be looking forward to the film."

"It's given him quite a burst of energy over the last few weeks. He's always had a tendency to burn the candle at both ends. It's lovely to see him like this, but I need to keep an eye on him and make sure he doesn't overdo things."

"It's good that he has you looking out for him. Will you be up here when we're filming?"

"Unfortunately not. I've got commitments in London and need to be there for the next few days. We'll drive back together tomorrow evening, then I'll put him on a train when the filming starts. I'll fret when he's alone in the hotel."

"Don't worry, Maggie, we'll look after him."

"Thanks, but don't let him lead you astray."

"Oh, I think I can handle a seventy-eight-year-old."

She gave me a look.

After the meal, Jason ushered us to a cosy, comfortable lounge and we settled into over-stuffed armchairs around a log fire. I didn't know where the bottle of brandy came from, but it was nice. Dick was the first to make a move.

"Well, ladies and gentlemen, it's high time I was in bed. Jason, thanks for your hospitality. May I also suggest that the evening should draw to a close soon? We have a full day's workshop tomorrow with a ten o'clock start. Any late arrivals will incur a fine of ten English pounds. We do that every day of filming, so keep it in mind. I think we'll have enough money to pay for a big night out."

We all cheered. Dick waved and left us to it.

Alice and Phil were next to leave. I'd overheard plans for a club, but decided my clubbing days were on hold for now. Jen was next, followed five minutes later by Jason. My heart sank at the thought of something happening. Maggie rose from her seat, kissed Roddy on the cheek, and pointed at me.

"You're in charge. Only half an hour."

"Scout's honour." Another look.

When it was just the two of us, Roddy leaned across.

"How about another bottle of that brandy?"

"You realise what Maggie would do to us both if we did?"

"Fair point. At least let's have a nightcap," he chuckled.

I caught the eye of the waiter and ordered two large brandies. I had a nice little buzz on and didn't want this to end. When the drinks arrived, Roddy raised his glass with a flourish.

"To Pennywise, long may she watch over me."

"Who's Pennywise." Roddy shook his head and raised a sad smile.

"Oh, I shouldn't call her that. She'd only stick another pin in the doll."

"Penny Peal, by any chance?"

"The same. My first love and biggest pain in the arse throughout the last sixty years. Brandy and Babycham was always her drink."

"That's a drink of its time."

"Very classy in 1958, especially to a wet-behind-the-ears teenager from the sticks."

"It must've been an exciting time."

"Christ, yes. It was brilliant most of the time."

"How did you meet?"

Roddy was now thoughtful. He sipped his brandy and then leaned forward.

"Through the band. Old Door-Open Dawson decided I was going to be the next big thing. He put me together with four gorgeous young women, and Roddy Lightning and the Thunderbolts were born. Doris Dickinson became Penny Peal, and a thunderbolt hit me. I fell in love with her on day one, if I'm honest, but Door-Open disapproved and had other plans for me. We saw each other, but we kept it a secret. Can't have the teen idol shagging his lead guitarist. Not good for the image."

"Why was he called Door-Open?"

"It was always a good idea to make sure the door was open if you were alone with him. He was always a bit of a hands-on manager, if you know what I mean. Knew how to pick a song, though. Who'd have thought *Ballad Of The Lonely Puppy* was a million-seller? He did. Debut single, bang. Number one all across Europe."

"Nobody sells a million these days," I offered.

"It did three million in the end. Changed my life, I can tell you."

"It must've been great having all that money at 18."

"What money? Dawson made sure he kept most of it. I was on a lousy weekly wage. Most of us were getting ripped off at that stage. It was only when he had his accident that things started looking up, for me at any rate. Did little for him."

"Accident?"

"Fell down the stairs. Several times." Roddy chuckled and took a sip of brandy. "Seemed he'd upset some of the wrong people, if you know what I mean. A silver lining for me, though. They took over most of his business but weren't interested in me. Kept the rights to *Lonely Puppy*, but ripped up my contract. I was free to sign with a big American agency. That's when the money rolled in. Also meant me and Penny were free to become the golden couple. The Yanks even encouraged it. Great publicity for my new audience. By the time I was twenty-one, we were married. Huge wedding, honeymoon in Monte Carlo, the works."

"I've seen some of the footage. Very glamourous."

"It was fantastic. We seemed to have everything. Turned out Penny could write songs. Used to bang out another hit for me every couple of months."

"So Penny wrote the songs?"

"Pretty much. Peal & Lightning is what it said on the credits, but I didn't offer much. Added some of the oohs and la las. Absolute genius; she could come up with a hook in seconds and know it would be a number one. Still does. *No More Morning Breath* — that's her."

He sang the tune to the latest chewing gum advert ear-worm.

"That was Penny?"

"Sure was. She's still got it."

I was trying to pluck up the courage to ask how Roddy ended up in a caravan while Penny was in the big house. Before I could, a young man in a cheap suit oozed towards us and passed a note to me. In block capitals was "*I SAID HALF AN HOUR*". I had to admit that Maggie was good at her job. Roddy knocked back his brandy.

"I take it that was the boss. Better call it a night."

He patted me on the shoulder and strode off into the night. I stretched my legs out in front of the fire and cradled my brandy. I was contemplating the wisdom of ordering another when the suit appeared at my side. This time, he just coughed into his hand. Then it dawned that Maggie's order applied to me as well. Best call it a day then.

13

The workshop was going well. The entire team, such as it was, was sitting around a conference table. Dick was in charge and walked us through each scene. The actors read their lines from the script. Jen and I took notes about what worked and what didn't read quite so well.

Jason seemed to spend most of the morning leaving the room, tapping his Bluetooth earpiece as he went. I'd always wondered what a producer did. This seemed to be it. As we broke for coffee, I followed Jason into the corridor, just in time to hear the end of the conversation.

"They can't do that to us. Look, Natasha, go around the loop again. There must be something we can do. Speak later." He tapped the earpiece again and almost leapt out of his skin when I spoke.

"Problems?"

"Christ, Frankie. Don't do that to me. I'd no idea you were there."

"Sorry. You just seemed to be worried, thought I might help."

"No, nothing for you to worry about. Natasha's my PA. We've got a few more certainties so she can update the budget. How do you think the morning's going?"

"Given that I have zero experience, I'd say it's going well. We're getting plenty of ideas for re-working the dialogue."

"It's certainly good that you and Jen are open to change. You wouldn't believe the battles we have with some writers."

"Yeah, we're okay with change. That's one of the many things Jen taught me. Another was oxyphenbutazone." Jason looked at me like I'd fallen out of a tree. "We play Scrabble. It's theoretically the highest score you can get—1785 points. Never got it yet, but you never know."

"She's terrific. You obviously get on very well together." I was uncomfortable with where this was going. Was he going to do the old territorial thing? Defend his woman? I needn't have worried. "How would you feel if Jen took on an extra role?"

"How do you mean?"

"It was Dick's suggestion. I spoke to him during dinner last night, and he made sense. He wants her to become an assistant director."

"But what about the script? We've still got loads to do."

"That's partly the point. She'd be working with Dick to shape the storyboards and how each scene needs to be shot. That would ensure that she knows exactly the changes that would work. It would be like bridging a gap between director and writer. Make it seamless."

"How does Jen feel about it?"

"We haven't asked her yet. I wanted you to be happy with the idea."

"I think it sounds great. My only concern would be if we spread Jen's time too thinly. Charley will always be her top priority, so there are limits. We'd have to make sure she could still devote time to the script."

"So, in principle, you are on board? We just need to help her manage the extra workload."

"Sounds like a plan." I headed back towards the room.

"Actually, while you're here. There's something else I wanted to discuss with you." Was he about to warn me off thoughts of romance with Jen? "I was wondering if we were to expand Jen's role, would you be open to something similar?"

"I know nothing about directing. Why would we both do that?"

"I didn't mean directing. As an investor in the film, how does co-producer sound?"

"But you're the producer. I know nothing about producing, either."

"It's basic project management. Given your IT background, I suspect that's something you know about?"

"Well, yes, but that's software, not a film."

"There are loads of similarities. It's just the finished product that's different. You still need to break it down into tasks, control budgets, manage risk and deal with people. I can teach you the specialist stuff. What do you say? We work on this together."

Well, this was not how I expected the morning to go.

"Can I use post-it notes on the wall?"

"You wouldn't believe what Natasha can get hold of from the stationery supplier."

"Then I'm in."

We shook hands, and I re-entered the room as co-producer, just like that.

I'd sat next to Jen for lunch. We'd both opted for a chicken salad. What I'd actually wanted was the chicken nuggets from the kids' menu, but I decided the salad was what a real film producer would go for.

"You look pleased with yourself."

"I believe you already know why," said Jen.

"Jason told me earlier. Congratulations, you'll make a

brilliant director."

"Assistant. I must admit, I'm looking forward to it. Thanks for agreeing to it."

"Don't be daft. Why would I object? Besides, you're looking at a movie producer now." I puffed myself up in the seat while retrieving a spinach leaf from the front of my shirt.

"So I gather. I can't believe how much has changed in the last couple of years. Congratulations."

"And all down to Ambrose's tweet challenge."

"Maybe not all. We've worked pretty hard and been lucky."

"Not to mention what a brilliant writer you are."

"Not so bad yourself." We both laughed and chinked orange juice glasses. "So, Mr Producer, what happens next?"

"I thought I'd have some of that cheesecake."

"Good idea. Get me a piece, then you can tell me what happens for the next few weeks."

I returned with two plates, one lemon and the other raspberry. In my head, I cheered when Jen took the red one. However, my understanding of what we had planned for the next few weeks was vague.

"I think Jason's got a slide later about what happens now. We have two weeks of rehearsals before Christmas. We film interior scenes in January, then move outside in the Dales in April or earlier if the weather is good. That gives us all of six weeks to get ready."

"I think Dick's already trying to bring those dates forward. He's got another project straight after this. He mentioned he wants to be storyboarding at the end of next week." I looked suitably puzzled. "It means drawing pictures for each scene, how we want it to look, that sort of thing. You and Jason get to work out where we will film and make sure everything is in the right place."

"Blimey, sounds like we're going to be busy."

"Don't forget, we've also got a script to finish."

"Best have another piece of cheesecake then; keep my strength up."

After lunch, we finished the read-through. Jason ran down the schedule. It confirmed what we'd discussed earlier, and, by four o'clock, hugs all around and a fleet of taxis waiting outside.

Maggie was standing alone by the door.

"Frankie, thanks for looking after us so well over the last couple of days."

"A pleasure. Where's Roddy?"

"I never let him leave a building without using the facilities first."

"Smart. Something I need to learn. Here he is." We shook hands again. "Right, look after yourself over the next few weeks. If I don't see you before. I'll see you in December for rehearsals."

14

An early night had done me a world of good. Saturday morning had that air of expectancy where anything could happen, rather than just wanting to go back to bed. We were due to meet in the office early on Monday to continue with the script, so I had an entire weekend to devote to myself. No work, just pursue my other interests. By the time I'd finished my second coffee, I still hadn't worked out what those interests were. Had I started being bored with my own company?

It was chilly, and I shivered. I had an idea. I could sort out the timer for the heating! How difficult could that be? Not only am I an IT consultant (retired), I'm a scriptwriter and film producer. A heating control panel holds no fears for me. The controller was in the big, scary cupboard. It was in the friendly, spacious cupboard when I moved in, but more and more crap had got shoved in there over the months. A floor-to-ceiling pile of boxes blocked my path to the controller. I could see the panel by removing two of them and peering over the rest.

I thought of Cheryl, the girlfriend before Robbie. She called it intuition, but she seemed to know how these things worked. At the opposite end of the evolutionary scale was me. I didn't have a clue. Maybe I should look on the internet for instructions, but how difficult could this be? I peered at the small white box with its displays and buttons. I reached out and had a pathetic tap on the keys. Nothing. Bugger all to suggest changing the timer or a temperature setting. I'd have settled for a picture of a radiator or a button that said "Make hotter"—anything. I read the logo on the box and cursed them for making it complicated. Only when I said it out loud did I realise it was the name of a power company. I was looking at the smart meter.

Bollocks.

Moving several more boxes, I located another small white controller. This looked more promising, if still confusing. It looked like the controls hid behind a small drop-down flap. I pushed another box to the left to clear a path to the flap. There was a curious, rumbling, scraping type sound. Half a second later, a minor avalanche of boxes, a sweeping brush and, to add insult, a hard hat left by the builders hit me square on the noggin. I rubbed my head.

"Fuck it. This can wait."

I shoved the two boxes back in and put my shoulder against the door to close it. I grabbed my jacket and locked the front door behind me. The cafe would be nice and warm with the bonus of a bacon butty on offer.

Before I got to the cafe, I spotted the bus trundling up the hill. On impulse, I jumped on, and ten minutes later, I was poking my head inside the door to Joe's cellar.

"Is that an extra pair of hands, I see?" said Joe, ushering me inside.

"Wow, this is…"

"A shit-hole?"

"You've done so much to it in the last couple of weeks." I laughed, taking in the full gravity of the shit-holery.

"To be honest, we've done bugger all. But I've got a

fabulous, all-over tan, thanks to a few cheeky days in Ibiza. It was just a shame that Rupert was still on the naughty step. I had some loose ends to tie up with the club. I'm never one to turn down a few days in the sun. "

"Very nice too. So where's Rupert?"

"Coffee and breakfast run. Text him your order. He's only just set off."

Kismet. Within seconds, my order was in, and I asked Joe what he wanted me to do.

"Well, anything that's not nailed down needs to go in the skip outside unless it looks like Ambrose could sell it. We'll pile that lot in the corner and move it to his stockroom later."

I put my jacket next to Joe's in the corner and rolled my sleeves up. It was ages since I'd done a full day's fair labour. It could be just what I needed. After ten minutes, Rupert returned, and we sat on the stairs to eat breakfast. No point peaking too soon. Seeing Rupert reminded me of when we had a similar day, clearing out the loft at the community centre to use as our office. Ambrose had been with us that day, but now he was working in the record shop next door. Right on cue, he appeared at the door.

"Room for another one? I've got two staff next door twiddling their thumbs so they won't miss me for the morning."

The band was back together. Let *Operation Shit-Shovelling* begin. Well, once I've finished my coffee, it can.

Over the next few hours, we all worked hard. I stopped to wipe the sweat from my forehead and considered the irony of the situation. I'd come here to escape from sorting out my messy cupboard and did almost eight hours of hard labour sorting out Joe's cellar. However, you couldn't escape the fact that it was pretty satisfying. Joe had accumulated tons of crap over the years, buying entire house contents and never getting the loot sorted and sold. He'd done a deal with

Ambrose that the records would get sold in the shop and split the profits. Several crates had already made their way through the adjoining door to the shop.

We'd talked earlier about rewarding my efforts. I'd tried to refuse, but Joe insisted I take something. We settled on a grubby-looking watercolour in a frame and a sealed packing crate, the contents of which were a complete mystery.

I was sitting on the crate when Rupert produced a crowbar.

"What the hell are you going to do with that?"

"I'm going to open the crate and see what's in it," said Rupert.

"No, leave it for now."

"Why?"

"You'll upset me if it's full of crap, and Joe'll feel bad. This way, as long as it's sealed, I believe it's worth having and feel excited about it."

"Weirdo."

Joe came forward.

"I like the idea. Leave it sealed." He produced a big marker pen and printed 'Schrodinger's crate' on the side.

"Just one question." They all looked at me. "How the hell do I get it home with me?"

Joe looked delighted.

"We can take you in Jean-Claude." He saw the look on my face. "Don't worry. Jean Claude is our new van, named after it broke down on its maiden voyage."

"As in Jean-Claude Damned Van?"

"You're good at this. I'll bring Jean-Claude round. We're just about done for the night. I can finish the rest tomorrow."

15

"Dad. What are you doing here? Where's Mum?"

I stepped out the front door to look for her just as an enormous truck pulled away, blasting a parting air horn. Dad waved.

"Thanks, Val," he shouted towards the parting truck. "Your Mum's at her yoga. She's been having a go at me to do more, so I thought, bugger it, I'll go see the lad. So here I am."

"Come in. Come in. You should've called me. What if I'd been out?"

"There's a pub over the road. I'd have been fine."

We moved through into the living room. Dad flopped onto the sofa, pulling the cushion from behind his back.

"How did you get here?"

"Val gave me a lift."

"You mean you hitchhiked?"

"Course. I did it all the time when I was younger."

"That was sixty years ago. Anything could've happened."

"It was fine. I had your address written on a bit of paper and I've got a tongue in my head. Not useless yet. Get the kettle on then."

I did as I was told, calling from the kitchen.

"So, did you tell Mum you were coming?"

"No. Like I said, she's been pecking at me all week. Better I'm out of the way."

"She'll be going spare. I'll give her a ring in a minute. You stay there. I'll bring the tea through."

"And biscuits - chocolate for preference."

That I could manage. Two minutes later, I had a mug of tea in each hand and a packet of penguins under my arm. Before putting them on the coffee table, I was stunned by what Dad said next.

"Euthanasia."

What the fuck?!

"You can't be serious?"

"Course I am. There're loads of 'em over here now. Val's a strange name for a bloke, but he was a good laugh," said Dad.

"What the hell are you on about?"

"I just told you. Val's from Euthanasia, but lives over here now." A very relieving penny worked loose.

"Could it be Lithuania?"

"That's what I said, didn't I?" My heart rate returned to normal. "Tell you what, it's bloody freezing in here."

"I haven't sorted out the heating controls yet." I waved a hand towards the big scary cupboard. "Cupboard's full of crap. I'll sort it out later. Just keep your coat on for now." My phone rang.

"Hi Mum, I was just about to call. No, don't panic. He's here, safe and well." Dad rolled his eyes and disappeared into the kitchen. "No, I didn't know he was planning to come." I picked up my cup of tea. "No, don't call him that. No, I'm sure he's not. He seems fine. Don't worry. We'll have our tea and biscuits… yes, penguins. I know." At least the choice of biscuit gained her approval. "Look, I'll find out what's going on, then drive him back this afternoon. Yes, and no. Yes, I'll stay for tea, and no, I can't stay over. I have to work first thing tomorrow. Okay, look, I'll see you this afternoon. No, I'm fairly sure Jen's busy today. Bye."

Dad returned, putting his hand on the radiator. Satisfied, he slipped his coat off and took a penguin from the table.

"Mum was beside herself."

"Why? I can look after myself."

"Yes, but you could've let her know what you were planning." He shrugged and unwrapped his penguin. I suspected that was the closest I would get to an acknowledgement that I had a point.

"Here, have a look at this." He reached into his coat pocket and pulled out a paperback-sized notebook. "I wanted to show you these."

He passed over the book and sat back, looking quite pleased with himself. I opened the first page. It was a pencil sketch of a face. I could tell straight away it was my mum. The light reflected from her eyes seemed to glow. He'd captured every detail perfectly.

"Wow. I'd forgotten how good you were at this sort of thing."

"It's something I'd meant to go back to for years, but I was always too busy somehow."

I tried to think of when I'd last seen him draw anything. I must've been a teenager. It hit me he gave up around the time of the fire. I flicked to the next page and was stunned to see my twelve-year-old face looking back at me.

"That's from my school photo. It's brilliant, Dad." The following page perfectly reproduced David Bowie's Pin-Ups album cover. "Have you thought about doing this professionally? You could make some decent money from them."

"Nah, who'd buy them?"

"I would, for a start." There were many more sketches, Frank Sinatra with Sammy Davis Junior, Bob Marley, and

John Lennon. There was even a version of the famous photo of the tennis player exposing her bum. "Don't tell your mum about that one."

"Okay. But I mean it, these are very good." I flicked through another couple of pages. "Would you do me a couple on a bigger scale?"

"I'd need to get a bigger pad, but why not?"

"We can go into Leeds after our tea and go to an artist supply shop. Get you all kitted out."

"I'd better make a note of what you want, memory like a whatsername these days." I laughed. "It's all right, you laughing. It's fucking annoying." Hearing him swear was a bit like a slap across the face.

"It's okay. We all forget words sometimes."

"But it's happening a lot. Sieve, fucking sieve. Knew it would come to me." He looked exhausted from the effort and sat back with a hand on his forehead.

"Sorry for laughing. I know it's easy to say, but try not to let it make you angry. You just proved that the words come in time. You remember the important things like who I am."

"I suppose so, Simon." I was about to correct him when I realised he was winding me up.

"Come on, Michaelangelo, you old goat. Drink your tea, and then we'll find you some artist's stuff. And thanks for sorting out the heating. I was going to do it this afternoon."

"Course you were, son, course you were."

Dad was fast asleep in his armchair, his fresh pad and pencils still in his lap. I was full of roast beef and Yorkshires and could do with a nap myself.

"Are you sure you won't stay the night, love? You look tired," said Mum, her head on one side.

"I can't, honest. Early start tomorrow. We begin rehearsals for the film in a couple of weeks, and we're still working on the script."

"I forgot to ask. What's it like working with Roddy Lightning?"

"He's brilliant. I expected him to act the big star, but he's just a normal bloke, excellent company."

"Did you remember me to him?"

"I forgot, to be honest. Promise I will when I see him next. He's due next month for rehearsals and some interior filming."

"Interior filming! My son, writing an actual film."

"Not just writing, Mum. I'm co-producing as well."

"What does that mean?"

"No idea. I don't even get paid more."

"Sounds impressive to me."

Steady rhythmic snoring was now coming from the chair. Mum looked at Dad, then back at me.

"What if he gets worse?"

"I honestly don't know, Mum. This is all new to both of us. We'll cope, don't worry. I would get in touch with the support group and see what help they can offer. Lots of people have coped with this, and we'll get through it too. I'll try to get over more often."

"But you've got a film to make."

"We're filming in the Dales, not Hollywood. I can be here in less than an hour from the set, assuming we find somewhere suitable next week."

"You could bring Jen and Charley to stay. Why haven't you got your finger out and snapped that woman up? She's good for you."

"How did this suddenly become about me? Besides, I've told you before, we're friends and business partners. She puts Charley before anything else. That's all she's interested in."

"But?"

"What do you mean—but?"

"It sounds like you'd quite like there to be more to it than just friends."

"I don't know. Maybe. It's complicated."

"Then uncomplicate it. Life's too short to bugger things up. Tell her how you feel, plonker."

"Should you be calling your only child a plonker?"

"Depends if he's a plonker. At the moment, he's a plonker."

"I think it's time I was off. Big day tomorrow. I've left him a note of the three pictures I want him to do for me. He might need a gentle reminder."

"Okay, love. Thanks for bringing him back home. I wonder where he'll wander off to next."

That was a worrying thought as I put the car in gear and headed for home.

Later that evening, despite being tired, I couldn't settle or concentrate on anything. Seeing how Dad's memory was causing him problems was hard to process. He seemed pleased with the supplies from the artist's shop, and by the time I got home, I had a text from him to say he'd started another drawing.

I tried the TV, but even David Attenborough couldn't get me interested, however blue the planet was. Then I thought of Schrodinger's crate. It was still in the hall, untouched, since Rupert and Joe had dropped me off in the van. I dragged it through to the rug in the living room. Attenborough got zapped, and I hit play on St. Vincent's new album. Returning to my seat, I grabbed a beer from the fridge.

As I settled next to the crate, I remembered I would need something to open it. Checking the lid confirmed several screws held it in place. I could do with Rupert's crowbar. Time to get my toolbox out. With what I can only describe as a grunt, I levered myself back to my feet. When did I start making a noise when I stood up?

My toolbox sounds very fancy. It's a red plastic storage box, last seen somewhere in the big scary cupboard. As I opened the cupboard door, my heart sank. One day, I had to clear this out. I picked the box at head height and pushed. It crashed to the floor. That's one way of making space. I used my foot to nudge a blue plastic crate out of the door. On top of it was my old action man. Why was I storing that? I picked it up and smiled at the empty sleeve on his uniform. He'd lost an arm in some epic battle involving my childhood best mate. We'd lost contact for years, yet the action man was still with me. What did that say about my approach to life?

I'd known Barney since we were five. That's not his real name. At that age, he had trouble pronouncing his real name and spelling it was right out. Getting his friends and teachers to call him Barney was a lot easier. The name stuck. When we were twelve, he told me the story of his parents arriving in Yorkshire from Kerala in the eighties. They'd loved the snow, fish and chips and, in his mum's case, televised snooker. The plan for their firstborn son was to become a doctor. However, when their fifteen-year-old offspring won a school investment competition, a future in the heady world of finance seemed to beckon. By twenty-three, he had his own company and a car that cost as much as my house. He even knows about OEICs (whatever they are). We'd lost touch after school, but I tracked him down when I'd started making money from my writing. Now, as well as being friends again, Barney was my financial adviser.

I told myself to focus on the task and shoved the action man back in the box. Shifting two more boxes opened a gap, and I could see the red plastic. Two minutes and one mini avalanche later, I hauled my treasure onto the kitchen table. The well-stocked toolbox of my imagination turned out to be a disappointment, if I'm honest. Two small screwdrivers, both the same size, a set of drill bits (but no drill) and a hammer. The hammer would do.

In my mind, one blow with my mighty Thor-like hammer would see the crate unfurl like a chocolate orange. As I feared, not a lot happened. I tried again, only harder. This time, I dropped the hammer and rubbed furiously at my wrist. That hurt. I followed Homer Simpson's advice to Bart. "If, at first, you don't succeed, bury the evidence and pretend you never tried." I attempted to lift the box, but a pain shot up my arm. Instead, I tipped the crate on its edge, planning to roll it back into the hall. I only noticed a small metal plate with a catch when I rolled it again. The bloody thing had been upside down all this time. I slid the catch to the side, and, to my immense pleasure, the top lifted off.

Several layers of newspaper covered everything inside. I felt a shiver of excitement as I saw that the top newspaper was from 1971. Had this not seen the light since then? I swigged my beer before pulling the first bundle towards me. It felt like a rectangular box. My heart leapt as I unpacked a record case for singles. I owned several of these already, but what was inside?

The first single was from 1965, a picture cover of Smokey Robinson and the Miracles' *Going To A Go-Go*. It was in pristine condition. This was gold dust. So was the next one. Another picture cover for Marvin Gaye's *I'll be Doggone*. It was the French import copy. Whoever had this collection knew his stuff. Third in the box was another picture cover, again from 1965. Martha and the Vandellas, *Nowhere To Run*.

By now, I was shaking. I had to call Joe and tell him it was too generous to give me this. Then a picture of me as Gollum came to my mind. I cradled the box in my arms—my precious. What else hid in the paper parcels? With a promise to return to the record case later, I pulled another package from the crate. They'd wrapped this parcel in the sports pages. A report on the Leeds against West Brom match distracted me. I'd seen Jeff Astle's controversial goal many times, but the actual match report was here. Feeling like a kid at Christmas who was more interested in the packaging than the expensive gift, I ploughed on, folding the newspaper and placing it to one side. It left me with a plain, brown envelope, about the size of my old school jotter. There were photographs inside. Black and white prints, taken in a nightclub. The first was a close-up of a singer in dark glasses playing the guitar. I couldn't believe what I was looking at. On the back, in neat handwriting - Roy Orbison, Batley Variety Club 1969. There were maybe a dozen more from the same night, some backstage in the star's dressing room.

I spent the next hour opening more envelopes. More incredible photos. Miles Davis at Ronnie Scott's, Bob Dylan at the Isle of Wight Festival, and Fleetwood Mac at a festival in London. Somebody had been very busy in 1969.

Next out was a small pile of wrapped LPs. The Beatles featured as well as The Small Faces and The Kinks. Happiness levels were now off the scale.

The bottom of the box held two small canisters. Again, the handwritten labels were in the same spidery script, and both had faded until they were almost illegible. From what I could see, they both said *Hockney - Bradford Grammar School*. There was no more information, and I had no way of viewing the film. A quick scan of Wikipedia confirmed my suspicion. David Hockney had attended Bradford Grammar School, less than two miles from Joe's cellar, where the carton had lived for years. My heart was pounding. Had I just unearthed two 8mm films by the world-famous artist? I couldn't believe I'd taken a hammer to my treasure chest. What I'd found almost overwhelmed me. What an excellent way to spend Sunday evening. Another beer was called for. I settled back with *The*

White Album from my new collection, sounding wonderful. It's amazing what you find in old crates.

16

Last night, Jen and I finished the latest re-write. At just before eleven o'clock on Thursday morning, I followed the road above the River Wharfe as it snaked its way into Kettlewell. The sun was shining, and life felt good. I even had the top down on the Eos for the last time before winter set in.

I was to meet Jason in the cafe in the village centre as we checked out a couple of film locations and reviewed the latest budget figures. This was proper, grown-up film producing, and I was nailing it!

The road curved to the right and dropped into the village. I turned left and pulled into a near-deserted car park. The cafe was opposite, and two minutes later, I was sitting in the sunshine at a picnic table with a pot of tea ordered. I got a text to say Jason would be another half hour, so I added a toasted currant teacake to the order. I'd offered to meet Jason in Leeds and drive up together. However, he'd had to be in Newcastle the night before, so meeting in the village made more sense.

I sat in the bright November sunshine, took in the spectacular view of the surrounding countryside and couldn't help smiling. This had always been one of my favourite spots in the entire world. Well, the bits of it I knew, which was not a lot, but anywhere else would have to go some to beat it. Contentment swept over me, especially when the toasted teacake arrived. Homemade strawberry jam added to the occasion.

The only nagging thought was that I was still no further forward with Jen. We'd worked hard this week and loved the changes to the script. We'd been so busy that there was no time for the heart-to-heart that everybody seemed to express the need for. Jen herself was very excited about getting started with her directorial duties. Dick was due at our office today for them to start work on the storyboards. It would have been good to be there, but I had essential producer things to do. A bite of the toasted teacake meant my good mood improved again.

I was looking forward to seeing the two locations that Natasha, Jason's assistant, had come up with via various agencies. One was a house in the village, the other an old farm building on the hillside above Starbotton. We'd already decided that beautiful though Hubberholme was, it would be tricky getting some of the production vehicles down the narrow approach road. So its next-door neighbour would be the likely location for the outdoor scenes.

As I drained the last of the tea, I spotted Jason crossing the road from the car park. His wax jacket looked very new. Had he bought it for the occasion?

"Sorry, I'm late. Didn't realise how far from the motorway this place is."

"Not to worry. I'll get you a drink." Jason eased himself onto the picnic bench.

"Great. San Pellegrino mineral water, please, or Perrier at a push. Actually, I'm starving. I could murder some smashed avocado on sourdough. Or sushi. Do you think it's too early for sushi?"

"I'll order." I went inside and walked to the counter

without looking at the menu. "Tea for two and two more toasted currant teacakes, please."

"Have a seat, love. I'll be out in a minute."

When I returned to the table, Jason was peering at his iPad.

"Natasha put together a deck on the deal with Flic. I thought we could start by going through it. I'll AirDrop the deck to you."

"Ah, sorry, no iPad with me. I didn't think I'd need it, to be honest."

"No worries. Look, I can tell you the basics, then you can go through the detail later when you've got the tech."

I felt chastised.

"Okay. To put it simply..." Is he having a dig? "Flic is buying the rights to make a film. They will release the money in phases, a bit like a self-build mortgage." I nodded, trying to hide that I knew nothing about self-build mortgages. "Each time we hit a milestone on the plan, we trigger another payment. Each payment gives us the funding for the next phase. I've inserted a clause that, should Flic pull out for any reason, we would have the first option to buy back the rights."

"Pull out. Why would they pull out?"

"Don't worry, they won't pull out," said Jason.

"So what's in it for them to structure it like that?"

"It means they can pull out."

"But you just said they won't pull out." I was panicking now.

"Why would they pull out? They won't pull out," insisted Jason.

"But..."

Our food arriving interrupted us.

"There you go, love, two teas and two currant teacakes." The waitress placed a tray in front of us. "Can I get you anything else?"

I could see Jason's mouth moving, but no sound came out.

"That's perfect, thanks," I said. She beamed at us both and went back inside. "Don't look so worried. You're in my world now."

"What in God's name is this? Where's the smashed avocado?"

"Trust me. This is better. How do you like your tea?"

"Would it do any good to say with a slice of lemon?"

"Not really. It was more a question of milk or no milk." I grinned. Jason looked like I'd just suggested he should walk around the village naked. I added jam to the teacake and tucked into my second breakfast of the day.

Jason shook his head but followed my example. He looked suspicious, but took a bite.

"Fuck me, that's good."

I felt like a parent when a child rode a bike for the first time.

"Now try the tea."

He took a drink, then another bite.

"What a perfect combination. Do you think you could ask that young lady for the recipe? This would be huge in Islington."

"I bet they'd charge an arm and a leg for it, too."

Jason returned to the iPad, but a solitary figure in full walking gear caught my attention, struggling under the weight of a vast rucksack and an even bigger bobble hat. He looked about my dad's age and stared at the sky through binoculars. He must've sensed an audience as he turned to me.

"Red kite, pair of 'em." My face betrayed my lack of a clue. He tried again and held out the binoculars. "Over there, a pair of beautiful red kites."

I took the binoculars he offered. I didn't even need to refocus, which worried me. It occurred to me that my eyes

110

were as bad as the old man's. I watched as two large birds swept over the hillside. I took it they were red kites. Jason coughed as a subtle reminder of his presence and I handed over the binoculars. The effect was instant. A huge grin spreading over his face. His shoulders relaxed. He tracked them across the sky until they became just a speck heading towards Kilnsey.

"Do you know? This place is fantastic. The budgets can wait." To my surprise, as he handed back the binoculars, he invited the old chap to join us for more tea.

"You must try these teacake thingies. They are quite remarkable."

We spent the next hour entertained with tales of many years walking the paths that crisscrossed this beautiful part of the world. The change in Jason was quite startling, and I almost expected him to stride off into the distance when his newfound friend decided it was time to move on. We almost reluctantly set off in the opposite direction to view the house we hoped would serve as Roddy's fictional home.

The owner met us at the front gate of a large stone cottage on the edge of the village. Within seconds, I was trying to work out how I could buy the place and move in. Ted, our host, explained that it had been an old farmhouse with an attached barn. The barn was now a spectacular double-height living room. The sun streamed through the enormous windows, and we stepped into a fabulous garden. I had a weird feeling that I'd been here before. Ted explained this when he reeled off the films and TV programmes made here over the years. It seemed he rented the place out regularly. The fees paid for his extended breaks in Spain and Florida and provided a steady income.

Having photographed everything in the house, or so it seemed, we were done. A flurry of handshakes on the doorstep sealed the deal. We would be back in a couple of months to make this our hero's home. We even had time for a fifteen-minute stroll around the village before we were due to meet the farmer who owned the second site. Bizarrely, he was also called Ted. I mused on the prospect of it being the same Ted with a different hat. It wasn't.

My dad would describe the man as a brick shithouse. Ted II was standing at the car park entrance when we returned. He looked exactly as you would expect a Dales farmer to look, except bigger. I felt like Jack, shaking hands with the giant.

"Hope you brought wellies," Ted II chuckled as he looked at Jason's expensive Italian boat shoes. I confidently opened the boot of the car and fished out two pairs. One pair was brand new, delivered to me yesterday thanks to Natasha's forward planning, and I handed them to Jason. I pulled on my mud-splattered pair but realised that the large yellow flower prints I was so pleased with at the Leeds festival didn't go down as well with a farmer the size of Huddersfield. Ted II let it go and motioned us towards a battered-looking motor. "We'll take t' Land Rover, and I'll drop you back 'ere later. Hate to think what state your cars would be in if not."

We bounced and clattered along in the ancient machine for the next five minutes. I was in the middle of the front seat with Jason clinging to the door as if his life depended on it. It probably did. Ted II swung extravagantly across to the right as the road bent to the left. The gate was open, and we entered the field. The bouncing increased noticeably, and I was soon in danger of seeing my currant teacakes again. We climbed steadily before coming to a halt by a stile over the wall. We all clambered out, and Ted II pointed out Kettlewell in the valley below us.

"Starbotton is down there, and Hubberholme is on the other side of the valley." He pointed out the villages on the spectacular landscape.

"It's stunning," I said. "But I don't see the shelter."

"It's this way."

Ted II climbed the stile and dropped onto the other side of the wall. We followed him and spotted the two quad bikes, side by side. It was only then that I noticed a short, skinny man of about thirty, sitting with his back to the wall.

"This lazy little bugger is my son, Ted Jr." He nodded and stood up. He wasn't any taller than when he'd slouched by the wall. I couldn't imagine a bigger contrast between Ted II and Ted III. I think I'd be investing in a paternity test kit if it was me, but I kept that to myself. Then it hit me they expected us to ride on the back of the bikes. Jason and Ted III were soon shooting across the field while I tried to squeeze into the space behind Ted II. I got to know him more closely than I wanted.

We skidded to a halt by the shelter. To my surprise, Ted II flicked a light switch as he opened the door and bathed the place in bright light. From the outside, it looked somewhat spooky. To say the location was remote didn't do it justice, but the views were stunning.

"We brought the generator up so you could see it better. You'd have enough power from it to run your gear, lights and whatnot."

I looked around and saw an empty building. Jason looked around and saw another world. He was so enthusiastic, criss-crossing the room, peering through the small windows and pacing out distances.

"Ted. I love it. What about transport?"

"There's a road from the other side of the building where we can move anything big with a tractor. It's just more fun on the bikes. We've got half a dozen of 'em, so getting people up here is no problem."

We moved outside and walked around the building.

"What do you think, Frankie?"

"It's spectacular."

"It's perfect. I think we've just found our primary location."

Ted II beamed as we all shook hands. Half an hour later, we waved to him from the car park in Kettlewell.

"Pint?"

"Pint," I nodded and walked back towards the village and the welcoming Blue Bell.

Today was the start of rehearsals, Monday, November 27th. Waking up early, I had a mix of fear and excitement churning in my stomach. We'd had the workshop where we walked through the script, but today was the day the actors would bring the words to life.

We completed the latest version of the script late on Friday night. Jen had invited me to spend Saturday evening with her and Charley, just like old times. Almost. There was still a little tension on my part. I knew I should open my heart to Jen, tell her how I felt, but I was a coward. We were working well together, and I was desperate not to change that. I'd even resisted asking why she wasn't out with Jason, although it was on my mind all evening.

It was strange being back at the community centre. It was where I'd met Jen, at the writer's workshop and, of course, Robbie. Robbie should've been my wife by now had she not committed fraud on a colossal scale, legged it with all my money and gone to prison.

We rented a big meeting room in the centre as a base for the two weeks of rehearsals. It was still the same tiny team we'd had at the script review. The script had parts for three principal actors with a handful of more minor roles. Dick wanted those to be played by locals with little or no acting experience, and we would cast them next month.

I'd driven the quarter-mile from home as I had two large

cardboard boxes full of scripts, freshly picked up from the print shop. I considered dropping the car back home and returning on foot when a red RAV4 Hybrid pulled into the car park. It was Dick. He'd magically transformed into a ball of pure energy, and, within seconds, I had a dozen jobs to do. The most important was to look after Roddy. Maggie had driven him up the day before and settled him into the small hotel a couple of miles away. She was like a nervous mum, leaving her four-year-old at school for the first time. She headed home after I promised to look after him.

Phil and Alice arrived together and seemed extremely friendly. They were as excited as I was, their exuberance helping set the atmosphere for the first day. Jason called to say he had some issues to sort out in London. Technically, that made me the producer for the day. As far as I could see, that meant, as well as looking after Roddy, I got to take notes for the scriptwriter (also me) and make the trip to the cafe for supplies.

Jen had adopted a very cool bandana for her role as assistant director and certainly looked the part. She seemed at home with the process, whereas I was in a permanent state of confusion. Was it my imagination, or was Jen flirting with Dick?

At the end of an exhausting day, the team dispersed. Dick lived ten miles up the road, so he was driving home. Phil and Alice had opted for a city centre hotel and were last seen in the back of a taxi. Jen had left to pick up Charley, and I drove Roddy to his hotel. We'd asked if he would rather be in the centre of Leeds, but he looked horrified at the prospect. He was reticent in the car. It wasn't like him to be quiet.

"Everything okay, Roddy?"

"Tired, I think."

"It's been a long day. Maggie made me promise to look after you so early night tonight. No sneaking off into Leeds and hitting the clubs."

"Ha. Once upon a time, not now."

He lapsed again into silence. Something was bothering him, so I tried again.

"What do you think of the hotel? It gets good write-ups."

"It's very nice. It's just…"

"Just what?"

"If I'm honest, I hate hotels. They can be lonely places. I miss my stuff, my routine. Even my ding meals."

The poor bloke looked totally forlorn. I spoke before I thought—again.

"Come and stay with me."

"That's very kind, but I couldn't put you out."

"Don't be daft. My house is four hundred yards from the rehearsal room. I've got a perfect spare room. I'd even look good, saving money by cancelling the hotel."

"I don't know what to say. Are you sure it wouldn't be putting you out?"

"Perfectly sure. We just have to promise to limit the brandy! Do we have a deal, then?"

"That would be fab, as the lads used to say. What about my stuff?"

"As soon as we get to the hotel, we'll pack up. How does fish-n-chips sound once we get home?"

"Sounds wonderful."

So, just like that, a bona fide music legend enjoyed his chippy tea and moved into my spare room!

17

From what I could tell, rehearsals had gone well. At least Dick seemed pleased with the first week. Roddy had settled into my spare room. Thanks to being so close to the rehearsal room, he could stick to his schedule. We ate at six, then I handed over the remote for the TV, and he dozed quietly in front of a succession of soaps until he went to bed at ten. A bit of an odd couple, I would keep him company for most of the evening before working on script notes. I even got into the habit of going to bed early, and, thanks to instructions from Maggie, we both stuck to drinking nothing more potent than tea.

Because of this abstemious lifestyle, I was up bright and early on Saturday morning. I had a plan. Maggie's latest suggestion was to make sure Roddy had some exercise. Her actual words were unnecessarily rude, but I took her point. It seemed, given a chance, Roddy would sit in the armchair all weekend but was actually capable of healthy walks. Maggie had packed walking boots and a very natty bobble hat. My boots had seen little action for the last few years, but thanks to the box that had fallen on my head in the cupboard, I knew exactly where they were. I drew my personal line at bobble hats.

With the promise of tea and cake to come, we stepped out into a bitterly cold but sunny November morning. We were on the canal towpath, heading towards Leeds in less than two minutes. The plan was to walk as far as Rodley, where the tea and cake awaited. From there, we could catch the bus home or, feet permitting, walk a big loop and follow the bus route on foot. I reckoned a couple of hours walking, plus a tea break, would see us arriving back home opposite The Crown at around opening time.

Roddy seemed in fine form.

"Any chance of a piece of cake on this walk?"

"Every chance. Like I said, there's a tea shop about an hour away."

"Great. I can't get enough cake. Maggie makes a lovely sponge cake." Roddy looked around at the scenery. "You live in a beautiful part of the world, Frankie, my boy."

"I must admit, I'm guilty of taking it for granted. I haven't walked down here in over a year."

"You should do it more often. I've always loved getting away from everything and breathing the fresh air. You won't believe it, but a love of walking was one of the first things that attracted me to Penny. That and her wonderful chest."

"That's a very impressive coat, by the way."

"Maggie bought it for me. Toasty warm and a million pockets. I find a new one each time I put it on." He did a twirl to emphasise the point.

"I would never have guessed that the rock and roll lifestyle included bright red coats, bobble hats and stout shoes."

"It did at first. Before the drink, drugs and general debauchery set in." Roddy's chuckle soon turned into a full-throated coughing fit. Once he'd settled down again, I continued.

"It must've been a different world at the start of the sixties."

"It certainly was. We were just kids. We had no idea what was going on most of the time. Penny kept writing songs, I kept singin' 'em, and the gold records filled more walls in the big house. They're still there, as far as I know."

"So the house that Penny's in now was your marital home?"

"Yep. Married in '61 and bought the house two years later. We'd basically lived in hotels for two years; always on the road. Then we bought our dream home. We loved it there, right until she slung me out on my arse. Mind you, I could see her point."

"Hope you don't mind me asking, but what went wrong?"

"The Crash."

I stopped walking, causing a young couple with a dog to swerve towards the water. After apologising to them, I looked at Roddy.

"You were involved in a crash?"

"Not so much involved in as involved with. Crash was the drummer in the band. Thunderbolt 3 - Connie Crash."

"Was that her real name?"

"No. Constance De'Ath, believe it or not. Certainly deadly for me being married to Penny."

I was pretty relieved when Roddy made for the bench just ahead. My boots were getting their revenge for spending so long in the scary cupboard. A steady stream of smoke came from the chimney of a brightly painted boat on the far side of the canal. The smell of frying bacon wafted across, and my stomach rumbled. Roddy continued his story.

"It was during filming on *Thunderbolts and Lightning*, the section in the south of France. Penny spent our days off in the hotel room with her guitar, writing songs. I got bored. Crash was fun. Totally potty, actually. She loved playing practical jokes and winding everybody up. I'd always quietly fancied her, but she was head over heels with some photographer when the band got together. He was actually on set with us, taking pictures for a book. One afternoon, she roped me into some prank on the beach. We were wetting ourselves laughing when she grabbed me and started kissing the face off me. I told her I was happily married to Penny, and this was wrong."

"That took some character to tell her that."

"It would if I'd said it there and then, on the beach. As it was, I said it two hours later in Crash's hotel room after an afternoon of frantic shagging."

"Slightly less noble," I said, watching a woman on the boat as she hung washing on a short clothesline.

"I felt like an absolute shit, to be honest. The trouble is I felt like a shit for two years before Penny found out what was going on. Hence, the out on the arse bit."

"I presume she didn't take it well?"

"You could say that." Roddy nodded when I suggested we set off again. "The divorce came through during the biggest bender of my life. It was the weekend that we won the World Cup. Got the papers Friday, match Saturday, woke up on Monday afternoon with two models and a well-known international footballer."

"Which one?"

"Never you mind. Not my proudest moment, and that's saying something."

We started walking again, Roddy stamping his feet as the cold set in.

"Hang on a minute. You went to the '66 World Cup final?"

"One perk of being an international star of stage and screen."

"Alongside three-day benders with a couple of models."

"Tough times."

"Sounds horrendous."

"No, seriously, I was dangerously out of control that year.

They booked us to tour Europe and then back to the UK. I wanted to call it off, but the legal fees would've bankrupted us." Roddy pulled off his hat to scratch his head. "Nearly ready for another sit-down, son. Is there a tea shop around here?"

"Almost there. You can see it up ahead."

"Any chance of cake?"

"I promise there'll be cake."

"I love a bit of cake. Maggie makes a lovely sponge cake."

"So I believe."

"Has she been bragging to you?"

"No. You mentioned it earlier."

Roddy looked at me like I was making this up and replaced his hat. A couple of minutes later, we bagged the last table inside the tea shop and soon had a massive piece of cake each. Once again, Roddy told me how Maggie made an excellent sponge cake. I realised this wasn't the only time he'd repeated things. Last night, he'd recounted how Penny had thrown his gold disc for *Lonely Puppy* across the room at him, leading to four stitches in his forehead. Half an hour later, the same tale, word for word.

The heat inside the tea shop contrasted with the icy blast outside. I rubbed at my cheeks before tentatively approaching my next question.

"You've got some great tales to tell, Roddy. Have you ever thought about writing them down? They'd make a brilliant book."

Roddy shook his head.

"Nah. Nobody'd be interested in me rabbitin' on. Besides, half the buggers would sue my arse off if I told everything. Mind you, more of 'em die off each year." I decided not to push it and changed tack.

"How are the rehearsals going, Roddy?"

"Okay, I suppose."

"Only okay? Is there something bothering you?"

"Don't worry about me. I'll be fine. It's just Dick. He's proper picky for sticking to the script. Jumps on me if I get the odd word wrong or dry up."

"I suppose we keep changing the script. Must make it difficult to learn."

"To be honest, I've never been good at learning lines. When we made *Thunderbolts and Lightning*, they wrote half the words down for me. It meant I could use a prop and just read my lines from them. I had them on the back of my hand, taped to the sun visor in the car, even on the back of somebody's hat. Think of how many scenes I'm in when I'm reading the paper or a book."

"Wow. I'd never have guessed from the finished film."

"Not getting wound up about memorising every detail is where a talented director comes in."

"Do you want me to have a word with Dick? I'm sure we could do something similar."

"That's the ticket. Are you going to finish that cake?" I grinned and pushed the half-finished plate towards him.

"I love cake. Maggie makes a lovely sponge cake."

18

We'd ended up walking all the way home. Thanks to a combination of exercise and an afternoon in the pub, I'd been quite content to join Roddy in his Saturday night routine. We replaced the microwave's ding with the doorbell chime as the pizza arrived. I'd confessed to my guest that I'd never watched *Strictly*. I think he was slightly ashamed of me, but he tried to hide it. He gave me a complete and detailed commentary on every performance. He made the same points as the judges would just a few minutes later on at least three occasions—very impressive.

By eight o'clock, Roddy had been fast asleep in the chair for half an hour. I'd picked up my phone. There was a text from Rupert asking if I fancied a club. I was relieved to reply that I needed to stay with my houseguest.

That turned out to be the highlight of Saturday night. Roddy had woken up at about nine and was on his way to bed by half-past. As a result, we were both up exceptionally early on Sunday morning.

"Can we go for cake at the tea shop?"

"Don't see why not. Are you up for another long walk?"

"Too right. Anything for that cake. Nearly as good as Maggie's. She makes a lovely sponge."

As a result, I'd eased my sore feet back into my boots at stupid o'clock on Sunday morning, and we were off again. Roddy set a fair pace.

"You seem keen."

"It just felt so good to be out and about yesterday. Good to get the heart pumping and a bit of sunshine on the back of the head."

"Do you walk much at home?"

"Not as much as I used to. Maggie chivvies me into it, but she's struggling with her hip these days. She's up to more of a shuffle than a hike."

"You two seem very close."

"She keeps me on the straight and narrow. Don't know what I'd do without her."

"Nothing romantic?"

Roddy let out an evil-sounding chuckle, drawing looks from the couple walking in the opposite direction.

"Not with me, mate. Wrong team, if you know what I mean."

"Ah, I'd no idea."

"No reason you should. Our Maggie's quite a private lady. She spends a couple of nights a week in London with her partner, has done for twenty years. Seems to work for 'em. She reads the news on the telly."

"How far back do the two of you go?"

"I'm her godfather." I paused and looked at Roddy in shock. "Knew that would surprise you. It was a strange choice, granted. Her dad was my manager. She was a bridesmaid when me and Crash got married."

"When was that?"

"It was just after Christmas, January 1967, I think. We did it in secret. Didn't want Penny to find out. There was a big enough stink as it was—after the divorce. We had the big tour to get through."

"Did the plan work?"

"Did it, bollocks. About six weeks into the tour, the shit hit the fan. Bloody *News Of The World* got hold of the story that we'd got married. All hell broke loose. The two of 'em ended up battering each other on stage in Liverpool, right in the middle of the encore. I got in the middle to split them up, and they both battered me. Ended up in the hospital with two broken ribs and concussion."

"They say there's nothing worse than a woman scorned."

"Trouble is, it wasn't the scorned one that did the damage. Crash brained me with a cymbal. Never saw it coming. Cheeky bastards for the *News Of The Screws* came to see me in hospital. Offered me a huge wad for an exclusive."

"Did you tell 'em where to go?"

"No. I took the cash. Needed it for the divorce. Can you imagine being married for six weeks, and she starts down the route of divorcing me? Lovely girl, but..." He shrugged and tapped the side of his head.

Conversation between us flowed freely. Roddy had a mound of stories. He was good at embellishing them just enough to keep them believable whilst ramping up the entertainment value. We should pull these stories together into a book. I wish he'd consider writing his autobiography. We'd reached the tea shop just as it opened, and we had our choice of seats. With tea and cake ordered, Roddy disappeared to the Gents. He'd been gone less than a minute when the woman I took to be the owner made a beeline for me.

"Excuse me. My name's Fran, chief baker and washer-up. I hope you don't mind me asking, but is the gentleman you're with Roddy Lightning?"

"Yes, he's a close friend of mine." I couldn't keep the smile off my face as I spoke.

"Do you think he'd have a picture with me? I'd like to put

it on the wall."

"I'm sure he'd love to. In fact, here he is. Why don't you ask him yourself? Roddy, this is Fran. She baked the cake you were raving about."

Roddy's face lit up.

"Fran. Lovely to meet you. I was telling Frankie that I thought your cake was the nicest I've ever tasted." Fran blushed.

A phone appeared, and Roddy immediately switched to celebrity mode. He posed for pictures with all the staff. It got even better when he was told that the tea and cake were on the house. Roddy went into detail about his favourite cakes, then asked Fran if she baked to order.

"Yes, I do. Special occasions, that sort of thing. My daughter tells me I should have a website, but I don't understand that gubbins. I could give you my phone number. Just give me a ring. I can always get them delivered."

Roddy's face lit up with the news and they exchanged phone numbers. Almost as an afterthought, I asked Fran if she could bake something special for the film crew this week. She added my number to her phone and promised to call later in the week to arrange the delivery. When the fuss had died down, Fran returned to the kitchen, and we tucked into the cake.

"Does that happen a lot?"

"Not as much as it used to."

"You don't mind when people ask?"

"Certainly not. Anyway, we got free cake." Roddy picked at a few stray crumbs on the plate.

"Actually, that reminds me. My mum says she met you. Blackpool Tower ballroom 1979. She was wearing—"

"A white dress? Looked like Debbie Harry. That was your mum? Stone the crows. She was a right—"

"Whoa. Time out. Are you saying you honestly remember

her?"

"Remember her? How could I forget? She was a—"

"Yes. You said. Anyway, she says hello."

"Does she live around here? I'd love to see her again."

"No. She's on the coast. With my dad." I was flustered and poured more tea for us both. A change of subject was in order. "I was thinking about all the stories you've told me. Are you sure you wouldn't be interested in writing an autobiography?"

"Nah. Who'd want to read that?"

"You're kidding. It'd sell loads."

"Are you saying there'd be money in it?"

"Definitely."

"I like the sound of that, but I wouldn't know where to start."

"If only you knew someone who could ghost write it based on what you said."

Roddy thought for a moment.

"I see what you mean. That might work. Do you think Jen would be up for it?"

To say I was crestfallen didn't do it justice.

"Oh. Err, I could—"

Roddy roared with laughter.

"Dozy twonk! It's too easy sometimes. Would you really do that for me?"

"Course I would."

"Do you honestly think there'd be coin in it?"

"Has to be."

"Must admit, that'd be very handy. You must've noticed that I'm in somewhat reduced circumstances these days."

"You mean the caravan?"

"What's wrong with the caravan?" Before I could apologise, the laugh came again. "Relax, it's a shit-hole. I was worried that another winter in it would finish me completely.

When do we start?"

"I think we already have. We'd need to crack on with it to release it alongside the film."

"In that case, we need more cake."

"Somehow, I thought you'd say that."

As we walked back from the tea shop, I got Roddy to tell me about his earliest memories, recording everything on my phone. The stories just flowed out of him. I realised that one of my biggest tasks would be to decide what to leave out. There was also a nagging thought that I may be about to take on too much. There were the inevitable script changes for the film, and whatever a producer had to do. My major fear was letting Roddy down. First, we needed to make the movie and autobiography a success. We had to make enough to set him up in a comfortable house and get him a pension.

Roddy looked at me as we dropped downhill towards The Crown. I had to point out that it was still early, and the pubs didn't open for another hour. We headed for home and were soon at the kitchen table. The stories continued once I'd plugged my phone charger in until Roddy yawned. I encouraged him to go for a nap, and I got to work on an outline for the new project.

It was after two when he reappeared.

"You look busy."

"I figured I needed to make a start. Why don't you take my iPad and read the paper on it?"

"I can't be doing with iPads. What's wrong with a proper newspaper?"

"Nothing, apart from we haven't got one," I said.

"Anywhere around here we can get one?"

"The cafe down the road sells them on Sunday. Give me half an hour, and I'll come with you."

"No worries. I'll pop out and get one, jobs a good 'un. Why

don't you carry on with that?"

"You sure you don't mind? You know where the cafe is?"

"Don't fuss. I'll be fine."

As the front started to close, I called out.

"And stay off the cake. That much sugar is bad for you."

"Yes, Mum." I realised I was mothering him, but I watched through the window as he made his way down the road; just to be on the safe side. He used the pedestrian crossing, a good sign as he must have remembered where the cafe was. He finally dropped out of sight as he went down the hill and over the brow of the bridge.

I returned to my laptop and continued to work. The sound quality on the recording was quite good, and I started making notes. Half an hour later, I stretched my back and wandered back to the window. Roddy should be on his way back, even allowing time for him to have a sneaky sticky bun. There was no sign of him. I was worried but told myself not to be silly as he was a grown man and could go out by himself. However, his memory was a problem. I tried phoning him. It rang for ages, but no reply, not even voicemail. Pulling on my trainers, I grabbed my jacket and headed for the door.

Ildiko was clearing tables on the pavement outside the cafe.

"Hi Frankie, have a seat and I'll be in to take your order in a second."

I explained I wasn't there for my usual coffee and told her about Roddy.

"Yes. He was here. Bought a newspaper and two pieces of ginger cake to go. Left a while ago."

"Did you see which way he went when he left?"

"No. I'm sure he'll be fine. Sorry, it's been hectic today."

"You're right. Roddy will turn up. If he comes back, could you call me?"

"Will do."

I made it official—I was worried now. Nobody had passed me coming up the hill. I checked each side street that led off the main road. Next, I walked down to the canal. He'd be feeding the ducks.

Nothing.

My search would be quicker in the car. I jogged up the hill towards home. The Crown! That's where he'd be.

I was gasping for breath as I burst through the front door. I spotted Ambrose and Stella straight away, with their daughter Olivia. They'd finished eating, and Olivia was colouring in an enormous book. Ambrose stood to get me a drink, but I waved away the offer. I explained about Roddy. He'd not been in. Stella said all the reassuring things you'd expect, but was worried enough to encourage Ambrose to help me with the search. While I ran home to get the car, he set off towards the housing estate to search the streets.

After twenty minutes of frantic searching, I was almost ready to admit defeat. I swung the car into the estate and saw Ambrose up ahead. He jumped in as I pulled alongside.

"Roddy can't just disappear," he said, as he climbed in.

"The old bugger seems to have managed it."

Should I call the police? He'd only been gone for just over an hour. Was I over-reacting? I should call Jen. She'd know what to do. Then again, she might give me a bollocking for misplacing our star performer. I tried Roddy's phone again. Nothing. Ambrose came up with the idea of checking the community centre. We rehearsed there every day. It was worth a try.

Inside the centre, there was a yoga class in the main hall. We headed down the corridor towards the rehearsal room and a locked door.

"I think I need to call Jen, let her know what's going on."

Ambrose agreed.

"It's going to be dark in the next half hour. I'll do another skirt around the side streets. Call me if Roddy surfaces."

"Okay, thanks, Ambrose."

I unlocked the rehearsal room and flicked the light switch. I wasn't sure what I expected to find, but it was undoubtedly a Roddy-free zone. Slumped on a chair, I took the plunge and called Jen.

"Hello, you. I presume your ears were burning. I've just dropped Charley at a birthday party, and she was asking if you could come to tea on Saturday. She misses you."

"I'd love to come. Trouble is, you might not want me when you find out what I've done."

"Who've you slept with?"

"What? No. Nothing like that." Wait a minute. Did she sound jealous? No. Concentrate, you idiot. "I've, sort of, lost Roddy."

"What do you mean, lost him?"

"He went for a walk to get a newspaper. Should've been ten, twenty minutes at most, but he's been gone an hour and a half, and there's no sign of him. Me and Ambrose have been checking all the side streets. He's disappeared. Do you think I should call the police?"

"I'm not sure they'd do anything after less than a couple of hours. Where are you now?"

"I'm at the community centre in case he'd come here. Ambrose is still out and about."

"Okay. Sit tight. I'll be there in five minutes. I'm sure everything will be fine."

She hung up. I pressed redial on Roddy's number, but it just rang and rang. I thought about calling Maggie but realised all that would achieve would be to make her worry. She was three hundred miles away. Best she didn't know. I locked the rehearsal room and went outside to wait for Jen. I was frantic when her car pulled into the space next to the door. She could see I was worried, and I avoided the bollocking, getting a hug instead.

"Thanks for coming. I was running out of ideas for where to try next."

"What about the memorial gardens? Have you tried there?" I shook my head. The gardens were just around the corner. Maybe he was sitting on a bench there? We left the cars and crossed the busy road. As we reached the garden, the traffic noise died away. We peered through the gloom. It was just about dark now, and there was no sign of Roddy.

"Try his phone again." I tried again. "If he doesn't answer, I think it is time to call the police."

"Nothing."

"Shh. Can you hear that?" I listened. Through the darkness, a distant phone was ringing. We started walking towards the sound. It got louder. Then, out of the gloom, a red-coated figure emerged. It was Roddy. I hung up the phone, and the ringing died. We rushed to our errant star.

"Hello, you two. Didn't expect to see you, Jen. How are you?"

"I'm good, Roddy. You had us worried there. Where've you been?" Jen was being very gentle, ushering Roddy to a bench. I wanted to throttle him. I almost shouted at him.

"Why didn't you answer your phone?"

"Well, I could hear the bloody thing ring, but I'm buggered if I know which pocket it's in. There's a million of the buggers." I couldn't help laughing, and the tension evaporated.

"So, where the hell have you been? We were worried."

"Ah well, I've been longer than I thought, granted." Roddy looked guilty and stared at his shoes. "To be honest, I couldn't remember how to get back to your place. I just went kind of blank. Then I saw the canal and remembered where we walked."

"You mean you've been all the way around the loop again?"

"Suppose it does. My feet are killing me now. The tea shop had shut. Lucky for me, I found some ginger cake in my pocket. Not sure how long it had been there, but it was lovely. What's for tea?"

Jen took over.

"How does beef casserole at my place sound?"

"Sounds lovely. I don't think I've been to your house. Have I?"

"No. Come on, the car's just over there."

The prospect of being looked after by Jen for the evening almost reduced me to tears. She looped her arm through Roddy's and led us back to the car park.

Half an hour later, Jen's kitchen was warm, cosy and smelt of casserole. Roddy was fast asleep in the chair.

"Thanks for this, Jen. As usual, I don't know what I'd have done without you."

"You and Ambrose were doing everything you could."

"Shit!"

"Charming."

"Sorry, it's just Ambrose. He's still out looking for Roddy."

"Call him quick."

I felt terrible, but not quite bad enough to tell him the truth, that he'd been out in the cold nearly an hour longer than he should've been. I called his number, and he answered on the first ring.

"Any news?"

"Yes, mate. Roddy's just this second turned up." I crossed my fingers as Jen looked aghast.

"Where are you? Shall I come and meet you?"

"No. I mean, you've done more than enough. Roddy's freezing. We'll get him back to Jen's and get him warmed up. You get back to Stella and enjoy the rest of your weekend.

Thanks for everything."

"No worries. Let's meet up for a pint later in the week."

"You bet. Thanks again."

I hung up and looked guiltily at Jen.

"I never knew you could lie so brazenly."

"It was only a white lie. This way, he feels good that he's done his bit in a crisis."

"Rather than wanting to kill you for forgetting about him. You're all heart. Open that bottle. I think we deserve it. Well, I deserve it. Not sure about you."

19

"And, action."

Just like that, two words from Dick Tate, and we were filming. We were ahead of schedule, but Jen was confident we could do it, which was good enough for me. We were all in the house in Kettlewell, filming the early scenes in Roddy's fictional home. Well, some people were inside. They consigned me to the garden, watching the action on a monitor. There just wasn't room for more than the actors, plus Dick and Jen inside. Jen had added the role of cameraman to her other jobs, another cost-saving that made sense. She'd just worked out how to get the angle to ensure Roddy's cue card wasn't visible once we taped it to the wall.

Even the icy rain couldn't dampen my enthusiasm.

"Cut! Roddy, you need to stick to the lines on the page. Please, let's go again, and, action."

I was worried about Roddy. I'd spent a lot of time with him over the last few weeks. It was a week since he'd gone walkabout, and I'd not let him out of my sight. His memory was a genuine worry. He could recall the most minor facts from thirty years ago and weave them into a sparkling story. Then tell you the same tale five minutes later. Remembering what he'd seen on TV last night was impossible. I felt guilty.

Guilty that I couldn't do more to help him, and guilty that Dad was going through the same experience. I promised myself that I would spend more time with my parents once we finished the film.

Jason flopped into the seat next to me and handed over a coffee. I hadn't expected to, but I enjoyed working with him, even though I knew so little about him. I'd avoided speaking to Jen about his online history. They kept public signs professional but still saw each other outside work. Our role as producers was still unfolding to me on a day-to-day basis. From what I could see, Jason was very good at his job. He watched costs like a hawk, pulling in favours, twisting arms, and being in control. It had been his idea for Jen to get behind the camera again. He'd also made friends with the local amateur dramatic society, filling the minor roles along the way.

Jason almost whispered. I had to lean towards him to hear correctly.

"I just looked at the weather forecast for the next few weeks. Looks like we could have quite a lot of snow."

"That's all I need. I'm bloody freezing as it is," I said.

"I was thinking more about transport. It's fine commuting when the weather's good, but I wouldn't fancy it in a snowstorm."

"What do you think we should do?"

"There's a holiday cottage complex just up the valley. We could get a deal on the job-lot before the holidays. It's worth checking out the pub as well. They do rooms, good food."

"What does that do to the budget?" I asked, pleased that I was thinking like a producer.

"We'd need a good deal, but cheaper than having to delay for a week if we get snowed off. Why don't I see what Natasha comes up with?"

"Sounds like a plan to me." Even better, I didn't have to do anything. Jason went off to phone his assistant, and Roddy slid into his seat.

"Give us a slurp," he said, pointing to the cup. I passed it over.

"Do you want me to get you one?"

"No. I'll be peeing all day if I have a full cup."

"What's going on in there?"

"Just setting up for the next scene. Told me to take ten."

"You sure you wouldn't rather be inside? It's bloody freezing out here."

"I live in a caravan, don't forget! Believe me, this ain't cold. Winter of '76. Now that was cold."

"Before my time, mate."

"I thought it was the end of my time, to be honest."

"Why? What was going on?"

"I was living in a squat in London."

"A squat? But you had the big house, all those hit records, the films."

"After the band split, everything went to shit. I met people who encouraged me to expand my mind. Spent most of the seventies off my tits."

"But you had the solo career."

"Very little memory of that. Besides, have you listened to the *Teddy Bears Of Your Mind* album? What a load of old bollocks. The record company could see that. Dropped me like a stone while I was in prison."

"Prison? What the f—"

"Drugs bust. They made an example of me, Keith, and a few others. I got thirty days, but it may as well have been thirty years. Came out with no record contract, nowhere to live, nothing. I spent most of the next few years kipping on sofas, working in pubs, and fucking up my life with drugs. Somehow ended up in an old Victorian house in London. There must've been ten of us squatting there. The place was better than the streets, but stunk to high heaven. Three of the young kids in there had a band. Well, sort of. Made a dreadful racket, but loads of energy. One night, they were trying to master some Eddie Cochran songs. It amazed them that this scruffy old bugger with no front teeth could actually sing when I joined in on *Something Else*."

"So that was The Rusty Stars?"

"Yep. I joined the band, and we got a couple of gigs in a local pub. Every record label wanted their own punk band, and we got snapped up. Papers made a huge thing about my comeback. I was thirty-seven, in a band with kids half my age. We went from getting a tenner a night to supporting Kiss in six months. Even got my teeth fixed. The trouble was that the management liked the toothless look, so I had to take them out whenever we played. We had an absolute riot for a year. Back and forth to the States."

"Then what happened?"

Roddy blew on his hands. I needed to get him back inside soon, but was desperate to hear the rest of the story.

"Benny, the bassist, reckoned that he was being tracked by the CIA. Took off one night. Too many mushrooms. Turned up in Iceland three months later. By then, we'd all fallen out and gone our separate ways. Suppose it worked out okay for me. The new profile meant I could put a new band together. Roddy And The Thunderbolts were reborn. We toured most of the seaside resorts that summer."

"That'd be when you met my mum in Blackpool."

"The white dress; looked like Debbie Harry."

"So you said. Not sure I want to know."

"You wouldn't believe what—"

"Roddy. Roddy, where the hell are you? We're ready to go again."

It was Dick from inside the house. Roddy was still chuckling as he disappeared through the front door.

* * *

At four o'clock, it was dark and cold. The novelty of sitting in my producer's chair had worn off, at least for today. I was trying to get some feeling back to my feet when I heard Dick wrap things up for the day.

"Okay, that will do for tonight. Can we just have five minutes inside? Jason wants a word, and I'd like to say thanks for a great effort. One day down, we are on our way."

There was a trickle of applause, and I was extremely grateful to make my way into the house. Although no heating was on, it felt a good ten degrees warmer than outside. I slipped my shoes off by the door to protect the carpets.

Jason gave his little pep talk, echoing Dick's thanks to the team before the local actors trooped out. With the core team remaining, Jason explained the weather forecast. Unfortunately, the cottages were unavailable, but Natasha had secured enough rooms at the pub in the village. The plan was to check in tomorrow for the next week. Roddy didn't look happy. I'd need to reassure him we could still have our routine. It should be easier without the long drive at either end of the day.

Jen was next to speak, running through the scenes we aimed to complete the following day. I made a note to print off Roddy's crib sheets later. I was getting quite skilled at secreting them on the set.

Dick wrapped the meeting up.

"Right, back here for an eight-thirty start tomorrow. Have a good evening, everybody, and well done." There was a round of applause, and everybody gathered their things and headed for the car park. Roddy waited by the door as I pulled my shoes on. Jason was busy inside, turning off lights and getting ready to lock up for the night.

"That seemed to go well. How did you enjoy being back on a film set?"

"I'd forgotten how much sitting around there was. Mind you, that's one thing I'm good at doing these days."

I looked at Roddy's slightly stooped frame. "You must be tired."

"Knackered, son. Bed after Corrie for me tonight."

His memory may be a problem, but he still knew the schedule for all his soaps. We were halfway across the village when I realised I'd left my script on a chair when sorting out my shoes. I gave Roddy the car keys, and Jen took his arm to escort him the rest of the way.

I set off at a pathetic jog; my legs were stiff from a day sitting outside in the cold. At least the lights were still on at the house. The script was where I'd left it, on the chair in the hall. I grabbed it, and several loose pages fell to the floor. Cursing fluently, I coaxed my stiff body to bend and gather the pages. I could hear Jason talking in the other room. He was on the phone. I couldn't help hearing the end of the conversation.

"Don't worry. I'll be home at the weekend. We can do something special with the kids then. I know they miss me when I'm away, just like I miss all of you. Look, I'll be back at the hotel before the kids go to bed, so I'll call again later. Okay, darling, speak to you at about seven. Bye."

I felt terrible for listening, but one thing seemed pretty obvious. Jason was married with kids. He was clearly messing Jen about and doing the dirty on his wife? What a twat. Deciding this was not the time to confront him, I sneaked out of the front door and hurried back to the car park. Jen was talking to Roddy beside my car. As I got closer, she kissed Roddy, waved to me, and set off to her car.

"Jen." I had to tell her. Then again, it was no surprise when it turned out I was a coward. "Be careful. Give my love to Charley." I waved as she drove off into the night.

"Come on, son, get the heater on. It's chuffing freezing

here."

"That's a quaint northern phrase you've picked up there."

"I'm an actor, darling. I do all the accents."

"Get in. Chippy on the way home?"

"Delightful idea, old boy."

I started the engine. Radio Four burst into life. There was a news report that scientists at Wuhan in China had traced the cause of the 2002 outbreak of the SARS virus to bats.

"Bloody depressing thought, let's have some music. I am a rock' n' roller, you know." I pushed the button for Radio Two, and Blondie's *Union City Blue* filled the car. "That's more like it. This reminds me of your mum in that little white dress."

"Behave, or it's back to Radio Four."

"This was out when I toured the states at the end of 79. I got to meet them after one of their shows. We shared a record plugger. Has to be said, he was better at plugging Blondie singles than he ever was with mine." Roddy reflected for a moment. "Maybe their singles were better than ours."

"How long were you over there?"

"Well, the tour was for three months, but I ended up staying ten years."

"How come?"

"One of the dodgy deals I had to thank a former manager for was getting me an American passport. Don't ask. Anyway, the band had to come home when their visas ran out, but I was sort of seeing somebody. She was married at the time, so no names."

"What a gent."

"Always. Anyway, I landed a nice little earner, singing jingles for TV and radio ads. Not as glamorous as I'd have liked, but it paid the bills. It also led to getting a toehold on US TV. It was a daytime soap. They needed an English actor. After doing it for two years, I got the call that changed everything."

It hit me I should record this for the book and fiddled with my phone while staring as the headlights picked out the first snowflakes. I nudged the radio volume down.

"So, who was the call from?"

"Rumble." I was about to question him when I realised that Rumble was Thunderbolt Four, the bass player. "Now, she was a stunning-looking woman. My soulmate, too. Renata Stich. Six feet tall, blond and beautiful. Since the band split up, she'd lost the German accent from living in the States. She'd made it big in the movie industry. Anyway, she'd landed the lead role in a series called *Black Gold*. It was a total *Dallas* rip-off, but they were looking to cast her British husband and did I fancy auditioning? I saw from the script that there were regular bedroom scenes with Renata, so nobody was going to stop me from getting that part. I woulda crawled over broken glass to get it."

The show was a genuine success. What I now knew also went a long way to explaining why my mum had been so obsessed with it. She'd watched all the repeats when I was a kid.

"We did five seasons, huge hit, made us both big stars. We coined it in. Do they do battered sausages?"

"What?"

We were approaching the chippy. Roddy pointed. It always impressed me how Roddy's stomach immediately overrode anything else that was going on. One second, he was telling me the story of how he worked with the love of his life. The next, totally focused on battered sausages.

20

Day two of filming was 'in the can', as we movie producers say. We had moved the entire team into the pub as planned. They had a booking for dinner at eight, but I was conscious of Roddy's schedule. As a result, the two of us were in the cosy bar awaiting homemade steak pie, to be served on the stroke of six o'clock. I told Roddy about the email that had arrived this afternoon.

"Good news! In principle, my agent has a publisher that is interested in your autobiography, as ghostwritten by yours truly."

"That is good news. How much?" Roddy was always good at getting straight to the point.

"That remains to be seen. The publisher has a couple of conditions, though."

"Oh yeah. What sort of conditions?"

"Nothing too bad. It'll be conditional on the film being released. They see it as crucial that it rides on the back of the publicity from the film."

"Best get your finger out and get it written, then!" Roddy let rip with that familiar, rattling laugh.

"No pressure."

"What's the other condition?"

"They want you to have a social media presence."

"What's one of them when it's at home?"

"You heard of Instagram?"

Roddy's face was utterly blank.

"Facebook?"

Same result.

"Twitter?"

"Now you're just saying random words."

"Don't worry. We'll take care of it. Lucky for you, I part-own a company that will set you up with all you need. I'll speak to my mate Spud in the morning. Speaking of spuds, look at that."

The waiter had arrived with the most enormous plates of food I'd seen in years. Roddy looked at the plate, then at me.

"I'll never get through that lot. You trying to fatten me up or something?"

I knew that conversation would be one-sided as Roddy tackled the enormous plate. It was almost twenty minutes before Roddy spoke again.

"Very nice, that. What's for pudding?"

"Thought you said you wouldn't get through it? You've polished off the lot."

"Hungry work, being a film star."

"How does spotted dick sound?" Roddy was about to say something smutty, but I silenced him with my best Maggie impression. He settled for a thumbs up.

"Heaven. You don't know how much I missed spotted dick when we lived in California all those years. Not much chance of getting a chef over there to make it for you."

"Is that where you filmed *Black Gold*?"

"Yeah. Home for five years. I proposed to Renata under the Hollywood sign. On one knee and everything. For reasons only known to her, she said yes. Bless her. She was the absolute love of my life."

Roddy was suddenly quite emotional and brushed away a tear with the back of his hand. The waiter arrived to take away the empty plates.

"Hope he's not bothering you, gents?" He grinned and nodded at the stuffed toy on the shelf behind me. "The landlord's daughter loves her elf on a shelf. She comes in and moves it to a different place every morning. You'd be amazed where it pops up."

"Cute. How old is she?"

"Twenty-seven." That threw me. I ordered two desserts, and the waiter wandered off. Roddy had composed himself.

"You were talking about your wedding. What year was that, Roddy?"

"1986 - I was 47 and getting married for the third time. All to Thunderbolts."

"And in the right order - two, three, then four. So what about five? How did she get left out?"

"Toni? Toni Truelove. She knocked me back, good and proper. An absolute genius with playing keyboards. Voice of an angel. Well, if angels drank whiskey and smoked forty a day."

"So you tried?"

"Oh, I tried. Nearly succeeded too. Then she got wind of me cheating on Penny with Crash. Told me I was immature and to go away and grow up. Not quite the words she used, but that was the gist. We lost touch when the band split. Not seen her for fifty years. The one that got away. Or rather, the one that told me to fuck right off. Still, I wouldn't change marrying Renata. A total joy, that woman. Even when they cancelled *Black Gold*, she just shrugged and said, 'What do you want to do now?' I told her I wanted to go home. We upped sticks to the Cotswolds and bought the manor - right on the banks of the Windrush. Became the country gentleman. Absolutely loved everything about that time."

"Renata obviously made you complete. Hope you don't mind me asking, but what went wrong?" Roddy welled up again. "Sorry, I shouldn't pry."

Roddy held up a hand and quietly slipped out of his seat. He gestured towards the Gents and was gone. I wondered about going after him, but decided he just needed a minute. Renata obviously still meant so much to him.

Within seconds, I noticed the smell. Please, God, don't let that be pudding or, even worse, Roddy in the loo. The source became apparent as the straggly beard slid into Roddy's seat. It leaned into eye-watering proximity. Even with my back arching to its full extent, I could feel the hot breath as it spoke.

"Sorry to bother you, but would I be right in thinking that your dining companion is 'im off the films? Singer. Shagged everything what moved when he was younger? He must be worth a fortune. What's he doing 'ere?"

I wondered how to remain polite but tell this thing to fuck off when the landlord did it for me.

"Sam Johnson. On your bike. Stop bothering my customers. You know you're barred from here. Sling your hook and leave this gentleman in peace."

"Just offering him a gift. Courtesy, like." With that, he opened his long coat. Two pheasants hung from a strap around his chest. They could've accounted for the smell, but I couldn't confirm. "Take your pick. I'll only eat one of 'em."

"Out. Now."

The landlord looked fierce. Sam Johnson slid out of the seat and made for the door, shouting as he went.

"Only being friendly. Well, you can forget that now. Shit pub anyway."

As the door bounced on its impressive hinges, all that remained of our visitor was the smell.

"Sorry about that, sir. Resident villain. Harmless, really,

except to the local wildlife. Bloody lethal if you're a rabbit or a pheasant. He won't bother you again."

Roddy emerged from the toilet, sniffed the air and gave me a very accusing look. I was about to explain, but the waiter returned with more huge portions. Roddy had recovered quickly and tucked in.

"Renata got ill. We'll talk about that another time, if you don't mind. Right now, I'm gonna enjoy this, then upstairs for Eastenders. Cheers."

He downed the last of his beer and returned to the spotted dick.

With Roddy safely in Albert Square, I was back in my room, directly above the bar. I propped myself up against the headboard and pulled my laptop towards me. Within an hour, Roddy had a brand new email address and profiles on all the major social media platforms. I emailed Maggie to explain what I was doing and asked her for help. Could she provide old photos from the years of the band and his TV career? The second favour on the list was from Spud. He agreed it sounded like the perfect project for the new trainee in the office and would get onto it first thing tomorrow. I put together a pack for him with account details, passwords and a rudimentary bio for Roddy.

After all of that, I decided I deserved a pint. There was no sign of the team in the dining room, but I heard laughter in the bar. Dick was holding court, telling some convoluted tale of film sets past. Jen obviously found the payoff hilarious and seemed comfortable sitting close together. Was there something being revived there? Dick waved me across and made a big show of getting a round in. I know it's childish, but as he went to the bar, I slid into the seat next to Jen.

Everybody was happy and wanted to know if Roddy was

okay. I explained his routine, and they all agreed I was looking after him well.

"No sign of Jason?" I asked, looking around the table. It was Jen who replied.

"He had some phone calls to make, then he's getting an early night. I'll be joining him after this drink." All eyes were suddenly on Jen. "Oh God, no. That didn't sound right. I meant joining him as in getting an early night, not, you know, joining him, in the same room or anything."

"Hey, it's a free country," said Alice. "Nobody would judge you. Jason, he's a bit of all right for an old bloke."

"Old? How old do you think he is?" I was a bit more indignant than I'd intended.

"I don't know. About my dad's age. Forty-two, something like that. Keeps himself in shape, though. He'll still look good when he gets to your age."

My mouth was opening and closing, but no words were coming out. Jen found this hilarious. She looked at Alice.

"How old do you think Frankie is?"

"About fiftyish, I think." Jen almost passed out; she laughed that much.

"I'll be forty next summer, thank you very much." Alice didn't miss a beat.

"The landlord says I can use the lounge to do my pilates in the morning. You'd be very welcome to join me."

"It's still not too late to remove the female kidnapper from the script, you know. We could give her a nasty illness or have her eaten by wolves."

"Ignore him, Alice. I'll join you if that's okay. I need to be done by eight to call Charley at her gran's. How about seven?"

"Perfect. What about you, Frankie?"

"Sorry, I've got grown-up work to do." I quietly sucked my gut in and willed Dick to get back from the bar. I needed a drink.

The conversation moved on, and Dick took a seat next to Phil. I couldn't help thinking about what Alice had said. Not so much that I looked older than Jason, although maybe I should do something about that. No, it was the fact that I was almost 40. What had I achieved? Things picked up in the last couple of years. The new writing career was actually earning me money. I now had a house, a share in an IT company, and I was making a film. The glaring bit, in big letters, was that I was still single, with no real prospect of that changing. I'd come close last year with Robbie, but now I was alone. I thought about my recent house guest, fast asleep in the room upstairs. By the time he was 40, he'd been married twice, divorced twice, had a career as a teen idol pop star, made films and was about to become a global TV star.

Right. The time was right to make some changes in my life. First, I was going to get fit and lose weight. I would cut down on my drinking. Not yet; Dick had just got a round in. First thing tomorrow, come rain or shine, I was going for a run.

21

The following morning, I was still fired up. Fair enough, we'd spent another couple of hours in the bar last night, but, even with a slight hangover, this was the new me. I pulled on my tracksuit bottoms. I'd brought them with me for slobbing around in the privacy of my room, but now they were my running kit. My trainers had seen better days, but my *War On Drugs* tee shirt was cool. I made my way downstairs, not wanting to attract any attention. The cleaner was busy mopping the bar floor as I opened the pub's front door.

"Fuck," I said, to myself. The snowdrift that came to the door must've been two feet deep. It covered the entire village in a thick white blanket of silence. There was a road and a river, but it was impossible to decide where.

"Bollocks to it. I'm off for breakfast."

I would start my fitness campaign with a full English and coffee that you could stand a spoon up in. These things take time.

Talk at the breakfast table at first was all about the snow. It was a relief that we'd planned for this and moved to the village. Phil was the first to notice he had a new, rather famous follower on Instagram.

"Roddy. Just noticed you followed me. I followed you

back. Never knew you were even on here."

"On what?"

"Instagram."

"What the f—"

I stepped in to save the delicate ears of the young family in the corner.

"I set you up on it, Roddy. Don't you remember? We talked about getting you a social media presence."

Alice took over.

"Here, let me show you how it works." I told Alice Roddy's password. Seconds later, Alice was giving him the full tutorial. I wondered how much of it would stick, but he seemed enthusiastic. I wished we could say the same for Dick. He looked decidedly grumpy. I picked up my coffee, moved to his table, and joined Jen and Jason.

"I gather from the looks on your faces we have a problem."

Dick nodded.

"You could say that. It's the snow. I know we are shooting indoors for the next couple of weeks, but there are windows. We set this in the summer. Kind of confuses things if it is deep and crisp and even outside. We're also shooting scenes out of sequence, so we're in danger of snow in one scene, disappearing in the next, only to return two minutes later."

"Shit."

"Spot on. It's always good to work with a true wordsmith."

I ignored that.

"So, what do we do?"

Jen was deep in thought.

"Could we bring forward the scenes in the barn? There are no windows to worry about if we shoot those scenes over the next week. Then we're taking a break over Christmas. The snow should be gone by the time we get back."

Dick nodded. "That's doable, but there must be three feet of snow on the hills. How do we get all the gear up there?

Not to mention our aged star?"

"Leave it to me," I said. "Let me make a call."

Ted II answered on the second ring.

"Ted, sorry to bother you. It's Frankie." I could hear a loud engine ticking over.

"Thought you might be calling. Do I take it you have some snow down in the village?"

"Tons of the stuff. What's it like up on the tops?"

"Clear as a bell."

"Yeah?"

"Is it buggery! It's up to my arse, and my arse is a long way from the ground. How can I help?"

In my best pathetic and pleading voice, I explained the problems and asked if there was any way we could get up to the barn.

"Well, I've already got the snowplough on the tractor. Just cleared the lane up to the farm. Reckon it'll take me a couple of hours to get the village opened up. We'd have to make multiple trips on the quad bikes, but I reckon it's doable. Be ready for 11, okay?"

"Cheers, Ted. I owe you one."

I hung up and went back to the breakfast table. Jen, Dick, and Jason had their heads together over a notepad.

"Sorted," I beamed. "Ted's going to get us up there with all the gear. He'll be here in a couple of hours. I reckon it's time for feet-up in front of the fire with coffee and more toast."

Jen gave me one of her looks.

"Nice try. We have props and cue cards to make. If Roddy is shooting scenes from later in the schedule, there's no way he'll remember the lines. We need to get creative with the prompts. Plus, we need a ransom note. We have one mocked up, but it's back in the office at home. Lucky for you, we've done a deal with the shop in the village. A sort of exchange. They're providing a pile of magazines, cards, glue and scissors."

"That's great. You said an exchange. Are they after a part in the film?"

"Not quite. We've volunteered you, Jason and Phil for snow clearing around the village. The shovels are by the door."

"Bugger. I suppose we should put something back. We need to be done by eleven. Come on, then."

22

We met in the bar on Thursday night for our early meal date. Roddy hunched over his phone, grinning as I slid into a seat.

"You're looking very pleased with yourself."

"It's this Insta-thingy. I love it."

"I spoke to my mate Spud. He's got somebody lined up to create content for you and manage the posts. He's on holiday this week, so he will get cracking when he gets back."

"No idea what all that means, but I've got three thousand and twelve followers. They seem to like my selfies."

"How did—"

"Alice helped me. Everybody's being so nice, sending me messages and stuff." The stuff bit was a little worrying, but he seemed more than happy and already had over three thousand followers. "Smile!" Roddy twisted in his seat and took a selfie, with me grinning in the background. "Now, a quick filter, caption and post."

I was open-mouthed. How had Alice shown him all this in a way that he could remember? At that moment, our lasagnes arrived. Roddy forgot the phone in a heartbeat. We chatted about how the film was going.

"I think you've created a great little team here. In films I've been in before, we had hundreds of people fussing with lights, cameras, and makeup. They'd spend hours setting up cameras and stuff."

"Don't forget the rest of the team that operates out of the big buses in the car park." I still had no idea what they all did, but Jason told me we need them. "I suppose the primary team is quite compact. Part modern technology making it easier."

"It helps that Jason's as tight as a duck's chuff," Roddy cackled.

"A rock-bottom budget helps too. I never knew Jen was such a wizard with lights and cameras. She seems to do about eight different jobs. The people from the village have been great as extras. We also dropped lucky with the local hairdresser being such a dab hand with the makeup."

Roddy was impressive, the way he tackled the huge portions on offer. He seldom paused between mouthfuls, then asked a question.

"Who was the bloke hanging around today?"

"How do you mean?"

"Some scruffy-looking bugger, big coat, beard. Like he was watching. Every time I went outside for a coffee or a breath of fresh air, there he was."

"I didn't notice. Maybe from the village, interested in the film. Not every day they get film stars in their midst."

"Suppose not. Warm in here tonight."

Roddy shrugged out of his jacket and hung it over the back of his seat. It slid to the floor, and several pieces of paper and a half-eaten KitKat fell from the inside pocket.

"Bugger."

"Here, let me." I leant across and started picking up the papers. They were copies of his lines, neatly cut up to be secreted on the set. I shoved them back in his pocket and replaced the jacket on the chair-back. I put the KitKat on the table. "The system with the cues seems to work well."

"Couldn't cope without it, to be honest. It's even better now. Jen made the print bigger."

I was enjoying the lasagne until a familiar evil smell erupted. Looking over my shoulder, I could see the scruffy black coat in the doorway. What had the landlord called him? Johnson? That was it. Sam Johnson. His host was currently blocking his route and instructing him in the ways of buggering off.

"Is that the bloke that was hanging around today?" I nodded to the door.

"What bloke?"

"The one in the doorway, scruffy, black coat."

"What about him?"

"Was he the one hanging around today?"

"Where?"

"At the barn."

"What barn?"

"Never mind. How was the lasagne?"

"Lovely, thanks. I'm stuffed to the gills."

The landlord came across and apologised for the floorshow. As he cleared the plates, Roddy barely missed a beat.

"What's for pudding, son?"

"Tonight, we have rhubarb crumble and custard."

"Lovely. Two of them over here when you've got a minute."

I looked at him and shook my head.

"What?"

"Nothing. I just don't know where you put it all. Don't think I didn't notice you scoff that KitKat, too. Look at you. There's not an ounce of fat on you."

"Can't fatten a thoroughbred son. That's what my old dad used to say. Toni, now she was different—always on a diet. Looked stunning, mind."

"I take it she avoided the carbs?"

"Carbs? We didn't have carbs in my day, son. Life was a lot simpler back then."

"What's that you've made?" Roddy had been fiddling with the silver foil from his chocolate.

"It's a flower. Thought it would make a nice buttonhole for your elf mate." I reached behind and attached the flower before putting the elf back on the shelf.

23

Not a cloud in the sky. A gentle breeze and the steady, rhythmic waves lap towards my feet. Running my fingers through the sand, waiting for Jen to finish her swim, I recognised the Style Council's *Long Hot Summer* drifting on the breeze. Roddy and Keith Richards were showing off, riding the quad bikes along the water's edge. Miss Banks, my history teacher, was starting up the bingo machine. The music was getting louder. I twisted on my sunbed, and as darkness fell, the music changed to *Chelsea Dagger* and was now very loud.

Shit.

I reached out into the cold air and snoozed my alarm.

Friday. We had a couple of days at home coming up. We'd discussed continuing through the weekend, but Jen wanted to get home to Charley. Better to have a break and get stuck in again on Monday. Besides, I would need to either do some laundry or go shopping for more underwear. I realised I would need to extend the offer to Roddy. Not sure how I felt about washing an old man's smalls. I told myself it was all part of being an international film producer and hauled my arse out of bed.

My 'running kit' was in the chair by the window. For a

moment, I considered starting my new regime, then assured myself it could be dangerous in the snowy conditions. Instead, I pulled on my jeans and threw open the curtains. The snow was almost gone.

Bugger.

In my defence, it was lashing down. A full English it was then. Phil was the only person in the dining room. I pulled out the chair opposite and sat down.

"Morning, Phil. Quiet today. Where is everybody?"

"Alice is just doing her hair." He almost knocked over his coffee. "I assume. I assume she's doing her hair. She usually does, in the morning, that is. I think."

"Relax, Phil. I assumed something was going on from the first script walkthrough."

"Please, say nothing to the others. I'd hate Alice to think I'd been indiscreet."

"Alice's honour is safe with me, don't worry."

Just then, Dick, Jason and Jen followed each other into the dining room and joined us at the long table. There was soon a steady buzz of conversation. Everybody was looking forward to the weekend off, but pleased about how things were going. As usual, Dick was grumpy about continuity. This time, the lack of snow was the cause, but Jen calmed him down. She finished her muesli.

"Anybody seen Roddy this morning?"

"Not like him to be late for food," I said, just as my full English with extra egg arrived.

"I'll give him a knock." I caught a faint trace of Jen's perfume as she slipped away from the table. Two minutes later, she was back.

"There's no sign of him. He'd left his door unlocked. He's not there." Jen sounded worried. I tried to reassure her.

"Hang on, I'll try his mobile." I picked up my phone in one hand and a piece of toast in the other. "No answer. He'll have it on silent again. Either that or he can't track it down in his coat of a million pockets. I'm sure he's just gone for a bit of fresh air. No need to worry."

"Who in their right mind goes for a bit of fresh air with rain hammering down like this?"

I had to admit to a slight concern. As a precaution against what I could see coming, I picked up the pace, demolishing my breakfast. I was less than halfway through when Jen spoke again.

"I think we should look for him."

Alice was first up.

"I'll check the lounge upstairs."

Phil was next.

"I'll check with the staff in the kitchen, see if they've seen him."

I shovelled half a sausage in as Jen raised an eyebrow. Seconds later, Alice and Phil returned, shaking their heads. By now, everybody was on their feet and heading to get coats. I looked at the egg and two rashers of bacon on my plate.

"Oy." Jen's look said it all. I grabbed a piece of toast and pushed back the chair. "That's better," said Jen. I dipped the toast in the egg yolk as she headed upstairs and followed her.

Five minutes later, our small team searched the village under leaden skies. Phil and Alice trekked over the bridge while Jason headed right on the road towards the barn. Dick was to check the car park. Jen and I set off to do an anti-clockwise tour of the village. The place was tiny. He can't be far away.

Fifteen minutes later, we were all back at the pub. Roddy had disappeared. We trooped back into the dining room, and coffees appeared almost instantly.

"Should we call the police or something?" I asked, once again looking to Jen to take charge.

"When was the last time anybody saw him?"

"I had dinner with him as usual. I haven't seen him since he went to his room about 7.30ish."

Alice was next to speak.

"He called me about ten minutes later. I've been showing him how to use Instagram and Twitter. During the day, I'd shown him Google. He was excited about it, but couldn't remember what it was called. I talked him through how to get on and heard no more from him."

"So," said Jen. "It's been twelve hours since anybody had contact with a seventy-eight-year-old man with dementia. I think we need to call the police." Jim, the landlord, nodded and pulled out his phone. It took twenty minutes for an officer to drive from Skipton.

Jim greeted him by name and ushered him into the dining room when he arrived. He took down the details and reassured us we'd done the right thing.

"So, will you put out an APB?" I asked.

"A what, sir?"

"APB - you know, all-points bulletin."

"We're in the Dales, sir, not Dallas. I'm sure there's a perfectly innocent explanation. We'll circulate the picture and get our patrols to keep an eye out for him. If he doesn't turn up this morning, I'll have a word with the big boys in Bradford."

Once the policeman had left, I phoned Ted II and explained the situation. He didn't hesitate to volunteer his 'boys' to use the quad bikes to scour the surrounding countryside. Jen and I did another couple of laps of the village, telling everybody we saw what had happened. There wasn't much more we could do.

After lunch, we agreed I would stay on at the pub for when Roddy surfaced, but everybody else may as well go home. Jen was keen to get back to Charley. Dick was going to edit the scenes we had already. Alice and Phil headed into Leeds. I waved them off and promised to keep in touch over the weekend.

24

By four o'clock, the light was all but gone. I called off my latest fruitless village tour and returned to the pub. The fire kicked out a lovely warmth as I sipped my tea. The homemade scone sat untouched. Where could Roddy be? I'd already thought the worst, but forced myself to be positive.

"Mr Dale. Good afternoon." The face was familiar, but took a moment to register. It was DI Cagney. His sidekick, Casey, was beside him as usual. "I understand you've reported a missing person."

"Yes. Please, take a seat. Can I organise tea, scones?"

Casey perked up, but soon realised his mistake and adopted Cagney's dour expression.

"No, thank you, sir. Just a few questions, if we may." I nodded. They both took out notebooks. "I believe you were the last person to have seen Mr—" He flicked over the page in his notes. "Lightning?" He looked at Casey. "Lightning?"

"Yes, sir. That's right. I believe it's a stage name. Mr Lightning was a singer in the sixties."

A look of triumph washed over Cagney's face. He returned his gaze to me.

"I thought I knew the name. What's he up to these days?"

"I'm hoping you can tell me; he's missing." Cagney stared

at me, and I apologised. "We're working together. Roddy is starring in a film that we're making. We've been filming here for the last week."

"We?"

I ran through the rest of the team's names and said I could provide contact details for each of them. Cagney continued asking questions about when I'd last seen Roddy, how he'd been and whether he had any enemies.

Then, a rather alarming bad penny dropped.

"Hang on a minute. Are you treating me as some kind of suspect?" I couldn't keep the edge of alarm out of my voice.

"Well, you have form in that respect, sir, if you don't mind me saying."

"Well, I do mind, actually. You may wish to remind yourself that I was a victim of serious fraud in that case. I also helped you put away a dangerous criminal and his daughter, who just happened to be my fiancée. Not to mention implicating the head of the council, unearthing corruption that went back years."

"Like I said, sir, form."

"As a witness, not a criminal." Exasperated, I looked at Casey for support. He shrugged.

"Morse would say the last person to see the victim was the killer," said Casey.

My heart rate went through the roof.

"Killer? What the f—. Have you found a body? Is it Roddy? Where?" If looks could kill, Cagney would be on a murder charge. Casey slumped in his seat and eyed my scone.

"No need to get agitated, sir. My colleague was not suggesting that Mr Lightning has come to any harm, merely that we must get a clear picture of how he came to disappear."

I made eye contact with Casey and slowly reached out for

the scone. I took a bite. The look of disappointment on his face was satisfying. Cagney continued.

"Look. We have all North and West Yorkshire patrols looking for Mr Lightning. I'm sure he'll turn up safe and well. In the meantime, we wouldn't be doing our job right if we didn't treat his disappearance as a potential crime."

"Makes sense, I suppose." I had to take a drink of tea. The scone was now stuck to the roof of my mouth.

"Right. I take it you have rooms here at the pub?" I nodded. "In that case, we'll need to search them, just in case. I suggest you go home and wait by the phone. As soon as there is news, we'll be in touch."

"I'll need to get my stuff."

"Afraid not, sir. You could remove evidence."

"I'd only be removing my dirty washing."

"We'll make sure no harm comes to it. Now, if you'll excuse us, we need to close the pub and begin our investigations."

They both stood up. Casey narrowed his eyes as I reached out and stuffed the rest of the scone into my mouth. They went through to the kitchens, presumably spreading good cheer and shutting down the pub. I poured another cup of tea and pondered what to do next. Two minutes later, Jim strode towards the front door. He slid home the central bolt and came over to join me.

"What a charmless wanker he is."

"I take it you mean the delightful DI Cagney?"

"Wanker."

"Look, I'm sorry about all this, having to close and everything."

"Don't worry about that. Not your fault. I just hope the old guy is all right. It's been great having you all here this week, especially Roddy. He's a lovely old bugger."

"He is. You're right. They want me to go home and wait there."

"That's maybe for the best. Don't worry about the rooms. At least if we're closed, I can join Ted and the rest of the villagers."

"Why, what's happening?"

"Hadn't you heard? Ted organised a search of the hills. Everybody's meeting in the car park at five, mountain rescue, cave rescue - the lot. You name it, they're coming. If he's out there, we'll find him. I suggest you get yourself off home, so you're ready for him when he turns up."

I shook Jim's hand, grabbed my jacket, and set off to the car park. Had I known what was about to happen, I suspect I would've stayed.

Looking back, I could remember nothing of the drive home. I suppose I'd been crawling along in the rush hour traffic, but my mind was racing all the time. What could've happened to Roddy? Could he have gone for a walk and forgotten how to get home? The last time he'd done that, he'd caught a memory of our weekend walks and simply retraced the familiar route. The road from the pub and the barn would be the only course he would know in the Dales. Jim and the searchers would've found him by now, wouldn't they? Could he have simply gone to the wrong pub? I pictured him sitting in the bar, wondering where we'd all disappeared to. The trouble with that one was the same as most scenarios. Somebody from the village would've seen him.

I let myself into my lovely warm house and ran a bath. As I eased into the slightly too hot water, my phone rang. Had they found him? It was Jen.

"Any news?"

"Not really. Oh, Cagney and Casey turned up."

"The two detectives from last year took all the credit for your work?"

"And they treated me as a suspect once again."

"Suspect? What do they think's happened?"

"No idea, but they were searching the rooms at the pub. Wanted me out of the way. I've just got home."

"It would've been good to invite you round for tea, but I'm staying at my mum's. Payback for looking after Charley all week."

The thought of a meal at Jen's was comforting, but I would have to wait.

"How is Charley?"

"She's bouncing off the walls. I suspect too much sugar and e-numbers while I've been away. She seems very pleased to have me back. Once Roddy surfaces, both of you come around for a meal. We should invite Maggie, too."

"Shit! Maggie doesn't know yet." I almost dropped the phone as I sat bolt upright, sloshing water over the floor.

"I think you need to call her before the police do."

"I'm on it. Speak later. Bye."

The bath was no longer having the relaxing effect I was aiming for. I dried myself off but left the sopping floor to look after itself. As I pulled my fleece over my head, I was already calling Maggie. The phone rang for ages. I was dreading the voicemail kicking in. What the hell would I say? Then there was a click, and Maggie was there.

"Maggie, hi, it's Frankie."

"Oh, it's lovely to hear from you. How was the first week of filming?"

"It's gone really well until today."

"Why, what's wrong?"

"Look, I don't want you to worry, but we've lost Roddy." There was a kind of shriek and whimper on the phone. "Oh, no, not lost as in lost him. Sorry, I mean lost as in misplaced him. He's sort of gone missing." Maggie was crying.

"How can he sort of go missing?"

"No. You're right; there's no sort of about it. Roddy's missing. I am so sorry, Maggie. I know you trusted me to look after him." Now I was close to tears as well. There was a pause, and then I heard a deep breath. Maggie was suddenly calmer.

"When was the last time you saw him?"

"It was about this time yesterday."

"Have you called the police?"

"Yes. They've got cars out looking for him. The villagers have organised a search of the hills. I wanted to be there with them, but the police wanted me to be at home in case he turns up here."

"Right. I'll throw some things in a bag and set off in half an hour."

"Are you sure, Maggie? It's getting late. There's not much either of us can do this evening. Besides, what if Roddy somehow makes his way home? Wouldn't you be better off down there?"

"Do you really think he could make his way down here?"

"You never know. He's very resourceful."

"By resourceful, you mean a sneaky bugger?" We both laughed, relieving a bit of the tension.

"Look, I know his memory's not good, but some things are ingrained. My Dad is going through the same problem, and just a few weeks ago, he hitchhiked across the country to visit me. He had no idea that my mum was worried sick. There's every chance Roddy is safe somewhere and unaware of the panic he's causing."

"If he is, I'll wring his neck."

"That's the spirit." Maggie laughed again before blowing her nose loudly.

"Okay, I'm in London at the moment. I'll stay here tonight, then check out the caravan tomorrow. Call me if anything happens. It doesn't matter how late it is. I suspect I won't sleep much tonight."

"Same here. I'll call as soon as there's any news."

I'd dreaded making the call, but speaking to Maggie made me feel more hopeful.

As I put the phone on the chair arm, it hit me how tired and hungry I was. Time to raid the freezer for emergency toast and open a tin of beans.

The used plate was beside me when I woke up with a half-drunk cup of tea next to it. I picked up my phone, but the battery had died. I plugged it in and looked at my watch. It was just after ten. I'd been asleep for a couple of hours. Without thinking, I turned on the TV. Huw Edwards was just handing over to their reporter in Kettlewell.

The familiar image of Cagney filled the screen. It was a full-blown press conference. Cagney had his concerned face on as he walked into the room and took his seat on a small platform. It was the same expression he'd used when he accused me of being in on the plan to steal all my money last year. I was struggling to understand what he was saying. I rubbed my face and concentrated hard.

"Roddy Lightning was last seen at approximately 8pm yesterday. We believe he may have been wearing a bright red, all-weather coat. He may suffer from short-term memory loss and could be confused. However, we are also following a line of enquiry that suggests he may have been abducted and held for ransom. We ask that any member of the public with any information calls the number currently on the screen."

Cagney loved being the centre of attention. I supposed that if he found Roddy, I'd forgive him for being a smug prick. Hang on. He was using words like kidnapping and ransom notes. He talked about the house-to-house searches of the area. Kidnapped? They thought Roddy had been abducted? The screen cut to clips from Roddy's career before returning to the reporter standing outside the pub in Kettlewell.

Kidnapped? What the actual f—kidnapped?

Once again, it looked like the plot of our script was happening in real life. My head was spinning. Could Roddy really have been a victim of kidnappers? No, no, no. It couldn't be. Could it? It would explain why he hadn't turned up in the searches.

The charger had brought my phone back to life. It started ringing as I tried to make sense of what was happening. I could see I had seventeen missed calls. Jason and Dick were amongst them but, so far, nothing from Cagney. I worked down the list, calling people back, but was at a loss to give them any information or reassurance. Ambrose offered to come around if I needed company. I thanked him but decided I would be better trying to get some sleep. I crawled into bed by about three o'clock, but sleep was impossible.

The loud knock on the door came at exactly seven the following morning.

25

By the second knock, I was out of bed and grabbing my tatty dressing gown. The third knock almost took the door off its hinges. Taking the stairs two at a time, I flung myself at the door. The key was in the lock. A tall police uniform stood before me while his much shorter female colleague was by the gate.

"Good morning, sir. I hope we didn't wake you." Was that a smirk? I thought that was a smirk. A raised eyebrow, at the very least.

"I was just getting up. Is there news of Roddy?"

"Perhaps we could come inside, sir?"

"Sorry. Yes, of course."

I stood aside, and the smirky one stooped under the door frame. His partner motioned me to go first and closed the door behind us. I shivered as I sat down. Smirky stayed standing and took out his notebook. After confirming my name and address, I asked again about Roddy.

"Our investigations are continuing. Would you mind if we were to search the house?"

"Search the house? This house? What on earth for?"

"Evidence, sir. We can always come back with a warrant. Maybe take you into the station while the paperwork gets sorted."

"No need. Do what you need to do."

Smirky went off to start his search while his colleague stayed to keep an eye on me. She took a seat on the edge of the sofa.

"Can I get you a coffee? Tea?"

"No thanks. It goes straight through me on chilly mornings like this. We always have to stop somewhere for me to tinkle."

"Fair enough." I tapped my fingers on the chair arm and wondered whether to make small talk. The officer looked very uncomfortable. "Is everything okay?"

"I don't suppose I could use…"

"Of course, just through there."

She went off to use the facilities. I wondered how they would explain it if I'd made a run for it at this stage. Then I reminded myself that I'd done nothing wrong and only wore a dressing gown, so making a run for it was right out.

Smirky was back and looked alarmed that his prisoner was unguarded.

"She's in the loo," I said, always eager to help the police with their enquiries. "Did you find anything?"

"No, sir, sorry for the inconvenience."

We heard the flush. "While we're here, do you mind if I go as well? Frosty mornings."

"Be my guest," I said.

Two minutes later, I was waving Smirky and Tinkle off with the promise to keep in touch if I heard from Roddy. I went upstairs to get dressed after putting the kettle on. Before I could make the coffee, my phone was ringing. I sat at the kitchen table, heart thumping in my chest.

"Jason, hi. No, no news yet."

"I just saw it on the TV. Do the police really think somebody's kidnapped Roddy?"

"Cagney seems convinced. Not sure what they're basing it on. I mean, who'd want to kidnap Roddy?"

"Look, it's probably nothing. I mean, it's ridiculous." Jason sounded shifty.

"What do you mean? Do you know something?"

"No. Not really. I could just be being silly, but there are rumours."

"Rumours? What rumours?"

"Remember when I was going to walk you through the finances for the film, and you said you wouldn't understand it? One thing I was going to point out was that Flic was only putting up half the money. One of her contacts put us in touch with another company who put us in touch with…"

"What are you saying?"

"We partnered with a firm that is based in the Caribbean. The source of the funding is a little hazy. As I say, there are rumours they get the money from, shall we say, nefarious activities?"

"Are you saying drug gangs? You partnered us with fucking drug gangs?" I was almost shrieking.

"I didn't know. Still don't, not for sure. As I say, it's rumoured."

"And what do these rumours say?"

"That they may have pulled this kind of stunt before. There's no proof, but conspiracy theorists say there was a film in the States where the star disappeared. Big insurance payout as the film never got made. Still, the company tripled their investment and walked away with the ransom as well."

"For fuck's sake Jason."

"As I say, somebody I trusted recommended them."

"What happened to the victim in this other case?"

"They released him. He was a bit shaken, but otherwise okay."

My heart was pounding even more.

"What the hell would that do to Roddy? He's seventy-eight, for Christ's sake."

I felt sick. Were we in business with some shady gangsters that kidnap pensioners? Was it all a con to claim on the insurance? Would Roddy be okay? What about the film? Jason sounded like a whiny child.

"What do you think we should do?"

All this before coffee.

"I've got no idea. I suppose we should call Cagney, but what would we say? Ooh, sorry, we seem to have somehow teamed up with the Mafia and got our mate kidnapped. I take it we have insurance cover? What the fuck am I talking about?" I was hyperventilating and did my best to calm down.

"It depends. We need to read the small print."

"Why don't you do that? I think we sit on this until we know what's happening. The police could be wrong. Roddy could turn up at the pub without a care in the world."

I didn't really believe that, but it was the best I could do. Bacon, coffee and some kind of miracle might help. The first two were easy. That would have to do for now.

Luckily, I got in and out of the cafe without awkward questions. I headed home with my takeaway. Two bacon and egg sandwiches were over the top, but I sensed it would be a long day. I was halfway through the second when the familiar knock at the door made my heart race again. It was Smirky and Tinkle.

"Sorry to bother you again, sir. Inspector Cagney asked us to call in to take you to the station. He has a few questions he'd like to ask you."

Thirty seconds later, I was again in the back of a police car.

After the mess with Robbie last year, this was becoming a habit. They even put me in the same interview room. I suspect they were trying to make me feel at home. It wasn't working.

"I don't suppose I could go to the toilet?"

Tinkle shook her head.

"Sorry, Inspector Cagney insisted we didn't keep him waiting."

I recognised the irony, but arguing was pointless. Anyway, Cagney burst through the door. He and Casey replaced Smirky and Tinkle. Cagney ruined the dramatic entrance as the folder he threw onto the desk slid straight off the other end. Casey sprang forward and gathered the escaping documents. Cagney sat down, and the interview began.

"Thanks for coming in, Mr Dale."

"My pleasure. I wish you'd call me Frankie. Mr Dale makes me feel ancient."

"Okay, Frankie. I wouldn't want to hurt your feelings." Casey handed him the folder. I noticed it was pretty thick. What the hell was in there? "Now, Frankie. Do you know of anybody who might wish to harm Mr Lightning?"

"No. Everybody loved Roddy."

"Past tense?"

"No, of course not. Everybody loves him."

"What about anybody taking an interest in his finances, watching him being where you wouldn't expect them to be?"

I hesitated. "No."

"Why the hesitation?"

"Just checking my thoughts." Should I tell them about the dodgy finance deal? What shower of shite would that kick-off? Then another thought hit me. "Now you mention it. One guy was hanging around, asking questions. A poacher in the village. Bit of a loner. He seemed to hang around a lot."

"Does he have a name?"

"Yes. Sam, something or other. Jim, the landlord at the pub, can tell you his last name." Cagney made a note. "Can I ask a question?"

"That's not really how this works, but, seeing as it's you, go ahead," said Cagney.

"What makes you think somebody's kidnapped Roddy, rather than he's just missing?"

"I'm afraid I can't divulge that at the moment. It's sensitive, as you are a person of interest to the case."

"Person of interest? What does that mean?"

"Means, motivation and opportunity, Frankie, old son. You were the last person to see the chap. He trusted you. That's means and opportunity, right there."

"What about motivation?"

"We're still working on that, but it's often financial or sexual."

For once, I had no words. Cagney ran through his list of questions, none of which appeared relevant. There was a knock on the door, followed by Smirky's head appearing. Casey listened to the whispering PC before relaying the message to Cagney.

"Right. I think that'll do us for now. Thank you, Mr Dale. You're free to go. I know we will be in touch soon."

Smirky and Tinkle returned and said they would give me a lift home. Before long, Smirky was sitting at my kitchen table, having accepted the offer of a brew. We heard the flush, and Tinkle joined us.

"That's better. What have I missed?"

"We were just talking about Roddy Lightning," said Smirky, who I now knew was PC Newhouse. He told me to call him Paul. I nodded, but he was still Smirky in my head. "My mum said this morning that he was a megastar in the sixties. Is that right?"

I rose to the occasion.

"He certainly was. As a singer, he was as big as Cliff Richard, even Elvis at one time." They greeted me with blank looks. "Please tell me you've heard of Elvis Presley."

"Was he the one that swore on the telly, mad scary eyes?"

"No. I suspect that was Johnny Rotten."

I trawled through the most prominent singers until the late nineties and got nothing from either. Then it hit me.

"*Lonely Puppy?*"

"The advert on the telly? That was him? Wow, I loved that advert." Now I'd animated Smirky. Tinkle looked blank. "It was mint. You must remember it. The puppy got lost and slept in a shed. It was snowing, and the puppy looked dead sad. Then a couple of kids found it and offered it a bit of mince pie or something. Ended up living with 'em and having its own turkey dinner, pigs in blankets, the lot."

Tinkle shook her head.

"Nope. Before my time."

"Blimey. It's a classic. Kids today know nowt about history. It'll be on YouTube. You need to watch it."

"Anyway," I cut in on the nostalgia-fest of five years ago, "that song was a big hit for Roddy. He was on TV, made films."

I was about to list his credits and realised it was pointless. I was around fifteen years older than Smirky, but it may as well have been a century.

Tinkle was obviously keen to join the conversation.

"So he was very successful? I take it he's worth a fortune. No wonder they're asking for such a big ransom. Do you think his family will pay?"

"There's been a ransom demand?"

Tinkle looked alarmed. Smirky took over.

"I'm afraid we are not at liberty to discuss the investigation details, sir. We'd better be going. Thanks for the tea." He looked at Tinkle.

"Do you need to go before we go?"

Tinkle did a weird little dance.

"No, I'll be fine."

We went to the front door, and I watched them walk down the path towards the car. After I closed the door, I thought about what I'd just heard. I almost got back to the kitchen before the urgent knock at the door. Tinkle rushed past me.

"Do you mind if I just…"

"Be my guest."

As soon as I'd ensured the house was a police-free zone, I flopped into my armchair. I had a text from Jen reminding me I was due at her place this evening. I didn't feel like socialising, but it would be great to talk things through with Jen. Given the revelation from Jason about the dodgy finances, maybe I should tell her my worries about the man she was seeing. Perhaps his appearance out of thin air a few years ago had a connection to dodgy dealings? I had to tell her what she was involved with. Then again, what did I know about what was going on? I could finally tell her how I felt about her, if nothing else. Was I lousy thinking that with Roddy being held captive somewhere, totally confused and in danger?

I texted Jen to say I was looking forward to it, just as a call came through from Maggie.

"Hello, Maggie. Any news?"

"No sign of him at the caravan. I take it the police have nothing?"

"Nada. How are you?"

"As you'd expect. No sleep and going out of my head with worry. I just wish there was something I could do. Would you mind if I came up there?"

"Of course not. Come and stay with me. Roddy's room is fr
—"

I felt terrible for saying that. I'd give anything for Roddy to be back in that room, moaning that he was hungry or couldn't learn his lines. Maggie was silent. I carried on. "Have the police been to see you yet?"

"They just left. They want me to stick around here today, just in case. I thought I'd see Penny next. I could come up tomorrow if she agreed to watch the caravan."

"Actually, that makes sense," I said.

"Apparently, there's a ransom note, but the police wouldn't tell me more than that."

"Do you have any idea how much they're asking?"

"No, but, to be honest, I can't see us being able to raise it. We're not exactly flush."

"Let's not worry about that until we know what's going on. Sorry, I've got another call coming in. I'd better take it in case it's the police. I'll call you later."

I answered the call, but it wasn't the police. It was Jason.

"Any news?"

"No more. The police were round again this morning. I've just been speaking to Maggie, and they've seen her. Do you think we should tell them what you told me? About this company that put money in."

"I've been worrying about that all night and have concluded nothing. However, the phone call I've just had with Flic might clarify things. Both parties are thinking of pulling the finances."

"Can they do that?"

"They can, I'm afraid. To be honest, I can see their point. They're citing potential damage to their brand if the police are interested."

"So, where would that leave us?"

"Fucked."

"Thought so. When will they decide?"

"Today. I've scheduled a call for seven o'clock tonight. I

think you should dial in."

"Okay. Send me the details. Let's hope the police come up with something. I'm not sure I can cope. Anything else?"

"Find Roddy?"

"That would be nice."

I hung up. What were we going to do? Poor Roddy. Who knew what he was suffering? The film and the autobiography seemed to be gone. There was no chance of the nest-egg to set Roddy up for the rest of his life. Jen might be involved with a criminal mastermind, and the police think I'm a suspect in the kidnapping.

I appeared to have hit rock bottom. Then the phone rang again. It was the hospital in Bridlington.

"Mr Dale. Your mother asked us to call. She's here, but she's a bit upset. Your father had a heart attack. We're preparing him for surgery at the moment."

I was in the car before the call ended. In a screech of tyres, I was heading towards the coast. The call had banished everything else from my mind.

Mum looked tiny, sitting patiently in the coffee shop.

"Hello, love. You didn't need to come dashing over. You must be up to your eyes in it."

"Don't be silly, Mum, of course I'd come. How's he doing?"

"They've just taken him to surgery. They're doing a heart diversion on him."

"Diversion? Do you mean bypass?"

"Oh, I don't know. I get mixed up."

"Did they say how long before we can see him?"

She just shrugged. There was no queue at the counter, so I went to get two teas. I piled sugar into Mum's. I'd read somewhere it was helpful for shock.

"Why don't we drink this? Then I'll find out what's happening."

We shared a packet of ginger nuts, but Mum was unusually quiet. I gleaned that he'd been out raking leaves from the garden this morning. They'd sat in the kitchen for a coffee at eleven, and he'd gone from feeling a bit unwell to clutching his chest. Luckily, she'd ignored his insistence that he would be okay and called the ambulance.

The sugar in the tea seemed to work magic, and Mum made more sense. We made our way to the ward and found a nurse who knew what was happening. She told us it would be several hours before he came out of surgery, and he'd be exhausted. She recommended I get Mum home and get her to sleep. The nurse took my mobile number and promised a call when Dad returned to the ward. We could come back in the morning.

Mum was reluctant, but I convinced her she could do practical things like packing pyjamas and slippers if we went home. She hardly spoke in the car on the way back, but soon fussed and defrosted a casserole from the freezer once we were back in her domain. While the microwave worked its magic, she went off to pack a bag to take to the hospital. I sat at the kitchen table and took out my phone. The first missed call message was from Jen. Shit, I should've been at her place a couple of hours ago. I called her.

I must've said sorry about ten times. Jen was calm and told me to stop apologising and tell her what had happened. I told her everything I knew.

"It sounds like things will look much better in the morning."

"I'm sorry about the spag bol and not getting to read Charley's story. I've missed our Saturday nights."

"So have I, to be honest. Let's get through this week and see where we are then."

"Have you heard from Jason?"

"Not yet. He said he'd call me after calling the backers."

"Crap. I'd forgotten about that. So, on top of everything else, we could lose our film by tonight."

"You just concentrate on your family for now. Actually, is that Sally I can hear in the background? Put her on. I'll have a chat."

"Thanks, Jen. You're special, you know that, don't you?"

"Give me a ring in the morning once you know what's going on."

I agreed and handed the phone to my mum.

26

The call from Jason came first thing Sunday morning. The film was dead. Both companies that were financing us were cutting their losses and pulling out. Jason was getting ready to call each member of the team.

When we got to the hospital, Dad was sitting in bed enjoying a slice of toast. He looked pale and tired, but he was still here. The operation had been a success.

"Why are you two looking so miserable?"

He was getting back to his old self. Mum started fussing with his pillows and getting glasses of water.

"You had us worried, you daft old bugger," she said as she kissed him on the cheek.

"There's no need to worry. It's all under control."

"It's okay for you. You were unconscious most of the time. It was me running around, getting ambulances and worrying myself stupid."

They could talk like this for hours. Anybody who wasn't used to them would assume it was a row. I knew better. It was done out of love to cope with the horror of what could've happened. I somehow got Mum to sit down and dragged another chair from the corridor. At last, I got a word in.

"How long are you likely to be here?"

"I'm hoping for a good few years."

I smiled.

"No, you know what I mean. The hospital. How long will you get to malinger in bed?"

"Doctor reckoned about a week. Should be home in time for Christmas. That's if Sal promises to look after me as well as these nurses do. Might stay here if not."

Mum bristled.

"You'll be in A&E for Christmas if you keep talking."

They were off again. At least their lives would soon be back to normal. I couldn't see a normal world for me anytime soon. We needed to find Roddy first. Was it too soon to think about rescuing the film? What if we didn't find Roddy? Had something terrible happened? What about my investment in the movie? I realised my parents were looking at me, waiting for an answer.

"Sorry. What did you say?"

"I knew you weren't listening. Your father asked about Roddy. What's happening with him?"

I explained he was still missing. Dad shook his head.

"That's terrible. You must be worried sick. Shouldn't you be at home in case the police need you?"

"No. Well, maybe. I don't know. I needed to come and see you. Make sure you were all right."

"Well, now you have, and I am. Your mum is going to fuss over me." He ignored the look he got. "You get off. Come back and see us when you've sorted everything, and bring Jen and Charley. That would help my recovery."

"What about you, Mum? Are you going to be okay?"

"I'll be fine. Your dad's right. You get off home and call me tonight. Gill, from next door, says there's soup in the fridge for when I get home."

I could take a hint and soon left them to it. As I opened the car door, my phone beeped. It was a message from Maggie.

"Making good time. Should arrive about 3 x."

Bugger, I'd forgotten that Maggie was coming. I looked at my watch. It was almost 1.30. I would have to get my foot down, but I should make it. I set off from the car park like a boy racer, only to grind to a halt as I edged my way into the queue of traffic crawling towards the temporary lights. Ten minutes later, I was through the green light and on the open road. It would be tight now, but still doable.

The phone rang when I was half a mile from home.

"Sorry, Maggie. I'm almost there."

"That's good news. I'm plaiting my legs here."

"You'll be inside in less than thirty seconds."

I gave a short blast on the horn as I pulled in alongside Maggie's car. Greetings were quick, and I ushered her inside, pointing to the downstairs toilet. I filled the kettle before dropping Maggie's case into the spare room. Some of Roddy's things were still on the bedside cabinet. Ten minutes later, we were sitting at the kitchen table with tea and biscuits. I apologised for not being here when Maggie arrived and explained my sudden dash to the coast.

"That must've been terrible. Is your dad okay?"

"He seems fine now. They're both more worried about Roddy, to be honest," I said.

"I'm worried sick. Where can the old fool be?"

"I'll never forgive myself if something awful's happened."

"Don't be daft. Whatever is going on, it's not your fault."

"But he'd still be safe if I hadn't got him involved in the film."

"And miserable. Getting the film was the best thing that's happened in ages. It's the first time I've seen Roddy animated in the last fifteen years. He's been pretty low since Renata died. Poor Rumble." I pushed the box of tissues across the table. Maggie took a sip of tea and composed herself. "Watching Renata go through the illness was awful, but seeing what it did to Roddy broke my heart."

"Roddy started the story but got a bit upset and never got to finish. He told me about the wedding in California."

Maggie smiled at the memories.

"They were the loveliest couple you could imagine. So happy, devoted to each other. The two of them weren't like the other Hollywood A-listers. Oh, they were big stars, but so down to earth. Roddy loved the bones of her. When they moved back to the UK, it was a big thing for me. The three of us spent a lot of time together. I didn't manage him at that point. Obviously, I'd known him for years. I even found their dream home through a contact. Got it before it came on the market, a lovely big place in the Cotswolds. River frontage, deer in the grounds, beautiful."

"So, how did you end up managing him?"

"That came much later. One of my biggest regrets is that I didn't spot that Roddy was being systematically ripped off for years. Let's just say he made some poor decisions."

"I must admit, I've never asked how he ended up in the caravan after all those big houses."

"It's quite a story. Any more tea in the pot?" I gave the teapot an optimistic swirl. "Bugger it. The sun's over the yardarm. Got anything stronger?"

I nodded and stood up. Maggie looked at me and could hold back the tears no longer. It was like I could see her being engulfed by unhappiness. Instinctively, I moved towards her and held my hands out. She stood, and we hugged each other as if the world depended on it. I suspect I sobbed more than she did. After a while, she patted my back and took a deep breath.

"I don't know about you, but I needed that," she said. It was Maggie's turn to proffer the box of tissues. She looked much older than when we'd first met. "There has to be something positive we can do?"

"The police are doing what they can. Half of the population of the Dales have been scouring the countryside. It's dark, and you're exhausted. Why don't we have that drink, rest tonight, and drive up to Kettlewell first thing tomorrow? We can join the search parties, knock on doors, whatever it takes. We'll find him. Right now, you need a drink."

Maggie nodded her agreement and sat down again. I took it as a sign of my growing maturity that I had a fresh bag of limes to go with the gin and tonics. Times had changed. Maggie had recovered her composure.

"How much did Roddy tell you? Cheers."

"Cheers. I know they got married and moved back to the UK when the Americans cancelled the show."

"That would've been around 1989. Life was good. They were both thrilled just to be together. Roddy did the sitcom for the BBC. They made an album together, which didn't sell very well but was excellent. They did a summer season together in Blackpool."

Maggie took a sip of gin and reached for the box of tissues before continuing.

"It must've been 1995. It was in the hotel there that Renata found a lump. She said nothing to Roddy at first. She told me, and I could see how worried she was. I helped her get tested. Only when the consultant confirmed it was cancer did she tell Roddy."

"How did he react?"

"It devastated him. He went into a tailspin. Renata asked me to help. We got her treatment organised like a military operation. Cancer treatments are tough now, but a lot more sophisticated than back then. Roddy couldn't face up to the reality. Renata wanted to protect him. She asked if I would be with her for the treatment. Roddy was almost living a double life. He was the perfect husband most of the time. On treatment days, he closed himself off. It was like the illness didn't exist for him then. I was with her for every appointment. It was brutal. The surgery, chemo, radiotherapy. The treatment almost killed her. But she pulled through." Maggie took another tissue and paused for a moment to compose herself. Maggie took a drink before continuing.

"We got the good news on a Wednesday afternoon, the day that England played Germany in the Euro semi-final. I watched the game with them at their house. Roddy was in tears when we got beaten. Then Renata gave him the good news that the tests were clear. The cancer appeared to have gone. The three of us just wept and hugged each other."

"So, if she got the all-clear…"

"The recurrence came about a year later. This time it had spread. The whole treatment nightmare started again, but this time Roddy stepped up. Held her hand through every appointment. I'd met Bridget by then."

"Your partner?" Maggie smiled and nodded.

"Yes, been together for over twenty years now. We both worked in London, so I saw less of Roddy and Rumble. When Renata got a break from treatment, we'd meet up, but it was Roddy that was with her all the way."

Maggie was still blinking back tears. The tissue in her hands was falling to pieces. I grabbed the kitchen roll and put it in front of her.

"Thanks. I blame myself, you know. For not being there."

"Surely, you couldn't do more than Roddy and the doctors did?"

"No, not the treatment. It was the scumbag of a manager that Roddy had. They were so caught up in fighting the disease, they didn't notice the money disappearing. Over about three years, he was bleeding them dry. The lousy bastard even defaulted on the health insurance payments. Roddy rang me in tears one night to say that he had a bill for twenty grand from the hospital and didn't have enough money in the bank. I dropped everything and drove over to the house. Roddy showed me the mountain of paperwork that had built up. The short version was that the manager had done a disappearing act and left Roddy with a mountain of debt and bugger-all in the bank."

"Did you call the police in?"

"Straight away. It was almost two years before they tracked the bastard down in Panama. He's now residing at her majesty's pleasure, but poor Roddy never saw a penny. We ended up selling the estate, the cars, and jewellery just to pay the hospital bills. Then, on top of everything else, Renata died in the summer of 2002. It almost killed Roddy. I've never seen grief hit anyone the way it hit him. He started taking drugs. Weed at first, just to relax, then they got him on the hard stuff."

"That must've been awful."

"It was. I'd taken over managing his affairs for him. As part of digging him out of the mess, I did a deal for a Greatest Hits CD."

"I remember that coming out. I've still got it."

"Well. The money from that paid for the clinic. Roddy got clean. Even bought a nice little house close to where he lives now. Then the pattern started. He'd fall off the wagon. We'd sell the house to raise funds, clinic to straighten out, buy a smaller house, get him some work. All would be well for a year, then bang. He'd meet a new dealer, and off we went again. It got to the stage where the money ran out, and Penny offered the caravan. I'm still unsure if she was doing it to look after him or get some perverse revenge for what he'd done to her all those years before. Anyway, he's been there near enough ten years. I get him the odd bit of work and, for all that time, he's been drug free."

"Do you think he's on a bender at the moment?"

"He could be. I told the police all this, then suddenly they're on TV with the kidnap story. We have to find him."

"I'm sure he'll turn up, despite the famous Cagney and Casey. They couldn't find their own arses without help."

Then the blue flashing light pulled up outside the front door.

"Speak of the devil. I'll let them in."

"Come in, officers. Any news of Roddy?"

"Good evening Mr Dale. Miss Windsor, I didn't know you were planning to visit."

I'd forgotten that Cagney had been south to speak to Maggie.

"We're still pursuing our enquiries, but nothing to suggest where Mr Lightning is being held."

As usual, Casey hovered while the rest of us sat around the kitchen table.

"You still haven't explained to us why you think someone has kidnapped him."

"All in good time, sir, all in good time." In his head, the idiot was Morse or Columbo. "Would you mind explaining to us why you were driving at high speed through the Yorkshire countryside earlier today?"

"I was late."

"You don't say. Not a valid excuse for breaking the law, I'm afraid."

"Hang on. Have you been watching me?"

"Should we be, sir? A lot of remote farm buildings in that area. Ideal for hiding something. Or somebody."

"You still seriously believe I'm... What the f—"

"Please, calm down, sir. You triggered a speed camera

between Driffield and York, doing 64mph. Quite the Ayrton Senna. So, would you mind telling me where you'd been that was so important?"

Maggie could see how wound up I was getting and stepped in to tell him about my dad and the dash back to meet her. Casey scribbled furiously, his tongue sticking out of the corner of his mouth. Cagney looked uncomfortable.

"I'm sorry to hear about your father. I hope he makes a full recovery. Now, if I can ask you to look at this. Sergeant Casey, if you will."

Casey stepped forward and proudly opened a manilla folder, extracting a single sheet of paper. He didn't quite say 'ta-da,' but he might as well have done. Cagney leaned forward.

"Have you seen this before, sir?"

"Yes. Of course, I have."

"Would it surprise you that your fingerprints are on this document?"

"No, not at all."

"So you admit sending it?"

"Sending it? What do you mean? Is this what your entire investigation is based on?"

"It's fairly important, don't you agree?"

"Yes. It was important to the film. It's a prop from the film we were making. A film about a kidnapping." They had the ransom note I'd made from cutting letters out of magazines.

"So, how did it end up in Mr Lightning's room at the pub?"

I was suddenly relieved but also trying to contain my rising anger.

"He struggles to remember his lines. We used crib sheets taped to various props so that he could read from them. He's a bit of a hoarder and collected them up every night. He must've picked this up as well."

A reasonably large penny seemed to drop deep in the recesses of Cagney's brain.

"So, in the film, the ransom demand would be one…"

"… hundred thousand pounds."

He shot Casey a look that suggested the junior officer would take the blame and a huge bollocking for this. My anger bubbled to the surface.

"So, your investigation so far stems from a ransom note made as a prop for a fictional kidnapping in a film?"

"We'll need to verify what you're telling us."

"But who would pay this ransom?" I asked, raising my voice.

Casey went on the offensive.

"The film's producers or Mr Lightning's manager."

"Right. Maggie is his manager. Does Roddy have a hundred grand that you could lay your hands on?"

"I doubt if he has a hundred quid to his name."

"And I am the film's producer, so I would extort this money from myself."

"That's what you want us to believe."

"Shut up, Casey, fucking idiot." We all looked at Cagney, open-mouthed. "It would appear we owe you an apology, Mr Dale."

"Again."

"Mmm. It also means that we are no closer to finding Mr Lightning."

"I wish you'd call him Roddy," said Maggie.

"And if I'm no longer a suspect, can I be Frankie? Mr Dale makes me feel so old."

"One step at a time, Mr Dale. We'll search the area again where Roddy disappeared, but is there anywhere else he may have gone?"

I told them about the cafe and how he hadn't remembered the route back to the house.

"Do you think he could have set off walking back from Kettlewell aiming for here?"

"I suppose it's possible. We drove that route several times over a couple of weeks."

"Right, given the new information, we'll leave you at peace for this evening. We'll be in touch."

I showed them out. As I closed the door, the last thing I heard was Cagney again questioning Casey's intellect, parentage, and future career prospects.

"Told you they were useless."

"You couldn't make it up," agreed Maggie. "But that still leaves us not knowing where he is or what's going on."

"I feel I should be out looking for him. What if he is trying to make his way back here?"

"All the more reason to stay here, just in case. There are hundreds of square miles to cover. Leave the search to the police for tonight at any rate. Like you said, we can join in tomorrow. At least now they know he's not likely to be with kidnappers."

"Imagine the battering their boss is going to give them for this. How the hell do they explain the telly story and everything?"

"That comes under the heading of not our problem. Might I suggest another gin and some takeaway menus?"

"Done. Then we should get an early night. Tomorrow we start again."

27

My head hurt. We were sitting at the breakfast table. It was the same table we'd sat at last night. Only then it had doubled up as a bar. Maggie had obviously needed to talk. By about 11pm, that simple skill had evaded me. A crazy memory came back through the alcoholic haze.

"Late last night—did you tell me Roddy had a daughter?"

"Were you that drunk?" I attempted to nod but soon realised that was a bad idea. "Lightweight. Yes, he has a daughter. Something that few people know, so can we keep it quiet?"

"I won't tell a soul."

"You will, because you tell Jen everything, but that's okay."

"Everything about last night is foggy. I'm sorry, but you'll need to tell me the details again. Can I offer you something to eat?"

"I've seen the inside of your fridge, remember? Don't worry, the coffee's fine. Polly."

"Polly?"

"Roddy and Penny's daughter. She was born just before they got divorced."

"So she's around fifty now?"

"Yes, with a grown-up daughter of her own, Amber."

"He's never mentioned them to me."

"Let's just say it's complicated. Penny never quite forgave him for not being around much when Polly was growing up. He missed her fifth birthday party because he was in prison. The infamous drug bust."

"That maybe explains why she still has it in for him."

"But there's still that bond as Polly's parents. I think that's maybe why she offered him the caravan. It's a sort of two-edged sword - punishment for what he did but being able to have him close. Like I said, complicated. He's had minimal contact with Polly for a long time. To my knowledge, he's never even met Amber."

My phone broke us off, belting out the intro to Blondie's *Hanging On The Telephone*. I apologised to Maggie and answered the call. It was Spud.

"Any sign of Roddy?"

"No. Nothing yet."

"I think you should come into the office. There's something I want you to see."

"Give me half an hour, and I'll be there."

Spud did the honours with his impressive new coffee machine, then joined me and Dev as we sat at my old desk in the corner. Dev looked about twelve, but had graduated from the Madras Institute of Technology last year. He was a junior software engineer, but he already knew more than I'd ever done. I'd been too much of a sleeping partner in the business in recent months.

"Dev returned from holiday this morning and started developing the social media stuff for Roddy. You haven't looked at Roddy's account since you set it up?"

"No. I know Alice has been showing Roddy how to post selfies. He was quite enthusiastic, if forgetful, even with the simple stuff. Why, what have you found?"

Dev tapped away at his laptop and turned the screen towards me. He almost whispered and I had to lean forward to hear.

"Roddy has already picked up around eighty thousand followers. Over a hundred of them have contacted him through direct messages. Many are bots and scammers, but he's been chatting with some of them."

"Please tell me he's not fallen for a scam."

"Not that I can see. Roddy tells a couple of them he doesn't have a credit card but could send something he calls a postal order."

"I'm not even sure they do them anymore. It was a way of sending money through the post when I was a kid."

"Why on earth would you do that? Why not just transfer it?" I appeared to have set off a minor explosion in Dev's brain.

"No internet in those days." The look on Dev's face suggested his brain had well and truly exploded now. Spud stepped in.

"Dev, I'll explain later. For now, we think there are three contacts to look at. Roddy may have been making plans to meet up with them, or at least, they've suggested it. Do you think we should tell the police?"

"Normally, I'd say yes, but my confidence in our friends Cagney and Casey is shaky at best. Can we do anything to track them down?"

"We thought about messaging them, pretending to be Roddy. We might get lucky and find the IP address of the sender. Trouble is, if they're crooks, they'd route things through a proxy server, and we wouldn't have a clue where they were."

"Got to be worth a try."

"Okay, but what do we say? Hi, it's Roddy here. Do you know where Roddy is?"

"Suspect that wouldn't work unless your name's Cagney. We need to give this some thought. Dev, could you start by doing some snooping on the user profiles? Cross-check with Facebook and Twitter to see if we can work out where they are." I paused. "Stupid question - do any of them give that sort of information on Instagram?"

"I'll get on it."

Dev picked up the laptop from the desk. Rupert had obviously been watching from across the office and replaced them as Dev and Spud went back to their seats.

"Hello, stranger. Come back to do an honest day's work?"

I resisted having a dig back.

"How's it going? Good to see you're still here. I thought you might end up working full time on the club conversion with Joe."

"Not on your life. It's bloody hard graft and plays havoc with the skin. I'd much rather tap away at a keyboard. To be honest, I help in the evenings. You should come down and pay us a visit."

"And get a paintbrush stuck in my hand?"

"Count yourself lucky we're past the sledgehammer stage."

"You're right. As soon as we find Roddy, I'll come down."

"Any progress with Roddy?"

"Just waiting to see what Dev turns up. He could be on to something."

"Okay. Give me a shout if I can do anything. Got to dash. Got a conference call starting in two minutes."

"Excellent. Keep earning money for me. Love to Joe."

I tapped my fingers on the desk. Everybody was busy but me. I wasn't used to that feeling, especially in this office. Maybe, if the film really was dead, I'd have a lot of time on my hands. I suppose we'd take a brief break and then brainstorm ideas for the next project. That was assuming Jen was still interested. She'd been spending so much time with Jason. Was I slipping out of the picture? It was only then that it hit me. How much of my investment had I lost if the film was gone? I might need to earn cash quickly. Would it be that bad to return to life here, writing code and designing systems? I never had to deal with kidnapped rock 'n' roll stars in my old life. Spud snapped me back to the present.

"Frankie, have a look at this." I pulled my seat across to his desk and stared at his monitor.

"We think we can discount this one. Looks like the guy lives in Australia. He's asking if they can meet up, but not until the spring when he's over here on holiday. We can see from his postings that he appears to be still in a place called Wollongong. There's a picture of him on the beach, and he's carrying yesterday's newspaper."

"Okay. Seems reasonable to rule this one out. What about the others?"

"That's where it gets interesting. Both appear to be from Yorkshire."

"I don't suppose one of them lists his interests as sixties films and kidnapping?"

"Not quite. However, this guy looks to be into any scheme to make a few quid. One of his enterprises advertises memorabilia. He specialises in the sixties and seventies—film posters, signed programmes, that sort of thing. Looks like he had some stuff he was trying to get Roddy to sign."

"What about the others?"

"The profile picture is a Yorkshire terrier," said Spud.

"Sounds like pure evil." Spud laughed. "I'm serious, mate. Can't stand the little sods. Of all the dogs that could take their name from God's own county, it had to be that yappy little bundle of shite."

"Not a fan?"

"Hate 'em. They always look like they're trying to pass a

pineapple," I said. "Why is this one interesting?"

"Nothing more than a feeling. They just seem quite chatty. Very comfortable with each other."

"Let's keep that in mind."

"What do you think we should do with the information?"

"I suppose we should pass it to the police. You did nothing illegal to get it, did you?" Spud looked shifty.

"Define illegal."

"Bugger. This is all public domain stuff, isn't it? We're allowed to access Roddy's account. We just tell them the absolute basics and see what they turn up. Send me relevant links, and I'll have a word with Cagney. Well done. This guy with the memorabilia sounds interesting."

I left the office and planned to head towards the police station. The thought of speaking to Cagney again didn't fill me with joy. Instead, I hopped on the bus and headed to Joe's. Given his background with the record shop, he may know this dealer. Besides, I wanted a nosey at how the club was coming along.

Peering from the top of the stairs, the place was amazing. I expected dust, noise and high-vis jackets. Instead, I saw wide open spaces and heard Miles Davis floating from huge mounted speakers.

"Frankie. My dear boy, welcome to the pleasure dome, soon to be El Sotano."

"Wow. This isn't what I expected. I pictured builders knocking down walls and plasterers with jeans exposing arses."

"Had you come a week ago, that's what you would have seen. Heady days indeed. Today is a brief lull in festivities. I've been cleaning for a couple of hours while the builders are all in town on Christmas shenanigans."

"On a Monday?"

"Only day they could get booked in at the all you can trough buffet. Dread to think what they'll be like in the morning, but they've been pretty good so far."

I looked around and nodded.

"This is a great space. What a transformation."

"They'll finish the stage tomorrow, then the bench-seating down two walls. Assuming the plumber doesn't get too pissed, we shall have running water in the kitchen tomorrow and toilets by the end of the week. Then they down tools for two weeks over Christmas."

"Have you set an opening date yet?"

"Your invite will arrive shortly for a small but exclusive private party on February 12th. Then we go for it on Valentine's day. Rupert is about to start his media campaign, whatever that entails. He assures me we will have a full house for the opening, which is good enough for me. Oh, I almost forgot. Major news flash incoming." You had to love Joe when he got this animated. "As of yesterday, Ambrose is now a partner. We decided to merge the two businesses. Makes perfect sense. The premises are in the same building, and I already miss the record shop. We'll knock down part of that wall and open up the whole cellar. During the day, Ambrose runs the record shop with a classy bistro and coffee shop on this side, and, at night, it becomes the supper club with a record shop attached. Both businesses open from early morning to late at night."

"That's brilliant. This is going to be huge," I said.

"Anyway, enough of me. What's the news about Roddy?"

"He's still missing. I'm very concerned about him. The police have been hopeless. We now think the whole kidnapping thing was bollocks. Rupert's team may have come up with a lead though. I thought you may help."

We perched on the edge of the half built stage. I passed my iPad to Joe.

"Have a look at the top link on that email. This bloke has been trying to set up a meeting with Roddy to get him to sign some record covers and photos. I thought you might know him."

Joe tapped the link to the profile.

"Blimey, it's Dodgy Alan."

"Dodgy?"

"Ironic nickname. The bloke is absolutely genuine. He's never done a dodgy thing in his life. That's why he's always skint. The slightest sob story gives you an instant discount on whatever you buy. Do you want me to call him?"

"You've got his number?"

"Of course. I've got everybody's number."

"What would you say? You can't ask him if he has recently kidnapped any film stars."

"Knowing him, it would work. He'd confess on the spot. Let me have a think. How about you nip down the road and come back with two coffees, and I'll come up with an excuse to call him?"

"All right, you're on."

On the way to get the coffees, I thought I'd call next door to congratulate Ambrose. Instead, there was a sign. "*Closed. Back in ten minutes.*" The pedant in me always wanted to point out that the wording meant nothing, as I had no idea when the ten minutes started. In Ambrose's absence, the philosophical rant would have to wait. I headed for the coffee shop. By the time I got back, Joe had made the call.

"I think you can rule out Dodgy Alan. He's been in Florida for the last two weeks, tracking down a signed Otis Redding LP. He reckons he could have a buyer lined up and stands to make five hundred quid. He seemed a bit upset when I asked how much the trip had cost. Seems he hadn't factored that in. Told you, useless, but lovely."

"So, you think he's a dead-end?"

"I think he's a bell end too. The other link, however, looks interesting."

"What, the one with the dog photos?"

"That's the one. Have you seen the username on the account?"

"Not really."

"It's Tonitru5." I looked blank. "One of the many benefits of a private boarding school. A thorough introduction to the friends of Dorothy being the highlight. Oh, I could tell you tales."

"Can we focus, please?"

"Sorry. We had a lot of time to kill and played endless hours of AdventureQuest. A favourite weapon in the game was a Tonitru. Couple that with an expensive and, up to this point, useless knowledge of Latin. Tonitru comes from the Latin for thunder."

My heart was pounding as I reached out and took the iPad. A quick Google search confirmed my thought.

"Antonia Stevenson. Stage name—Toni Truelove. Also known as Thunderbolt 5. Roddy was obsessed with her in his younger days. I think we're onto something. Surely he has to be with her?"

"Trouble is, there's nothing on the profile to show where she is."

I started typing.

"What are you doing?" asked Joe.

"Sending her a message."

"What, have you kidnapped Roddy?"

"More or less. I just pointed out that Roddy is missing; we're worried about him, and has she seen him?"

"What next?"

"We wait?"

"What about the police?"

"Fuck 'em."

"Seems fair. Listen, I'm meeting Rupert for a few drinks this afternoon. Why don't you join us?"

"Normally, I'd love to, but I've got a mystery to solve."

"Okay, Shaggy, keep in touch."

I called Maggie while I was waiting for the bus.

"Toni? Do you think he's with Toni? But where?"

"No idea at the moment. I was sort of hoping you might know where she lived."

"That would be handy, but no. Sorry. The woman seems to have disappeared altogether."

"I've sent her a message through Insta. Hopefully, she'll get in touch with good news. By the way, how are you feeling? I had a thick head today."

"Don't worry about me; I'm in perfect health, but I have a problem. I got a call from Bridget. She's had a fall. They think she's fractured her hip. She needs me."

"Well, go. Look after Bridget. There's not much you can do here. We'll find Roddy. I'm sure of that now. When we do, I'll bring him back home to you."

"If you're sure?"

"Yes. Just lock up when you go, and keep hold of the spare key. I can get it back when I deliver Roddy. Don't worry, it's going to be fine."

As I hung up, the bus appeared, and ten minutes later, I was in our office. I felt a pang of disappointment that Jen wasn't there. There was little reason she should be. She must be busy preparing for Christmas since we had no script to work on. I felt guilty that I had bought no presents yet, but there was so much going on. I needed to call Mum to get an update on the patient. Most urgently, I had to track down the fifth Thunderbolt.

I powered up my Mac and started online stalking Tonitru5.

I compiled a file with all her photographs going back almost three years. She was obsessed with her dog. It appeared in every shot. No people, no names and no places. After twenty minutes, I set up all the photos to play on a slideshow. I sat back with my feet on the table and clicked through. The dog had a wonderful life. There were pictures of it eating ice cream, drinking beer outside a pub, walking by a river, and asleep in front of a log fire. Not a bad way to live. I was in danger of being envious of a dog's life.

Hang on. Back up a bit. I clicked back to the picture outside the pub. There it was, sitting in the window. Just above the dog's head, staring out at the world. An elf. Not just any old elf, but one with a tiny silver foil flower in its lapel.

Just then, the office door opened. It was Jen. The sight of her, coupled with the excitement of seeing the elf, made my heart leap.

"You okay? You look odd. No offence."

"None taken. I'm just pleased to see you."

"I thought you'd be miserable with Roddy missing and the film being canned."

"I was until just now. "

"Maybe these will help." Jen pulled a sheet of paper from a thick envelope. It was a picture of Roddy with the word *Missing* in red letters and my phone number at the bottom. "I thought we could distribute these in the villages around Kettlewell. Somebody must've seen him."

"That's a great idea. You're not the only one that's been busy though. Look what I've just turned up."

I sat back and proudly pointed at the screen.

"Very nice. What is it?"

I realised Jen had missed the rest of the day that had led up to this point. I brought her up to speed.

"So, let me get this straight. You think Roddy has hooked up with this Toni from the Thunderbolts and that this photograph proves she was in Kettlewell this week?"

"That's about right."

"Have you told your old friends Cagney and Casey?"

"I decided against it. The police seem determined to treat me as a suspect. Every time I help them, I end up in jail."

"You didn't end up in jail."

"Okay, but it was a smelly interview room."

"Hardly Papillon." I ignored the sarcasm. "So, what do we do now?"

"I assumed you were going off to make Charley's tea."

"She's at her gran's for the night. I was calling in to see if you fancied Tesco's finest and a bottle of Chianti at my place. Now it sounds like we're going on a road trip to the Dales."

"You up for a bit of Miss Marple-ing?"

"Too right, but it'll be dark by the time we get there."

"You think we should go in the morning?"

"No. We should grab a bag each and use our rooms at the pub. We can make a start this evening. If we find Roddy - result. If not, eat in the bar and pick up the search first thing in the morning."

"Sounds like a plan. I'll pick you up at your place in half an hour."

28

We were on a mission to find our friend, who I desperately hoped was okay. Over the last few weeks, I'd dreamt of sweeping Jen away for a weekend in the countryside. I hadn't entertained the idea that it would be like this. Now we were headed for the Dales. Jen threw her overnight bag on the back seat and climbed in beside me.

"This is exciting. Riding off to find Roddy. I suppose you've got a soundtrack lined up for the drive."

"Joni Mitchell okay?"

"Perfect."

As I pulled away, the headlights picked out the first snowflakes from a darkening sky. We should be there in under an hour, but it would be nice not to have a blizzard to contend with. I realised it had been a while since I'd been alone with Jen outside work. She'd been spending more time with Jason while I'd been with Roddy or Maggie. It felt good to be close to her. I still loved her subtle perfume. Within minutes, we were chatting away just like we used to. She brought me up to date with Charley's adventures.

"She misses you, you know. We need to make time for you to come around for dinner soon."

"I'd like that. Things always seem to get in the way at the

moment."

"True. You must miss Roddy. You seem to get on so well."

"We do, and, yes, I miss him. I'm scared something terrible happened."

"Don't think like that. You've found a plausible explanation, and we're on our way to check it out. Well done. I knew you being so intimate with the internet would come in handy one day."

"Intimate?"

"All right, expert. That better? I'm just amazed at what you've turned up in the past. What other gems have you discovered?"

"Just people with mysterious pasts. No past at all sometimes."

"Oh yeah? Spill the beans. What have you found?"

I squirmed. Why had I said that? She was looking at me, waiting for an answer. I dived in.

"Actually, it's Jason."

"Jason? What about him?"

"How much do you really know about him?"

"Strange question. Quite a lot, as it happens."

"I know in a physical sense you've doubtless discovered a lot, but what about his background?"

"What the hell are you talking about?" She sounded annoyed. That wasn't part of the plan. Plan? If only I'd had a plan. I'd blundered into this conversation by mistake.

"Well, I, erm, I suppose when you sleep with someone, you get to know quite a lot."

"Hold on. Who said I was sleeping with Jason? And if I was, what's it got to do with anybody else?"

"Nothing. Exactly. What? You mean, you're not sleeping with him?" There was hope, but she was now quite angry.

"No, if you must know. Why would I be sleeping with him?"

"Well, you spend a lot of time together. You've had dinner together several times. I just…"

"Idiot. I spend a lot of time with you, and we've had dinner many times. Did I miss the moment I couldn't resist you any longer, and we fell into bed together?"

"So you're not in a relationship?" She glared at me as we sat at the traffic lights. Joni Mitchell still sang happily, but my discomfort was growing. "It's just that I'm not sure I trust him."

"Why on earth not?"

I explained about the dodgy company that had financed the film and the way I'd sort of stalked him and found nothing online before three years ago. She said nothing for what seemed like ages. The piano intro to *River* filled the car. I couldn't help but think of *Love Actually* and how Alan Rickman behaved. I had a soft spot for Emma Thompson. At Christmas, I always watched *Die Hard* straight after *Love Actually*. That way, Rickman got what was coming to him. Jen cleared her throat before continuing.

"It's a professional relationship, if you must know." Shit. That sounded even worse.

"How do you mean, professional?"

"I'm helping him to write a book. He asked me to keep quiet about it, but he agreed I could confide in you if I wanted."

"A book?"

"An autobiography. Jason wants to tell the story of why he had to reinvent himself. He didn't feel confident enough to write it all, so he asked me to ghostwrite it. The same as you've been doing with Roddy."

"So, what's his big secret?"

"I'll tell you more later. You're still in the doghouse for assuming I was sleeping with him. I thought we understood I wasn't ready yet for that sort of thing. Everything is still too raw after Sean died. Charley comes first. I have my eye on someone if my feelings change."

Was that Dick? He was an old flame trying hard to ingratiate himself, and she was always laughing at his jokes. I didn't have time to ask as my phone rang. It was my mum with the latest hospital bulletin. I explained she was on the speaker and Jen was with me. That was like the magic word, and they chatted happily for the next half an hour. It was almost like I wasn't there. To cut a long story short, Dad was fine. Mum was fine. It was all fine.

I concentrated on the road ahead, covered in a layer of snow. Mum and Jen remembered I was there just as I pulled into the car park in Kettlewell. At least Jen seemed to have forgotten her annoyance with me. We said our goodbyes to Mum and made our way to the pub.

Jim was pleased to see us and soon settled us into our old rooms. Cagney had forced me to abandon my dirty laundry, but it was all clean, neatly folded and put away. Made a change from everything being stuffed in my holdall. The police had allowed them to re-open the day after Roddy disappeared. I realised we still had all the rooms booked for this week and another two weeks after Christmas. I'd have to cancel them if the film funding had evaporated.

The snow was still falling. It was clear our search would have to wait until tomorrow. Besides, I was hungry. Jen was already in the bar.

"Blimey, you're keen," I said.

"I just knew if I sat in the room, I'd crash and burn. I feel like I could sleep for a week. Anyway, I seem to remember you promised lasagne and a bottle of something nice."

Jim was listening and took that as his cue to step out from behind the bar and deliver two menus.

"Jim, while you're here, could you have a look at this?" I showed him the photo on my phone.

"Horrible rat thing."

I turned to Jen.

"See. It's not just me that doesn't like the horrible little things."

"Of all the dogs that Yorkshire could give its name to," said Jim.

"Exactly what I said."

Jen cut in.

"Can we focus, please? Jim, do you recognise this dog?"

"Of course, Yorkshire terrier. Can't be doing with the little —"

"No. I don't mean the breed. What about the actual dog? Do you know who owns the dog? They took the picture at a table outside here."

Jim looked again at the picture.

"Can't say I do, no. Sorry. We don't let dogs in the main part of the pub where we serve food. They're allowed in the back room, but it's mainly farmers calling in for a quick pint before tea."

"It was worth a try. We think the owner might know something about Roddy's disappearance." I took the phone back.

"Tell you who might know. Sam Johnson knows every animal in this dale and the next."

"You mean the smell—" I corrected myself. "You mean the bloke you warned off the other night that was asking about Roddy?"

"That's him. The smelly one."

"How do we get in touch with him?"

"He lives in a little cottage out towards Hubberholme. Bit remote, not the place to be going on a night like this. Mind you, it wouldn't stop him coming down here if he decides he's got a thirst on."

"Didn't you bar him last week?"

"I bar him every week. Makes no difference. He still turns up like nothing's happened. Quite a comforting routine we've got going. One of life's constants you can rely on. I'll give you a shout if he comes in. Now, two lasagnes, is it?"

We nodded and handed the menus back.

"Oh, and a bottle of—"

"Something nice. I know. Give me two ticks."

"You're good at this. You should do it for a living."

"Nah, money's shit." With that, he strode off towards the kitchen.

"What do we do if this Johnson character doesn't show up tonight?" asked Jen.

"No idea. I suppose I haven't thought this through. Maybe we should've called Cagney in."

"What, and let him mess things up, then take all the credit when we find him?"

"Now you put it like that."

"Well, the aim is to find the dog's owner, yes?"

"Yes," I agreed.

"So, one possibility is Sam Johnson. He'll know the owner if he knows as much about the dale as Jim says. I'm sure Jim can give us directions to the cottage. We can drive up there tomorrow unless we have six feet of snow."

"What if he knows nothing?"

"Then we get copies of the dog's picture printed off and start knocking on doors. We can distribute them at the same time as the fliers I printed. That's what Cagney would do."

"You're right. We can do this." Jim had returned with a bottle of something nice and two glasses.

"Food'll be with you in a minute. Enjoy."

We spent most of the meal with me tip-toeing around the subject of Jason. Jen noticed and put me out of my misery.

"I take it you want to talk about Jason?"

"Only if I don't get into trouble." Jen took a deep breath and then a sip of wine.

"You were right. Jason has a dodgy history." I was about to celebrate being correct, then decided that would land me in it again. "Or at least he did when he was younger. Even then, it wasn't really him. It was his dad. At the risk of understating, he was a bad lad. He was part of a gang that broke into several wholesale jewellers. They got away with millions over the years. As a result, Jason had a very privileged upbringing. Private education, big family house, trust fund, the lot."

Jen paused as Jim came and collected the plates.

"Can I get you two anything else?"

"No thanks. That was lovely. We could both do with a good night's sleep. I don't suppose Sam Johnson's been in?" Jim shook his head. "In the morning, do you think you could do us some directions to his cottage? We'd like to pay him a call."

"Will do. I'll see you in the morning." Jim returned to the bar. I picked up my glass and focused on Jen.

"You were saying about the big house and everything. What happened?"

"One of the gang shot somebody. Killed a security guard who disturbed them one night. Jason's dad freaked. Said that's not what he'd signed up for and wanted out. The other gang members decided that retirement wasn't on the cards. They threatened him and his family if he didn't carry on. Eventually, he went to the police. Did a deal. He gave up the house, cars, the lot. They were all put in the witness protection scheme for giving evidence."

"How old was Jason at the time?"

"He was fifteen. And it wasn't Jason back then. It was Wayne. In his GCSE year, they pulled him out of a very nice public school, transported two hundred miles to Cheshire, and into a big comprehensive. He had quite a tough time at first. He still sailed through his exams and got a place at University in the States. Life was peachy for years. He started climbing the corporate ladder at a marketing firm in New York. Then he got a call from the witness protection people. There'd been a data leak. His identity was no longer secret, and they believed the gang knew where the family was and were out for revenge. Two days later, his dad's body turned up on a building site, and Jason was on a plane with another new name."

"Jesus. That's quite a story. So, why tell everything in a book if this gang is after him?"

"The police caught up with the other two gang members. One died in a shoot-out, they arrested the other and got life. That sentence ended last year."

"Ended? You mean they let him out?"

"No. He died in prison. The police are happy that there's no longer a threat to Jason or his family, hence the decision to tell his story. He's got an eye on making a film about it as well. In fact, he'd like us to write the script if he can get it off the ground."

I was stunned. None of this was remotely what I'd expected. Especially the bit about Jen not being in a relationship with him. Then I remembered what she'd said about having her eye on somebody. Was Dick the one? He was older than Jen. Then again, so was I. They'd spent a lot of time together over the last few weeks. At least if the film was dead, she wouldn't be working with him every day. Silver lining and all that. Jen's chair scraped on the stone floor as she stood up.

"Sorry. I'm done in. Do you mind if I call it a night?"

"Not at all. Early start tomorrow. We've got a star to find."

Jen put a hand on my shoulder and kissed me on the cheek.

"Night."

Then she was gone. Except that scent lingered just for a few seconds. I sighed and stared into the log fire.

Hours after getting into bed, I was still wide awake. I felt powerless on so many fronts. My thoughts were on a loop, getting faster and faster until they blurred and merged. Where could Roddy be? What kind of financial mess had I created for myself? Would my mum and dad be okay? Who did Jen have her eye on? Did I need the loo, or would I last until morning?

I fumbled on the bedside table for my phone. It was almost half-past two. I definitely wouldn't last until morning. Sighing, I threw aside the warm duvet and, using the dim glow from my phone to navigate, made my way to the bathroom. Seconds later, I was mid-flow when the phone threatened to vibrate its way off the edge of the washbasin. I had an incoming call. I reached out with my free hand before realising I didn't know the etiquette for this situation. If I answered, it would be apparent from the background noise what I was doing. I knew that after eight rings, the voicemail would kick in. We'd reached five, and there was no immediate sign of an end. I didn't recognise the number. At seven, I had to risk it.

Lifting the phone to my ear blocked the ambient light from the screen, and my world plunged into jet-black darkness. This had two immediate consequences. The darkness somewhat compromised my aim, and I had no actual idea where the light switch was. I could hear that the voice on the other end sounded quite formal, but my mind was elsewhere. I ended the call of nature and turned to where I assumed the door was. It wasn't. My knee connected instead with the corner of what I later realised was the heated towel rail. I cursed my attacker, but the phone escaped my grasp and crashed onto the tiled floor. I bent to grab it and cracked my head against something solid. Luckily, it turned out to be the bathroom door, which burst open. There was now enough ambient light for me to crawl across the floor and switch on the bedside lamp. What stopped me from doing that in the first place?

Grabbing the phone, I apologised before realising the call had ended. I sat on the bed and looked at the call log. It was an unrecognised number. Great. I almost killed myself and had no idea who was trying to get in touch. Deciding that sleep was not coming soon, I switched on every light I could see and flicked the switch on the kettle. While it was boiling, I checked for damage, both to me and the bathroom. The latter was acceptable, but a bruise was forming above my right eye.

Cup of tea made, I was just getting back into bed when the phone vibrated again. It was Jen.

"Are you awake now?"

"Wide awake. I just had a phone call, but—"

"I know. It was the police. They assumed you were pissed and called me. Frankie, they think they've found Roddy's coat. They want us to go to Skipton police station as soon as possible. I told them we'd be over the driving limit, so they're sending a car. It'll be here in fifteen minutes. Meet me downstairs."

Jen had sounded anxious. Finding the coat can't be good news. Heart pounding and stomach-churning, I got dressed.

When I got downstairs, Jim was already there.

"Sorry Jim, did I wake you up?"

"No. The police called me to let me know they were coming to pick you up. I came down to unlock the doors. I hope everything's okay with Roddy. Do you need a bit of a stiffener before the car gets here?"

"No thanks, mate, better not. Might feel differently when we get back," I said.

"Give me a ring when you leave Skipton, and I'll make sure the doors are open for you." He looked past me to the window as a pair of headlights came over the bridge. "Your ride's here."

Jen joined us. She looked frail, but beautiful. I wanted to hold her close and protect her from what may be about to come.

We held hands in the back of the police car all the way into Skipton. Before long, we were passing the castle and driving through the marketplace before turning left, pulling up on the double yellow lines outside the station. Our driver got out of the car to open the back door for me. He explained he had another call to answer, and his colleague was waiting at the front door. We thanked him, walked towards the station, and the hovering Sergeant Casey. He only sounded a little bitter when he explained his boss was at home in bed. He led us down a corridor to a small meeting room.

"As my colleague explained on the phone, our search team discovered a coat. It matches your description of the one the victim was wearing."

Oh no.

"Victim?"

The word was enough to panic Casey.

"Sorry, not victim. Not yet anyway. The erm, the… Roddy. It matches what we believe Roddy would have been wearing. We asked you to come here to identify the coat."

The door opened, and a young uniformed officer entered and placed a clear plastic bag on the table. I could hear Jen's intake of breath when she saw the coat. Instinctively, I reached out and took her hand. Casey opened the bag and took out the waterproof jacket. It looked like Roddy's coat of many pockets. I nodded at Casey and blinked back the tears. As he folded the jacket back into the bag, Jen sat up straight.

"Hang on. Look at the logo."

I wiped my eyes with the back of my hand and stared at the Ruckoats logo. They'd been our sponsors for The Woman In The Yellow Raincoat.

"Surely we would've noticed if Roddy's coat had been from Ruckoats?"

I agreed.

"Can I look at the inside?"

I took the coat from Casey. There was a large, zipped pocket at waist level on the inside and two on the outside. But that was it.

"It's not Roddy's coat," I said. "His had at least three pockets on the inside, maybe more. It even had them on the sleeves. He never even knew how many it had. It's not his."

Casey looked at Jen.

"Frankie's right. It's not Roddy's."

I wasn't sure whether to feel relieved or more worried. At least he hadn't lost his coat in the depths of winter, but we were no closer to finding him.

29

We were both exhausted on Tuesday morning. We'd managed showers and coffee, but no sleep. Jen was peering at the map Jim had drawn, and I was peering at the narrow tyre tracks through the snow. There was a lot of peering going on.

"Just up here. There should be a road off to the right." I clicked the indicator and pulled across. "No. No. Straight on."

"I thought you said there was a road on the right?"

"There is. It's just that we don't take it," said Jen.

"So why…?"

"It was just to prove that I knew where we were."

"And do you?"

"What?"

"Do you know where we are?" I felt that maybe we'd found the one thing in the world that Jen wasn't great at.

"Yes. We've just passed that road off to the right."

My heart pounded as Jen started shouting.

"Stop. Stop."

We slid to a halt. I looked at her, trying to keep a smile on my face.

"You should've turned left there."

She pointed at the lane that we'd just passed. There was no

other traffic on the road, and I reversed, trying hard to keep to the furrow made by my tyres. Soon we were bumping down a very rough track.

"This is it," said Jen, with more confidence than I thought it merited.

"Can you be sure?"

"Yes. Look. Jim's written on 'bumpy as f–.' Actually, I can't quite read his writing, but it definitely says bumpy."

I feared for my exhaust and the possibility of sliding into the ditch alongside the road. After what seemed like hours, we arrived at a tiny, tatty cottage. A small cobbled yard at the side of the house contained the remains of a motorbike. I parked next to the bike. Had I seen the shotgun pointing towards us, I wouldn't have bothered getting out of the car. My first reaction was to put both hands in the air, as I'd seen in many films.

"This is private land. No parking!"

The shouting was coming from the open window of the cottage, just behind the shotgun. Fear silenced me. Jen took over negotiations.

"Mr Johnson. My name is Jen. I work with Roddy Lightning, making the film. We're trying to find Roddy and thought you may help us."

The window closed. Seconds later, the front door opened, and the shotgun poked out, followed soon afterwards by Sam Johnson.

"Step away from the car, where I can see you," he shouted.

The shotgun waved around as I stepped sideways and slipped, hitting the cobbles hard. It knocked the wind out of me. There was more shouting, but this time it was Jen. The gist was for me to stop messing about and get up. I did. I was breathing hard as well as being wet and cold. Jen tried again.

"We believe Roddy might be with an old friend. She may have a dog. We were hoping you might know where she lives. We have a picture of the dog. Frankie, show Mr Johnson your phone."

I lowered my hands, eyes glued to the shotgun, and went to my pocket for the phone. I was mindful of the potential assassin following my movements.

With the iPhone stretched out in front of me, I stepped forward.

"Stop right there." I froze. "I know you from the pub. You're the one that gave my name to the police. Came up 'ere, sniffin' round. Carted me off to the nick. For questioning, they said. Now you want my help. Well, bugger off."

That was rude. For a moment, I forgot the shotgun and protested.

"I'm sorry about that. Could you just—"

"No. Bugger off."

"It's just—"

"No. Bugger off. Bugger right off. Then, when you've buggered off, let me know. Then I can tell you to bugger off again. Now bugger off."

We buggered off. At least we got back in the car. I started the engine, but my leg shook so violently that I couldn't control the accelerator. We jerked through the first five turns of a three-point turn before Jen spoke.

"Stop. Give me your phone."

"You heard him."

"His argument appears to be with you. Let me try the charm."

"I'll keep the car running, just in case."

Then I stalled the engine. I unlocked the phone and handed it over. Jen got out and moved towards Johnson. What if he turned violent? I should call Jen back and speed off towards civilisation. The car was at an angle. I had to turn in my seat to see what was going on. Hang on a minute. They were both laughing, and Jen was nodding her head, agreeing with something. I suspected it was about me. They chatted for the next thirty seconds, pointing and waving arms. Then a handshake and Jen was on her way back to the car. With a cheery wave, the shotgun disappeared back into the cottage.

"What a sweetheart."

"Sweetheart. He could've killed me."

"He's just not keen on unexpected visitors, that's all. Anyway, I think I know where Toni lives. Fancy going to see her?"

We reached the main road without a genuine threat to our lives. My legs were still shaking as I edged the car left towards Buckden. We passed the road to Hubberholme, again triggering the fears about what had happened to Roddy. Jen had been scribbling on the map Jim had drawn. She looked at me and seemed concerned.

"Are you okay? Only, you look pale."

"Being threatened with a shotgun will do that to you."

"You were fearless." Was she taking the proverbial? "Especially when you fell over."

The sniggering started.

"I could've damaged myself."

"Did you hurt yourself?"

"I'm wet through." The sniggering turned to almost helpless laughter. "And I grazed my knee," I protested. This was a heartless response to my brush with death. I was seeing Jen in a new light.

"Does it hurt?"

"Yes."

"Aww, I'll kiss it better for you."

That's more like it. She was still laughing at me, but the thought of Jen kissing me was worth it. Shame it was my knee.

"Anyway, what were you scribbling?"

"I was making a note of the directions, so I wouldn't forget."

"Do you think your new mate really knows where the dog lives?"

"I don't see why he'd make stuff up. Like Jim said, he seems to know everything that goes on around here. Slow down. Take the next right. We're looking for a green door somewhere up… there. Pull over."

My mind was racing, trying to work out a way to get Jen back onto the subject of kissing it better. When I needed my brain to be clever, it came up with nothing. Jen jumped out of the car.

"Come on. Let's find Roddy."

Easing out of my seat, wet jeans sticking to my legs, I affected a slight limp. I wasn't beyond a cheap bid for sympathy. I needn't have bothered, as Jen was already heading up the short path to the green door. She reached out and rapped the ornate brass knocker.

Immediately, there was mayhem from behind the door. It sounded like a pack of giant, wild dogs that wanted to rip us limb from limb for daring to knock on the door. Being brave, I stepped back a bit and hid behind Jen. She seemed unruffled. Behind the door, a deep voice boomed out.

"Shut up. It's only the bloody door. Stupid animals, get in there, go on."

The door opened. Two sets of eyes peered out. The first set was almost level with the top of the door frame and surrounded by a grey, bushy beard. The second set was at floor level and shaking like every other Yorkshire terrier I'd ever seen. Before either of us could speak, the terrier suddenly came over all brave and started yapping. A massive hand reached down and scooped the animal up.

"Shh. It's okay, sweetheart." The giant looked at us. "Hello, how can I help?"

I was about to demand that he take us to Roddy, then realised that there was no way that this was Toni Truelove. Jen rescued things again. She explained we were looking for Roddy and Sam Johnson suggested that the Yorkshire terrier lived here.

"Why don't you come inside? You look like you could do with a cup of tea."

He looked at my bedraggled jeans. Jen accepted and followed the man inside. I stared through the door, looking for the hell hounds that had been making all the noise. He noticed.

"Don't worry, you're safe. I locked the daft buggers in t'back room. Come through."

He led us into a spacious, homely kitchen.

"I'm Bernard, have a seat." He waved a hand towards the oak table as Jen introduced us. I took the end seat next to the toasty warm aga. Within seconds, a teapot and plate of scones had appeared on the table.

Jen explained the whole story. Before she'd finished, I realised I was steaming. Gently at first, then like a kettle coming to the boil. I was a bit too close to the aga and tried to shuffle my seat away. The screech of chair on tile set the dogs off again. One boomed word from Bernard quietened them down, and on the pretext of showing my phone to our host, I swapped seats.

"This is the photo of your dog that brought us here."

"It's a photo of a dog, granted. Just not mine. Looks totally different."

I looked again at the picture and then at the dog, quivering in a small basket in the corner. The dogs looked identical. I was about to voice my opinion when Bernard played his ace.

"Not even the same sex."

"Really?"

"Aye. Dozy Boris over there in his basket is male. This little beauty in the photograph is female. Obvious when you look."

I looked again at the head and shoulders photo of the dog. Before I could ask, Jen cut in.

"Lovely scones Bernard."

"Thank you, Jen. Just made a fresh batch this morning. Must've known I was going to have visitors."

"Do you live here by yourself, Bernard?"

"No. The boss is at work this morning. Annie, she's a vet out at Leyburn. If anybody can tell you more about yon dog, she will. Most of the vets around here spend their time with farm animals. Annie specialises in pets. If that dog is from around here, Annie's seen it. She'll be back for dinner in an hour or so. Are you in a rush, or can I offer you more tea while you wait?"

"We don't want to be any trouble," said Jen, eyeing up another scone.

"No trouble at all. I just need to pay a call. Help yourself. Back in a minute."

As the kitchen door closed, I leaned closer to Jen and whispered.

"How do we know he's not some sort of murderer that's got Roddy tied up in the cellar?"

Jen looked at me as if I was mad.

"Why would a murderer tie Roddy up in the cellar," she hissed. "Why wouldn't he murder him?"

"Okay, maybe a kidnapper, then."

"Would a kidnapper invite us into his home and feed us scones? They're delicious, by the way."

"Agreed, they're very nice. It could all be part of a fiendish plan."

"Or he could be a delightful man who thinks his wife can help us find the bloody dog!"

I rubbed my knee, thinking that might elicit some sympathy. It didn't. The door opened, and Bernard returned.

"I just had a thought. If you're in the film industry, you might be interested in what I have in the cellar. I'm a bit of a geek. I love the cinema. Come on, let me show you."

Jen stood up and followed him. I grabbed her sleeve. Wide-eyed, I whispered, "we can't go to the cellar. It's a trap."

Jen gave me one of her looks and headed for the cellar steps. Looking around for a weapon, I picked up the butter knife from the table and set off after them.

"Mind the first step. It's a bit bigger than the rest."

I couldn't believe we were doing this. Had Jen seen no horror films in her entire life? Rule one is - you never go into the cellar. Yet here we were, GOING INTO THE CELLAR!

"Hang on a minute. The switch is down here."

There was a click. I closed my eyes, expecting some kind of cage to fall from the ceiling. Instead, the cellar transformed thanks to a soft sheen of light. Jen summed it up well.

"Wow."

Wow indeed. Instead of some imagined torture chamber, I was looking at a small cinema. Ornate theatre seats, five rows of six in each. Bernard pushed a button, and a red velvet curtain retracted to reveal a screen the size of the wall. There was even a tiny ice cream counter in the corner. Brass wall lights added to the atmosphere, but the auditorium lights came from a rig in the ceiling.

"Have a seat," said Bernard.

I was like a small child and couldn't take my eyes off the screen. I pulled down the seat nearest to me and sat next to Jen. Seconds later; the lights went down, and the screen came to life. Laurel And Hardy's Sons of the Desert followed an old Pathe News film about the Yorkshire Dales. We sat open-*mouth*ed. I don't know how long for. When Jen spoke, I realised we'd been holding hands again.

"I've never seen you look so happy," she said. I looked down at our hands, and she didn't move hers away. "Still think Bernard's a serial killer?"

"Worth it if he is," I laughed and returned to the film.

The reel finished too soon, and the house lights went on.

"Bernard, this is fantastic. Did you do all this yourself?"

"I did. Some people have train sets. I've got a cinema."

A chorus of dogs barking came from upstairs.

"Sounds like Annie's back. Come on, let's see if she knows your dog."

It wasn't just the contrast with her husband's size that made Annie look small. She was tiny. We were sitting at the kitchen table. Older and wiser than this morning, I had taken a seat further away from the aga. I couldn't believe that more food had arrived. We were being encouraged to tuck into the large bowl of salad, cold ham, smoked salmon and, best of all, homemade pork pie. I was thinking I'd died and gone upstairs.

Annie was cutting slices from the home-baked bread as she spoke.

"So. I gather you're looking for a dog."

Jen explained about Roddy and the Instagram stalking, culminating in the picture of the Yorkshire terrier.

"I remember seeing the story on the news. So you're saying they didn't kidnap him?"

This time, I answered.

"We don't think so. We think Roddy may have met an old friend. His memory isn't what it was. There's a fair chance he's forgotten he was in the middle of making a film. The alternatives don't bear thinking about, to be honest. He's been missing for four days now. With the weather like this…"

My voice trailed off as the enormity of what could've happened hit me again.

"Right, let's see the dog then."

I passed Annie my phone and accepted the slice of bread she offered in return. Annie pushed her glasses onto her forehead and screwed her eyes up in concentration.

"Ah-ha. Clunk." I must've looked very confused. "I think the dog's name is Clunk. It was a man who brought him into the surgery."

"I suppose Toni could be married. It's been years since anybody heard from her. Clunk's a strange name for a dog."

"It used to jump up into the armchair but never made it. The owner thought it was hilarious to call it Clunk. Bitch."

"Bernard said he thought it was a bitch."

"She is. But that bitch tried to bite me once. Yappy little bugger."

"So you know where she lives?"

"Can't remember off the top of my head, but I can find out, no problem."

"What about, you know, client confidentiality?"

"I can't see a Yorkshire terrier navigating the court system to sue me."

Annie considered for a moment.

"Tell you what. Rather than giving you the address or phone number, I'll take you on a sightseeing tour. If we should park outside a house and you need to knock on a door to ask directions…"

"Sneaky. I like it," I said. "But aren't you busy this afternoon?"

"This morning I was treating a St. Bernard with food poisoning and a Doberman with halitosis. Light relief is what I need. Besides, this is important. We need to rescue your friend, Roddy. Eat up. When you've had some of Bernard's rhubarb crumble and a cup of tea, I'll pop upstairs to my office and do some sleuthing on the practice database. Then we'll have ourselves an outing."

More food! I could get used to being a detective. I'd need to buy oversized trousers, but it would be worth it. Jen told Annie they had a lovely house while Bernard was making custard. My mind drifted back to the events in the cellar. The cinema still impressed me, but the hand-holding was wonderful. I couldn't remember how it had come about. Was I the initial holder, or the held? Either way, Jen hadn't objected or pulled her hand away. We both seemed wrapped up in the cinema's joy. It was a very welcome development. Now that I realised Jason wasn't a rival, I would just have to see off the attentions of Dick. Was she considering a relationship with him? She said she had her eye on somebody. What if it wasn't Dick? What if there was another rival lurking out there? As my mum says, that would be a real kick in the ya-yahs. I'd have to console myself with the steaming hot rhubarb crumble and custard.

Just when I thought I could do with a nap, Annie emerged with a piece of paper.

"Found it. I'm pretty sure this is the right address."

We said our goodbyes to Bernard, promising to return to try his Victoria sponge. Jen jumped in the back, with Annie navigating from the front. She directed me back down the road we'd arrived on a few hours before. Darkness was already gathering, but the skies had cleared, and snow would not be a problem. A few moments later, we were turning right towards Hubberholme. The coincidence struck me that Roddy may have ended up in the same village as our film location. Annie pointed to a car parked on the left.

"Pull over here. Parking is a nightmare further up. Let's stretch our legs."

As we walked, I mulled over what was coming next. I turned to Jen.

"What do we do when we get there?"

"What do you suggest we do? I imagine knocking on the door would be a start."

She was deadpan, and then playfully punched my arm..

"Knocking seems like a plan. It's just, you know, a bit…"

"A bit what?"

"Dangerous."

"How do you work that out?"

"She may be a vicious criminal that's kidnapped Roddy."

"She's a woman in her seventies. I think you could take her."

I drew myself up to my full height and puffed out my chest.

"You think so?" I said proudly.

"Yes. *Even* you could take her."

My shoulders slumped again. But she was right. What was the worst that could happen?

We turned into a narrow lane, and Annie pointed at the first house.

"There you go, the home of Penny the bitch Yorkshire terrier."

I looked from Annie to Jen and back, but the door knocking was my job. In the end, I rang the bell. Silence. No dog barking. Nothing.

"There's no answer."

"Try again. If she's anything like my mum, it will take her a while to get to the door," said Jen.

I tried again. Same result.

"What now?"

Jen thought for a second.

"No idea."

We trudged back to the car.

"Can I help you?" I turned to see the woman coming from the opposite direction. She wore a bright yellow raincoat. In one hand, she held a dog lead attached to a Yorkshire terrier.

In the other, she had the hand of an ancient, tiny man. Both of them looked like they were Chinese. Neither of them was Toni Truelove.

We left the very confused Chinese couple and returned to the car.

"I'm sorry. I convinced myself that was the right one."

"Hey, it's not your fault," said Jen. "We wouldn't have known where to even start without you. We've taken up most of your day. You've fed us and navigated us around North Yorkshire."

"Jen's right. Thank you so much," I added.

"So, what will you do next?"

I sighed. I was tired, worried sick about Roddy and totally out of ideas.

"I feel like I'm beaten, to be honest. What made me think we could solve this better than the police? I suppose we call Cagney. Give him the photo of the dog. See what he can do. Knowing him, he'll probably arrest the dog."

Jen looked at me through the rear-view mirror.

"No feeling sorry for yourself. We'll find Roddy. We're exhausted. Neither of us slept last night. There are still things we can do. In all the excitement, we never got to distribute the pictures. Things will look different after a hot bath and a good night's sleep. Tomorrow we get out to the neighbouring villages. If that turns up nothing, then we get hold of Cagney. How does that sound?"

Jen must have seen the silent tears rolling down my cheeks. She reached out to me and passed a tissue. That simple act of kindness almost finished me for the day. I wanted to curl up in a ball and make all this disappear. It was all my fault. I wanted Roddy to be in the film. If I hadn't pushed it, he would still be safe in his caravan with his ding-meals. Then there was the money I'd invested. I needed to talk to Jason to see how much I'd lost. Barney had warned me it was risky, but I'd convinced myself we couldn't fail. Wrong again.

Before long, we were pulling up outside Annie's house. We all climbed out of the car. Annie could see how despondent I was. She hugged me, told me to listen to Jen and that things would be better tomorrow. A hug for Jen. Then we were back in the car and doing a u-turn back towards the pub, leaving Annie with Bernard and the cosy house full of dogs.

30

Jen was right, as usual. After a relatively good night's sleep, I felt renewed and ready to find our star. The plan, such as it was, started at the visitor centre in Grassington. We spoke to a lovely lady who put three of our small posters on noticeboards around the centre. She also gave us a list of neighbouring villages to try, and the address of her neighbour who owned a Jack Russell. I wasn't sure that she quite appreciated the relevance of the dog. We thanked her and left.

We had similar conversations in the library and around the marketplace. Eventually, Jen turned to me. She looked pretty dejected.

"Do you think this is going to work?"

"Honestly? Probably not. Most people here are tourists doing their Christmas shopping. I know they are all wonderful, warm human beings, but there's no way they'll recognise a dog or know where Roddy is," I said.

"I think it's time to call Cagney. It's not as if we're giving in. We just need more help. Why don't we head somewhere quieter, get a cup of tea, and make the call?"

Reluctantly, we trudged back to the car. It had taken less than an hour to go back to being at rock bottom. I started the engine and turned to Jen.

"Where to?"

"Keep on going." I smiled as I recognised the line from Thelma and Louise.

"I'm not sure I'm ready to go over the edge of a cliff. How about a cup of tea in Arncliffe?"

"Good enough for me. But no cake. I've put about a stone on since we got here."

I was about to say something complimentary, but my phone rang. I pressed the hands-free button. It was Annie.

"I hear you two are out looking for Roddy."

"Good guess," I laughed.

"Not a guess. Grassington's a small place, and the network is buzzing. You sound like you're in the car. Where are you now?"

"Just heading out of Grassington towards the tea shop in Arncliffe."

"Any chance I can tempt you to the Red Lion in Burnsall? I've got something for you, and I'm between calls in the area. Got to go. Another call coming in."

"We'll be there in ten minutes."

The call went silent. We agreed we wanted to see whatever Annie had found. Just over ten minutes later, I was edging into a near-deserted car park in Burnsall. Sleet was blowing across the village as we strode towards the pub. Inside, it was warm and cosy. Annie waved from a corner table. A large teapot and three cups sat in front of her. We chatted as Annie poured.

"Sorry I can't stay long. Got a horse with toothache to attend to. I made a couple of calls this morning, and one vet at another practice came up with a dog to try. Matches the description in the photo. The owner is a widow living alone. Her surname is Stone, but we think she is a musician. Jackie remembers talking to her about where to buy sheet music in the Dales."

"That sounds very promising," I said, sneaking a biscuit from the plate on the table.

"Unfortunately, I can't come with you and the house is quite remote. I take it you have satnav?"

"Yes."

"That's a relief. I was dreading having to describe how to get to the place." A text message lit up Annie's phone. "Sorry. The visit has to be short and sweet. The horse is getting twitchy, apparently. Got to go. Tea's paid for. Good luck. Call me."

With that, she was gone.

I picked up the business card that Annie had left on the table. It had a postcode written on the back. The weather was getting worse; the sleet turning to snow from a leaden sky. We drained our cups and headed back to the car.

Within minutes, we were out of the village and climbing steadily. The road was getting narrower. I half expected the satnav to ask if we were sure and wouldn't we be happier at the seaside? We pushed on as big snowflakes blew across the windscreen. I could see a lone light on the horizon and was quite relieved when the car told me to turn right. We had reached our destination.

"Are you ready for this?"

Jen nodded, and we climbed out of the car. Against the wind, we headed towards the door of the large cottage. A tall, glamorous woman watched us from the kitchen window before stepping towards the door. As she moved aside, I could see into the kitchen. Comfortably at home and asleep by the open fire was a famous singer and film star.

Once again, we found ourselves at a kitchen table, being force-fed tea and cake. Roddy sat opposite me, not making eye contact, concentrating on the orange drizzle cake. I could almost understand him; it was delicious. We'd introduced ourselves to Toni and explained how we came to be standing on her doorstep. During all that, Roddy never said a word. He just stared at the ground. It was very odd. Jen took up the conversation.

"So, Toni, do you follow the news on TV?"

"Not these days. Too many books to read to bother with a television. Haven't had one in the house for fifteen years."

"What about radio?"

"Ah, now there, I'm a very high-tech consumer. I discovered an app. BBC iPlayer. Marvellous. Wall-to-wall Radio Three and Desert Island Discs going back years."

"It's excellent, isn't it," I ventured. Jen gave me a look, and I shut up.

"Mind you, I have to go into the village to get an internet connection. Nothing like that here."

"Newspapers?"

"Too depressing."

"So basically, you don't follow the news."

"No. If it directly affects me, I figure I'll hear about it in the village. If it doesn't, I don't need to worry about it."

That seemed like a decent theory to me.

"So, you don't know who we are or any of the fuss about Roddy disappearing?"

"Disappearing? But he's right there, aren't you, darling? More cake?" Roddy accepted another slice. I perked up, but the offer didn't extend to me. Could I help myself anyway? I did.

"Sorry, Toni. You don't understand. We were in the middle of shooting a film. The police convinced themselves that somebody had kidnapped Roddy."

"Kidnapped. Good lord, that's terrible. Did you hear that, Roddy? Kidnapped." Roddy was now back in the room.

"I once made a film about being kidnapped," he said, a look of bewilderment on his face. "Not sure if it was any good. Remember bugger all about it, to tell you the truth." Roddy went back to his cake. Jen had been quiet so far, but turned to Toni.

"How did you two meet up again, Toni?"

"I sent him a message on that Instagram thingy. He said he was in the area and at a loose end, so he came over. He's been here ever since." Toni brushed the mountain of crumbs from Roddy's jumper.

"How much do you use social media?"

"What's that?"

"Well, Instagram, Facebook, Twitter."

"No idea about Twitter. Been on Facebook for years, but don't check that often. Heard about Instagram on Desert Island Discs and thought I'd give it a go. I looked for this young man and sent the message. Easy. Not used it since, though. Didn't see the point. Too much to catch up on, if you get my drift." Toni winked at me.

"In other words, no contact with the outside world for the last four days?"

"I suppose that's true. Come to think of it, it's time Roddy had his nap: he needs to keep his strength up."

Saying nothing, Roddy stood up, kissed Toni, and moved back to the armchair by the fire. He was asleep in seconds. I was relieved that we had found him safe and well. It worried me he didn't seem to know who we were or have any concept that he'd been on a film set just four days ago. It was as if he'd made the film years ago. Jen was thinking along those lines and asked Toni about last week.

"We'd been swapping messages for a few days. I suggested we meet up. Roddy said that he'd finished filming and was free."

"That would be Friday morning."

"Yes. I picked Roddy up from the car park in Kettlewell. I don't drive that much these days, but the old Jeep behaved itself and started first time. We hit it off straight away. It was as if the last fifty years hadn't happened."

"Did you think it was strange that Roddy could just drop everything and stay with you all weekend?" asked Jen.

"I asked him about who he'd been with. Roddy said he'd finished filming but had to ring Frankie to let him know he was safe and would be back in a few days."

"He rang me?" I panicked a bit. Had I missed something?

"Yes. You didn't answer. I was with him when he did it. There was a whatchamacallit, voice thingy."

"Voicemail?"

"Yes. Voicemail. Roddy left a message. He said he was taking a few days off and would see you when he got back. He was insistent that he let you know so that you wouldn't worry."

Jen looked at me. Did she think I'd forgotten that he'd left a message? That was ridiculous. Wasn't it? Or was it? I'd overwhelmed by work. Could I have forgotten? No. Could I have missed the message or deleted it by accident? Had I caused all the flap? Bugger, that sounded much more plausible. I looked across at Roddy, snoring by the fire. At least he was safe and happy.

We sat around the table and talked for another half an hour. Toni was quite concerned when she learned the complete story.

"I'm dreadfully sorry if I've caused all this trouble. We just wanted to catch up after all these years. I didn't expect the sort of weekend we've had."

"There's no wonder he's tired." Two pairs of eyes were staring at me. Had I said something inappropriate? "I mean, being out of his routine has been a lot for him. Must be exhausting."

At that point, Roddy let out a huge snort and woke up.

"Frankie, Jen. I didn't know you were here. So good to see you. Maggie, any chance of a cup of tea and some cake for these people? I'm parched."

"Roddy. It's Toni, not Maggie," said Jen, gently. "Do you remember?"

"Course it is. Toni, love, I'll put the kettle on." Roddy appeared to be back with us. "Is young Alice here? I've got stuff to ask her about my Social Media whatsits."

We explained Alice had gone home for Christmas. We used the same story when he asked about the film—a Christmas break. Without the financial backing, there was no film. More than likely, Roddy would've forgotten all about it by tomorrow.

31

It was already dark when we got back to the pub. I'd offered to go straight home, but Jen thought I looked exhausted. We agreed on another night in our digs and would head home in the morning. Jen went off to phone Charley while I flopped onto a seat in the bar.

It was a strange feeling. Roddy was safe and happy, which was wonderful. The relief was mixed with sadness. Roddy was struggling with his memory, but also that our film was dead in the water. To celebrate Roddy being safe, Jim delivered a pint on the house. I realised I needed to make a few phone calls. I started with Maggie.

"He's fine. We found him this afternoon. He's been with Toni Truelove all weekend." I told her the whole story. She was still at the hospital, visiting Bridget. I could tell she was crying, but sensed it was with relief. At least she didn't have to worry about Roddy anymore.

Next, I tried DI Cagney but was told he'd left for the day. I explained that we'd found Roddy, and they could call off the search. I gave the officer Toni's address and hung up. Jason was next on my list, but I decided it could wait. It was almost like not speaking to him meant he couldn't confirm the project was dead. There was still hope.

Jen arrived, followed by a teapot and cups, thanks to Jim.

"I phoned Jason while I was upstairs," she said. So much for my plan. "He's delighted that Roddy is okay."

"What news about the film?"

"Not good. He confirmed the finance has gone." I let out a long sigh. "There's more. Dick's out as well. I called him. After all this time, it's been great hooking up with him again, but Film 4 has offered him a script."

I resisted the urge to giggle at the phrase 'Dick's out'. This was too serious. Besides—hooking up? Did that mean, you know, hooking up?

"So the film's dead."

"Never say never. We've got a script. We've even got half the footage we need to finish it." Jen poured the tea while I sulked.

"So we just need a shitload of money, get Flic to agree to release the rights and find a director. It's dead."

"I thought you were excited about this?"

"But without the money, we're sunk."

"How much would we need?" I shrugged and held my hands up.

"No idea, to be honest."

"Might I suggest we need to meet Jason ASAP to find out? We could look at where we could make savings, get the total as low as possible, and start using Jason's contacts to come up with the cash." I took a long drink from my pint. "Of course, you could revert to the old Frankie and give up. Or you could turn up tomorrow afternoon and see what can be done."

"How do you know Jason can make it tomorrow?"

"Already arranged. Two o'clock at our office. You in?"

"Seems rude not to."

"Good. Now, are you going to order a bottle of wine, or do I need to drink tea all night?"

I looked across the bar; Jim was already taking glasses

from the shelf. My phone rang. It was Fran from the cafe by the canal.

"Frankie. Sorry to bother you. We've just got back from a weekend in Paris."

"It's all right for some."

"It was lovely, but we saw in the paper that Roddy was missing."

"Actually, he's turned up this afternoon—the panic is over. He'd gone off with an old friend and forgotten to tell anybody."

"But that's why I'm ringing. We got home to a voice message on the landline. It was Roddy explaining that he was going away for the weekend. He said not to worry, and he'd be back in a few days."

"But why would he call you?"

"I think he just got the wrong number. He thought he'd called you when he left the message. Fran would be next to Frankie on his phone."

I thanked Fran and promised to call in for cake in a couple of weeks. Who'd have thought something as simple as a mis-dial had caused all the panic? I thought I might keep that bit to myself if I spoke to Cagney again.

Later, much to Jim's surprise, we both turned down desserts. We were onto the last of the wine when Jen excused herself and headed for the Ladies. Jim got over his disappointment and returned with a bottle of Patron chocolate tequila.

"With my compliments. Celebrate Roddy being safe." He left the bottle and two glasses on the table. This could get messy. I downed the last of my wine and poured two small measures of the tequila. Apart from the film, everything else was looking up. Roddy was safe. He hadn't just wandered off telling nobody, but had left a message for me. Okay, so he left it on somebody else's answer machine, but the thought was there. Then there'd been the hand holding. The first sip of the tequila added to the warm, rosy feeling. What did the hand holding mean? Where did I fit into things if Jen was eyeing up a return bout with Dick? At least they wouldn't be working together in the short term. Work. That was a bit of a downer. We'd have to find a source of income soon. Maybe we'd come up with something at the meeting tomorrow.

"Who's daft idea was that?" Jen was back and pointing at the bottle.

"Compliments of Jim. A thank you for being good customers and not getting any film stars killed. A small one won't harm. Go on."

"It's the way he left the bottle that's worrying me." Jen took a sip. "Ooh, that's nice." She topped up both glasses and giggled. "I could get used to this."

"Stick with me, kid. I'll show you the world."

"You seem to have cheered up a bit."

"Life's too short to be miserable for long." I raised my glass. "To you and Dick. I'm sure you'll be very happy."

"Me and Dick? What makes you say that?" Jen looked and sounded annoyed. Panic. I thought I was being all grown up and giving her my blessing.

"But… I just thought… I just thought… you said … you… that he'd asked you out and that you had your eye on someone."

"You've already proved that thinking isn't your best attribute. Idiot."

"So you're not interested?" There was new hope in my voice.

Jen sighed and folded her arms.

"I thought we'd had this conversation already? Charley is my priority. Everything is still too raw after Sean. I'm not ready for a relationship yet."

"But you said you had someone in mind if that changes."

"I do. If it does. It's not showing any sign of changing short term, particularly when some people are as thick as mince."

"Eh?"

Jen downed the shot of tequila and poured another for herself, but nothing for me this time. She took a deep breath and sighed again.

"Like I said, I'm not ready yet. When I am ready, I kind of thought me and you would, you know. Assuming you don't prove to be a fuckwit, which, at the moment, is looking unlikely."

"Me? Do you mean you and me? A couple? Assuming I'm not a, you know."

"Fuckwit?"

"I was trying to be polite, but yes. Wow," I said.

"Hardly a Clark Gable response."

"Wow."

"You said that already." I just sat and grinned. Jen leaned across the table and covered my hands with hers. "Now, don't get carried away or big-headed or anything. I say again - I'm not ready yet. But, if I feel differently at some as yet unspecified date in the future, if you are still interested and available…"

"Wow."

"Fuckwit." We both collapsed in floods of laughter.

I poured us more drinks. This could get messy!

32

We'd left Kettlewell early, before breakfast. I'd been floating on air since last night. Fair enough, Jen had stressed that she wasn't ready for a romantic relationship. But when she was, I was in pole position. No Jason, no Dick, just me. That would do for now. It was over a year since Robbie disappeared from my life, and there'd been nobody else since. Yes, at the risk of going all Mills & Boon, I had 'needs'. But this was a glimmer of hope.

We'd driven back from Kettlewell quite early and went straight to our office. Jen headed upstairs while I clicked the music on. Immediately, The Artistics boomed from the speakers. *This Heart of Mine* seemed appropriate. I continued floating and got busy making coffee. I usually slouch on a stool and wait for the interminable delay to be over and my magic coffee was ready. Today I was in full-on song and dance mode, with the squeezy tomato sauce bottle as a microphone. The playlist clicked over to *My Girl*, and I tried to remember The Temptations shuffle.

"Somebody's had a perky pill." I hadn't heard Jen come downstairs.

"I'm just in a good mood."

"Better than being a miserable git, I suppose."

"It certainly is. Come on. Dance with me." Jen stepped back.

"Sod off, you dozy beggar."

"Come on, you know you want to."

"What were you doing, anyway? You had a whole routine going there."

"Classic Temptations. I'll show you." It was all coming back now. The step, the finger clicks, arm in the air, and turn. Within seconds, we were giggling like school kids. The song ended, and I sprinted back to the office to start it again. "From the top."

"From the top? Who do you think you are? Bob Fosse?"

Jen controlled her laughter, and we went into a semi-competent routine. All went well until the third time we executed the stepover and turn. I must've started with the wrong leg or something. I crashed into Jen, and we both hit the floor. Well, I hit the floor. Jen landed on top of me. We were both helpless with laughter. In that split second, everything felt right. Jen was in my arms. We were laughing, and we felt close. Time seemed to stand still.

Then she started screaming.

"Oh, my god. Blood! Lots of it. You're bleeding."

Only then did I notice the pain. I felt the back of my head, or more accurately, the enormous soggy golf ball-sized lump rapidly growing. Jen sprang into action and got me sitting up. She even knew where the first aid kit lived and was ready to swab within seconds. At that point, I realised I could smell tomato sauce.

Sure enough, on the floor behind me was the sauce bottle. Most of the contents were on the carpet or on the back of my head.

"Want a taste," I said, holding up the remains of the bottle.

"Idiot. I thought you'd really damaged yourself." She rubbed at the sauce with her cotton wool.

"Ow."

"It's only sauce."

"Yes, but the lump is real."

"Does it hurt?"

"Yes."

"Good. You frightened me to death." Jen looked at the mass of tomato and cotton wool in her hands and laughed. She daubed the sauce all over my face in one swift movement. Again, the world stood still. Neither of us moved. Then I remembered the sauce bottle and decided it would make an excellent weapon. Jen shrieked and leapt to her feet. She held her hands out in front of her. "No. No. Good suit. I'm wearing my expensive suit. Do not shoot, please." I dropped my hands to my side. "Thank you. Now hand it over." How could resist that smile? I did as she asked. She took the bottle.

"Sucker!"

The remaining sauce left the bottle as she squeezed hard, aiming right between the eyes. Another shriek and she was gone. I followed her into the office.

"I can't believe you did that. Look at the state of me."

"Funny, though."

"Child."

I laughed and sat at my desk.

"I think you probably need to get cleaned up a bit," said Jen.

"D'you think?"

"Tell you what. You clean yourself up, and I'll get us both a bacon butty from the cafe. How's that?"

"Sounds fair."

"Tommy sauce?" Before I could reply, she was out of the door. I could still hear her laughing outside.

I was regretting using the washing-up liquid as shampoo. It

was all I could find to remove the sauce from my hair. I was now itchy and smelt of lemons. At least the headache had gone, and the lump was receding. Jen had even bought a replacement sauce bottle, so life was good.

Jason arrived for our meeting just before two. We were all subdued at first. The film we'd worked so hard to bring to life was now unlikely to get finished. I leaned back in my chair, hands behind my head.

"Can they just walk away like that?"

Jason replied. "They can, and they have. There are rumours they would've pulled the funding even if Roddy hadn't disappeared. It always seemed that they decided incredibly quickly."

"That's what I thought," said Jen. "He'd been gone a couple of days when they pulled out. What do you think happened?"

"As I say, rumours at the moment, but, as we thought, the second company was dodgy. The US authorities have frozen their assets. The FBI has been investigating the source of their revenues and doesn't like what they found."

"Are we under investigation?" Cagney and Casey were one thing, but the FBI was scary.

"Apparently not. I spoke to Flic earlier. She's been speaking to the investigators, who are happy that it was a genuine investment. It just means that all future payments are out of the question. Without them, Flic felt she had no choice but to pull out. She reckons they will get their cash back via the insurers. It could take a long time, though. She's getting a lot of grief from her bosses. It will be a big write-off if the insurers don't pay up."

"But they could get their money back, and we're left with nothing to show for all the work?"

"Not to mention a bloody good script," added Jen.

"That just about sums it up."

"Hang on," I said, sitting upright. "If the only reason Flic is pulling the plug is the loss of half the money, why can't we just raise the money? How much are we talking about?"

"Just short of half a million to get us to the end of the film," said Jason.

I almost choked on my coffee.

"Why on earth do we need that much?"

"It's quite complicated. If you remember, I tried to take you through the numbers…"

That sounded familiar. I apologised to Jason for not taking an interest sooner.

"Would we need all of it?"

"We could work through the plan, see where we might save some money, but we'd still need most of it. There'd be the director and the actors to pay. Location fees, accommodation, post-production and editing. We earmarked a chunk of the money to get a distribution deal. We'd still need to convince Flic to see the project through to the end."

"She might be up for that if the insurers are proving difficult. I'm keen to try if you two are," I said.

Jen and Jason looked at each other. Jen nodded, and just like that, we launched into the numbers to make savings where we could.

In four hours, we covered a lot of ground. I discovered several roles in film production that I never knew existed and how much they cost. We trimmed the budget to the bone. Even then, the shortfall was scary and a significant number. Jen excused herself as her phone lit up with a call from her mum.

I went off to the kitchen and returned with fresh coffee. Jason then pointed out a big hole in the plan.

"Don't forget, we don't have a director. Dick quit and signed up for this new project with Film 4."

"We don't need him," I said. "Jen would do a brilliant job."

Jen had just ended her call and appeared to disagree at full volume with this suggestion.

"Hang on a minute. I've done nothing on the scale we're talking about here. I was an assistant to an old tutor from university, not Martin Scorsese."

"That's just detail." I ducked as the screwed-up sheet of paper headed towards me. Jason saved me.

"Hang on, Jen. I think he's right. Nobody knows better than you and Frankie what the film should be. You were doing a lot more than just assisting. You'd do a great job. As a bonus, you'd help the budget figures no end."

"You mean I'm cheap. Thanks a lot."

"I think he means you're free. We've worked on this for months. Come on, Jen, what else are we going to do?"

"Even if I agreed, we're still a long way short, and we need Flic to change her mind about pulling out."

Jason looked shifty at this point and removed the pen from his mouth.

"Flic might be less of a problem than we thought. When you were talking to your mum and Frankie was making coffee, I called her. She wants to discuss options."

"Let's get her on a conference call right now," I said.

"Actually, we're meeting her tomorrow evening over dinner in London. Technically, when I say we, I mean you, Frankie. It appears she enjoyed your company so much she wants to wine and dine you. We're relying on you to turn on the charm and win her over. I suggested all three of us go, but she insisted on just Frankie."

Jen giggled.

"She's after your body."

"Hey, if it saves the project, she can have it," said Jason. I wasn't sure if he was joking or not. Now, Flic is a beautiful woman, and we hit it off, but this felt like I was being offered as a sacrifice.

"We can't be serious that the future of the entire project relies on me charming Flic. It feels wrong."

"Come on, man. Grow a pair." Jen seemed to find it funny. "Look, if you can clinch the cash, I'll take on the director role," said Jen.

"In that case, I'm off to pack a bag. London, here I come."

33

It felt odd being back at this hotel. I wasn't in the same room, but it was where I'd stayed with Robbie last year and ended up proposing. That seemed like a lifetime ago. Bizarrely, I was here to have dinner with a beautiful woman with the approval of the other beautiful woman in my life. I told myself not to be silly. This was a business meeting, pure and simple. I was still telling myself that when my jaw dropped as Flic glided into the restaurant later that night. She was wearing the most glamorous black dress I'd ever seen in real life. Slashed to the hip at one side and low at the front. I was glad I wasn't here to play poker, as concentration might be challenging.

"Flic, you look fantastic." I stood and went for the kiss on both cheeks. For once in my life, I got it right. No clash of noses or kissing ears.

"You scrub up well yourself."

The days of jeans and a music tee-shirt in this kind of place were well behind me. Fair enough, I was still wearing a tee-shirt but plain black topped off with one of my few indulgences, a Valentino suit that fit almost everywhere. A waiter swooped to pull back Flic's seat, producing menus. Flic's first question was about Roddy.

"He seems perfectly fine and happy, to be honest," I replied.

"Is it true he'd skived off for a bunk-up with an old bandmate?"

"I suspect he'd couch it in more romantic terms, but yes. To be fair, he'd tried to phone me to let me know but got a wrong number."

I explained the mix-up. There was a pause while we selected from the menu. I winced when I realised the wine price I'd looked at was by the glass. I forced my eyes to the other column. Even scarier, but best to buy in bulk.

I'd forgotten how well we'd got on when we'd met. The comfortable conversation meant two courses flew by, not to mention a bottle of wine. Flic turned down dessert, and we both settled for brandy and coffee.

"I suspect you're wondering why I asked to meet you tonight."

"I was hoping you would tell me you'd reconsidered pulling out of the film. There isn't a reason to pull out now that Roddy is back."

Flic leaned forward, resting her elbows on the table and her chin on her hands.

"Apart from the big hole in the finances because of the unfortunate circumstances our partners find themselves in."

"There is that, I suppose."

"I confess, I really believed in this project."

"So, why not up your investment to cover the shortfall?"

"If only it were that simple. To be quite honest, the risk is just too big. I feel exposed enough as it is." It took every fibre of willpower not to look at the bared cleavage at this point. Flic continued. "My boss is very twitchy and sees an insurance claim as the easy way to get back our investment."

"But you believe in the film…"

"I do. I think you and Jen have done a great job. You've

developed an excellent script, and I'm confident you could write many more. People are talking about you a lot." I must've looked alarmed. "I've been doing my homework on you. It confirms that you have a happy knack for quickly getting things up and running. You've got great ideas. I'd love to invest in that."

"I sense there's a but."

"There is. As I say, I'm under a lot of pressure from the States. We've looked at the numbers in great detail. Jason says that you can shave the budget, but we still have a significant gap even if we keep our investment there."

"And you're not willing to bridge the gap?"

"It's more that I'm unable rather than unwilling." The waiter arrived with the coffee and brandy. "I have a couple of proposals for you to consider."

Jen's words were in my head about her being after my body. I told myself it would be a sacrifice, taking one for the team. Flic took a business card and pen from her clutch bag. She wrote on the card and pushed it across the table. "I'm allowed to extend our funding if your production company can provide a sizeable investment. Increasing your skin in the game if you like. Come up with this much and we'll fund the rest. We can work out precise details later, but I need to know your response within a week."

I reached out and took the card. Fuck me - that was a big number.

"That's a lot of money."

"It is. But you believe in the film. You think it's going to be a gigantic success. The sky is the limit for what you make."

My heart was racing. I was trying to work out how much I could scrape together. It wasn't enough. Jason and Jen would have to match my investment. Even then, it would be a push. Maybe I could sell my body after all.

"You said you had a couple of proposals. I must tell you, if you're after my body..."

"I am," said Flic with a smile. "But not like that. Film or no film, I believe in you. I want to offer you a job."

"A job?"

"Yes. We're creating a starter division to create content across new media. Streaming platforms, social media, and new markets that we haven't even defined yet. You have the ideas and technical insight to make a great success of it."

"But I have a job, writing with Jen."

"And you're very good at it. You'd be even better at this. The number on the card that I want you to invest in the film is also what we're offering as a basic salary. You'll have a car, bonuses, stock, all the usual."

My heart was racing now. I sipped the brandy and imagined the lifestyle on offer.

"What's the catch?" I asked.

"No catch. Well, maybe one. We want you to start in May, and you'd need to find somewhere to live. We want you based in New York. Two weeks to decide on that. Dinner is on me. Sorry, I must dash as my fiancé is waiting in the bar."

Flic shook my hand and was gone. What an offer. Could I do the job? Could I turn it down? What about Jen; could I leave her and go to New York? Should I have had a pudding?

I got back to the hotel after eleven. Jen would be fast asleep by now. I desperately wanted to speak to her, but I wasn't sure what to say. In the lift, my finger hovered over the button for the rooftop bar. In the end, I changed my mind and headed for my room. As I opened the door, a text arrived. It was from Jason asking how things had gone. I replied, asking if he was okay to talk. The phone rang as I pulled a beer from the minibar and flopped into the armchair.

"Do you have good news?" asked Jason.

"Sort of. I think."

I explained the investment being back on the table if we could come up with our contribution.

"That's a lot of money."

"But it would allow us to finish the film. It could still be a success. Flic would give it everything to push the distribution deal."

Jason seemed to hesitate.

"I think we could do with some success. The bank is getting twitchy. They're not willing to make any more cash available. Without the film, the production company goes under."

"And without cash, the film goes under. Don't suppose you're a secret millionaire that can invest private funds."

"Not so you'd notice."

"What about your contacts for potential investors?"

"Difficult. Word is out about the FBI investigation."

"But that's nothing to do with us." I sounded a bit like a child denying blame.

"I know that, and you know that, but how can I put it? Shit sticks. All people can see is a rotten deal. I'm doing everything to distance us, but it will take time."

"We've got a fortnight. So, unless Jen and I can come up with the cash between us, we're back to being dead in the water?"

"Afraid so. If you know of any buried treasure, it's time to dig it up," said Jason.

Then it hit me. Did I have some buried treasure? The rolls of film I'd found in the crate. I'd been so busy I'd done nothing with them. Early work by a genuine genius had to be worth something? I made a mental note to dig the tapes out as soon as I got home.

I looked at the bottle in my hand. How much should I tell Jason about the final bit of tonight's conversation with Flic? I decided I needed advice.

"Can I tell you something in confidence?"

"If you've murdered somebody, I have to go to the police."

"Fair enough. It's something Flic said. She's offered me a job. Mega money—I mean ridiculous."

"That's great. Isn't it?"

"Well, yeah, sort of. It would be a fantastic opportunity."

"But?"

"It's in New York. It would mean leaving all my family, friends, everything."

"You mean Jen?"

"Am I that obvious?"

"Pretty much. Look, I know it's complicated between you but, for my money, you belong together. As writers, but also as a couple. I don't know all the details, but Jen told me she wasn't ready for a relationship. I suppose it comes down to whether you're willing to wait or cash in and take the job. It is a great opportunity. That said, people like Jen don't come along very often."

"I think I need another beer."

34

I gave up trying to sleep at stupid o'clock, and by seven, I was in my first-class seat to Leeds. I welcomed the coffee and bacon sandwich before texting Jen. She replied within two minutes, and we agreed to meet for lunch. There were two questions in my head all night. Could we raise the money to finish the film? New York - should I stay or should I go? It may have been good enough to name it twice, but was it sufficient to leave Jen behind? As Alexandra Palace slipped behind us, I opened my iPad.

The person behind bellowed into his phone. I thought about pointing to the 'no phones' sign, but couldn't face the conflict. I slipped on my headphones. The Clash seemed a sensible soundtrack to my morning, and the *Combat Rock* album blocked out the annoying man.

I pulled together a list of all the places I could lay my hands on cash. I could sell my house. Maybe impractical, as I'd still need somewhere to live. Unless I went to New York. But that would mean not seeing Jen. After a few laps of my brain, I discarded selling the house. I could take out a mortgage. This earned an asterisk. I created a side column - How much could I raise by mortgaging the house?

I had savings from the children's books selling well. How

much did I have left in my OEIC (whatever that was)? I guessed an amount. Another asterisk and another question - How do I access my OEIC (whatever that is)? Could I get an advance against Roddy's autobiography? Without an advance, could we finish the movie? This was a catch-22. Without the film, the publishers weren't interested in the book.

What about the films I'd found in the crate? It was ages since I'd found them, and I'd done nothing with them. What if they were genuine films by David Hockney? Could I raise some of the money by selling them? Was I obliged to give them back to Joe if they proved valuable? Joe's mate could help to sell them. What was his name? Honest John? Bent Bobby? No - Dodgy Alan, that was it. I suppose before I approached him, I should get to see what was on the films. Bernard! He was a film nut. He was bound to have the means of viewing the reels. Two quick phone calls later, I'd sorted it. Bernard was happy to verify what was on the films, and I'd booked a courier to deliver them to him this afternoon. How organised was I getting now that I was a proper film producer?

Looking at the list was more problematical. I was adding more asterisks and questions than anything else. What if I took the job and commissioned the film as part of the new role? Not even I had the balls to do that. I didn't even bother with an asterisk for that one. I stared out of the window. In the gap between songs, I could still hear the bloke behind droning on to his client on the phone, about investment returns. Hang on. He was some kind of financial adviser. I had a financial adviser. Barney was the one that set up my investment plan. He could do things like give advice on how to raise money.

I called him now and explained what I needed. He made a lot of worrying noises, pointing out that we'd been around this loop before. He agreed to pull together a picture of what I could raise. He was less than impressed that I asked him to get back to me before he packed in for Christmas. He pointed out that he was finishing this afternoon as Sunday was Christmas Eve. We were wrapping up the call when the steward tapped me on the shoulder and pointed at the no phone sign. I was about to protest and pointed at the bloke behind, only to find that he was fast asleep. Any protest was futile as the steward was already lumbering down the carriage.

Yawning, I contented myself with the thought of a boozy lunch with Jen, then sleeping it off at home. Then it hit me: I realised I'd ignored Christmas. I was going to spend the day with Jen and Charley. I had shopping to do. Even worse, if today was Saturday, I was due tonight at my parents' house. I had to join the hordes in Leeds for shopping and then a late afternoon drive to the coast. So much for a boozy lunch.

Merry Christmas.

By half-past eleven, I was hot, sweaty and laden with Christmas presents for Jen, Charley, Mum and Dad. The pubs and bars were already filling with my fellow shoppers. We hadn't factored in that it was going to be so busy when we'd suggested lunch. I called Jen.

"Hello, you. I was wondering where you were."

"I'm in Leeds, about to jump in a taxi," I said.

"Great. It just occurred to me that pubs will be crazy today. How do you fancy picking up some sushi and coming to my place?"

"That sounds perfect. I'll see you in an hour."

Ten minutes later, I had a massive bag of sushi containers and I was in a taxi. A quick pit stop at home, then off to the calm of Jen's house. From there, I could head straight to the coast to see my parents. I yawned and wondered if I could fit in a nap. Maybe not, but at least Mum would fuss around me tonight.

Feeling much better after a shower and changing clothes, I dropped the films at the post office for the courier. I arrived at Jen's, finding the table set and candles lit.

"Candles at lunchtime? Are you made of money?"

"I just thought it was nice and relaxing. Making the most of the tranquillity before the Christmas whirlwind gets back from her friend's party."

"I take it she's excited."

Jen laughed and spread her arms wide.

"You could say that. I'm worried she might explode before the big day. Speaking of which, are you still happy to come and spend it with us?"

"Only if there's going to be booze and chocolates."

"Done, but I was also hoping you might put together the doll's house that arrived this morning. I hadn't realised it was going to be flat-pack."

"Tell you what. If somebody were to be ordering pizza on Christmas Eve, I could help distract Charley, then build the house when she's in bed."

"That would be great. We've missed having you around. We can even watch your two Christmas films. Make sure Rickman gets what he deserves."

"You're on."

Jen took the carrier bag of sushi and told me to sit. As she unpacked the various containers, I wondered whether this was the time to talk to her about New York.

"Beer?"

I think we were both surprised with my answer.

"No thanks. I'll stick to coke, please."

"Are you okay? You've never turned down a beer before."

"I'm in the car because I need to drive to the coast later to stay with my parents. Plus, I got next to no sleep last night.

I'd be dopey all afternoon if I had a beer."

"So it went well with Flic? I knew she was after your body."

"Nothing like that, I promise. It was business. Besides, you know I'm sort of spoken for, I think." Jen smiled, almost shyly. She passed me a can of coke and I continued. "Flic came up with some interesting proposals. She's prepared to maintain her funding if we can come up with the shortfall."

"How much are we talking?"

"A lot! I don't suppose you've got a small fortune lying around looking for a home?"

"Far from it. Your mate, Barney just helped me set up a trust for Charley in case anything should happen to me," said Jen.

"Like what?" Alarm bells were ringing.

"Anything. Don't worry, I'm not ill. As a single mum, I just worry about Charley. What if anything happened to me? All my cash went into the fund. I've just about got enough to live on until I finish Jason's book. In fact, I've just taken on a couple of commissions from a magazine. Sorry. Does that make it difficult?"

"Not sure, to be honest. I don't think we can raise the money in time."

"Something will come up: it always does. You got anything in the pipeline if the film doesn't happen?"

I took a deep breath. It was time to explain about New York. Then Jen's phone rang.

"Hi, Mum. No, just having lunch with Frankie." Jen pulled the phone away from her face. "Mum says hello."

"Hello, Geraldine." I waved and helped myself to a piece of sashimi, feeling ridiculously proud for enjoying the small rectangle of salmon and rice. A choice I would never make in my previous life. Thanks to Jen's civilising influence, I was a regular at this kind of thing. I still drew the line at fish with heads, but they didn't build Rome in a day.

Jen finished her call and attacked the sushi. She was an expert with the miniature chopsticks, handling the whole ginger and soy sauce business with ease. My approach was more basic and involved fingers. Even then, three drops of soy sauce appeared down the front of my shirt.

"Bugger."

"Don't rub at it. You'll only make it worse. Hang on." Jen sprang into action, grabbing a bottle from the cupboard under the sink and a cloth. She grabbed a handful of my shirt and squirted some foul-smelling liquid on me without asking. As she leaned in and dabbed at the fabric, I breathed in the aroma of Jen's shampoo.

"Mucky pup."

I protested my innocence.

"Not fair. I didn't even think anything bad!"

"The soy sauce. I was ignoring the fact that you sniffed me again."

"All I did was breathe in. If you go around sticking your head under somebody's nose, you're gonna get sniffed."

"Pervert."

"It's just a nice smelling shampoo."

"Thank you, I think. There: all done."

I looked down. Apart from a damp patch, I was pristine again.

"How did you know about that?"

"I'm a mum to a five-year-old food spraying machine. I believe you've met her? You get good with stains in this job." Jen resumed her seat and looked at me, head on one side.

"What have I done now?"

"Nothing." She smiled but looked sad. If I was in writing mode, I'd have said she was wistful. "It's just that Sean used to do that."

"What, sniff your hair."

"Ha, I knew you were sniffing me! No, he used to chuck food down whatever he was wearing."

"Ladies tell me it's a desirable feature."

"They were lying." Jen pointed at the neat pile of serviettes that had come with the takeaway. I took the hint and grabbed a couple.

"You still miss Sean, don't you?"

"What's the saying? It gets easier, but it never gets easy."

"He'd be very proud of what you've achieved. Charley is a great kid. Your writing career is going well, and even though you miss him so much, you hold it all together. Did he like sushi?"

"No. Sean would run a mile before he'd touch it. He's like you used to be. Fish had to be battered and come with chips and mushy peas." I dabbed at the single tear on Jen's cheek with the serviette. "Thanks."

"It was nothing."

"I didn't mean the dabbing. Thank you for asking about Sean." She picked up the coke can but didn't take a drink. "It's so rare I get the chance to talk about him. When he died, that's all I wanted to do, but friends and family just wanted to cheer me up. Every time I said anything about him, they'd change the subject. It drove me up the wall. I let things fester. In the end, I just gave up."

"Do you talk to Charley about him?"

"I do, but I'm unsure how much it means to her. Sean's just a picture on the bookcase. She knows he's Dad, but has no real concept of what Dad means. He never got to take her to school or the park. Tucking her up in bed or reading stories is what Mum does, or Gran. Uncle Frankie too, when he's around."

"I'm sure she understands more than you think, and as she gets older, you'll make sure she knows how much her dad meant to you."

Jen smiled again as another tear rolled down. She reached across the table and put her hand on mine.

"What would I do without you?"

"Make twice the money from being Vince Taylor?"

"Suppose there is that." Jen laughed and blew her nose. Not the time to mention New York.

35

Christmas seems to be a big punctuation mark in my life, chunking it up into manageable pieces. I was with Mum, Dad and Cheryl two years ago at my old childhood home. Within days, Cheryl left me, and Ambrose issued his five-tweet challenge. It's fair to say that changed my life. So much so, that I was marrying Robbie last year at Christmas. Then she legged it, taking just about everything I owned. Instead of a wedding reception and happily ever after, she ended up in a prison cell, and I was back to being single.

Now, it felt like Christmas was a critical junction again. I craved a committed relationship with Jen. I understood her reticence and the devastating effect Sean's death had had on her. Then again, Flic was offering the chance of a lifetime. The salary alone was ridiculous. Throw in the exciting job and life in New York—was there any wonder my head was spinning?

"Sorry, Mum, what was that?"

"I asked what you wanted to drink with your meal?"

"What are you having?"

"Advocaat."

"With Turkey?"

"It's Christmas. Do you want one?"

"I'd prefer to chew my own toenails. What about you,

Dad? What're you having?"

"I fancy a beer," he answered without looking up from his sketch pad.

"I'll have the same then."

"No, you won't," said Mum.

"Why not?"

"There isn't any. The shopping delivery isn't coming until tomorrow."

"Okay. I'll have a glass of wine." Mum looked at me as if I was being awkward on purpose. "Let me guess. Shopping delivery tomorrow?"

"No, smart arse. I forgot to add some to the order. Advocaat?"

"God, no. Hang on, I've got a couple of bottles in the back of the car that I picked up for emergencies. I think this qualifies."

At least the wine had chilled on the drive over. I shivered as I returned to the nice, warm kitchen and got busy setting the table. Mum had insisted that we have the entire Christmas dinner. Sprouts had been boiling when I arrived, and she still doubted they were ready. The smoke from the oven suggested the turkey might be. The smoke detector screamed. Mum was nowhere to be seen. I turned off the oven, retrieved the singed bird, and opened the kitchen window. After some emergency tea towel wafting, the alarm went quiet. It made a tiny beep two seconds later, as if it was just making a point, and then peace returned. Dad looked up from his artwork.

"Everything all right?"

"Fine, Dad. Where's Mum?"

"I think she went to watch the telly."

I walked through to the other room. Sure enough, Mum was watching *Pointless Celebrities*.

"Hello, love. Just putting my feet up for five minutes."

I went back to the kitchen to deal with the rest of the meal. Dad put his pad down and almost whispered.

"She's doing that recently, leaving pans on and forgetting about them. Good job you were here."

"But you heard the alarm, you could've…" I stopped myself. As if it hadn't entered his head that he could do something in the kitchen, Dad looked confused. Forty years of it being Mum's domain had conditioned him. I poured us both a glass of wine and joined him at the table.

"This dementia thing that the doctor says I've got…"

"It can't be that bad if you remembered you've got it."

He considered this for a second, then laughed and raised his glass.

"Aye, happen you're right, son. The trouble is, I think your mum's as bad as me.She plays hell with me for forgetting stuff that I'm pretty sure she hasn't asked me to do in the first place."

"Has she seen the doctor about it?"

"Refuses point-blank. Gets quite arsey if I suggest it. Says it's me that's forgetful and leaves it at that." I wondered if any pensioner in the country still remembered anything. Dad continued. "Anyway, I was talking to the doctor about me, and he asked if we'd set up power of attorney yet."

"What's that?"

"It's a legal thing, but it means once we've signed it, you'd be able to take control of the bank account, decide for us, that sort of thing."

"Shit, that's miles off yet."

"That's the whole point of these things. You never know. Besides, it doesn't kick in until the doctor says we're both gaga or snuff it. It's all set up. We just need you to sign it. There's some other stuff to look at, but your pan's boiling over."

I jumped up and rescued things just as Mum re-entered.

"What on earth are you doing? Here let me."

Within seconds, the crisis was over, and she was straight into finishing the Christmas dinner, just as she had done for the last forty years.

By eight o'clock, we were in the front room. We'd agreed that we could do presents tonight as I would be at Jen's on Christmas Day. The meal was lovely, although the sprouts could've improved with about three days less boiling.

The smelly stuff and hand cream had gone down well with Mum. To be fair, it did every year. I got socks and a fiver again. The pattern hasn't changed in twenty years. I thought about asking for a cost-of-living increase but decided against it. Dad was very pleased with the vinyl re-issue of Bruce Springsteen's London gig from 1975. Ambrose had got hold of a copy. It was extravagant, but the look on his face was worth it. We agreed we'd listen to it later when Mum went to bed.

Mum was onto her third advocaat. I suspected bedtime wouldn't be late for her tonight.

"There's something else for you, Dad, but it is selfish of me as well."

"How does that work?"

I produced the extra parcel. It had two framed enlargements from Schrodinger's Crate. The prints of Roy Orbison and Miles Davis. Dad held them up.

"This is great. Thanks, Frankie. Why are these selfish?"

"Because I want you to draw them for me. I thought pencil drawings would be more personal than photos. I want to get them framed for Joe and Rupert's club."

"That's not selfish. I'd love to. I'll get cracking tomorrow."

"Oh Mum. I spoke to Roddy about Blackpool. He remembered you well."

"Told you he would," she said, with a slight slur. She

smiled to herself. "How's the film going, now that Roddy's back?"

I sighed. "It's not really."

I explained about the backers pulling out. I wondered whether to tell them about New York. Could I leave them as they both showed their age? Dad pointed at the mantlepiece.

"Grab that envelope, Frankie. It's for you."

I stood up and took the white envelope.

"What is it?"

"Well, I told you we'd seen the solicitor to get advice about the future. As well as the power of whatsit, he told us to start some financial planning. By gifting some of our savings, we can avoid you paying tax on it when you inherit. The catch is we have to live long enough for it to qualify." Dad waved away the start of my protest. "Don't look like that. We're not planning to go anywhere just yet. We're just preparing, so that's for you."

"The solicitor says you should get some financial advice to invest it. It'll make a nice little nest egg for when you retire," said Mum. "Ooh, this advocaat's going right through me." Dad looked at me and winked. Mum disappeared into the bathroom.

"Bugger a nest egg," he said. "If that means you can finish your film, use it. You'd make me so happy. Plenty of time to worry about retiring. This film could be huge for you. Do it."

I opened the envelope.

"Jesus, Dad, this is too much."

"Rubbish. You'd get it anyway when we peg out. Now get that film made. We've got plenty left to live on."

I looked at the cheque in my hands. Things were looking up.

36

The call from Bernard came at bang on nine o'clock. This was exciting. We established we were both fine and Roddy was fine. Then I took a deep breath. This could mean the end of any financial worries.

"Go on then, Bernard. Did you watch the films? Are they the buried treasure we need?"

There was a pause. It felt like Bernard was mulling over his words. He might have been building tension like they do on the telly.

"I hate to be the bearer of bad news."

Bollocks. So much for building the tension.

"How do you mean bad news?"

"Well, I've looked at the films. Both of them are fascinating. It seems the PE teacher was a bit of a film enthusiast and very proud of his teams."

"But what about the label? Surely it said, Hockney?"

"I think the 'k' just has a bit of an extravagant flourish. It definitely says Hockey."

I had to laugh. Talk about seeing what you wanted to see rather than what was there. I apologised profusely for wasting Bernard's time. Still, he assured me he loved every minute, apart from crushing my dreams. We promised to meet up in the New Year and wished each other a Merry Christmas.

I was back to square one, but had one last chance. I had no time to worry, Barney was calling.

"Have you lost your fucking mind?"

He'd definitely read last night's text.

"Hello, Barney. Good to talk. How are you?"

"I'm fine, mate. Just worried that you've lost it."

"I take it you are referring to my proposal to further invest in the film I've poured my heart and soul into for the last few months?"

"I don't mind your heart and soul. They cost nothing. I'm more worried about you risking everything you've got on an investment that will most likely fall on its arse."

"I'm touched by your confidence in me," I said with a grin.

"How many films make a profit? Especially by first-time writers who are also producing."

"Jen's going to be directing as well."

"Oh, that makes all the difference, then. Silly me, thinking you'd got Simon Spielberg lined up."

"Steven."

"What?"

"Steven Spielberg. You said, Simon."

"Sorry. My mistake. Maybe you're not crackers after all." I tried to decide if pleading would alter Barney's attitude. Then he surprised me. "For what it's worth, I think you and Jen are fabulous writers. If anybody can pull off something as mad as this, it would be you two. It's risky. Even with your house as security and all your savings, you'd still be short."

"I've got an OEIC too."

"Like you know what that is. I've included it. Still short."

"Even with the cheque from my parents?"

"Yes. That's all that stops you from being totally screwed."

"So that's it then. We scrap the film and walk away?"

"I didn't say that, did I?" I suspected Barney was taking a drink. "How about if your uncle Barney made up the shortfall? I'd like to invest."

"You? What happened to films not making a profit and all that stuff?"

"Are you trying to talk me out of this? It's been a good year. What can I say? I believe in you guys. All I ask is a credit as associate producer and a plus-one for the premiere. Wait a minute, that's not all I'm asking. I want a return on my investment, but I'll work out the numbers later. In principle, are we partners?"

"Too right we are. We won't let you down."

"Thing is, I'll still have a house even if this goes tits up, but I'm not sure you will. No pressure."

The line went dead. I jumped from my seat, punched the air, and shouted at the top of my voice.

"You fuckin' beauty."

Everybody in the cafe stared at me, but I didn't care. I had a film to make.

37

I was like a kid at Christmas. It was Christmas, and I've always been a big kid, so it was not surprising. I'd been frantic for the last twenty-four hours. All I wanted to do was get filming.

"For the fifth time, it was the holidays," said the voice of reason, Jason.

Everybody was concentrating on celebrating rather than thinking of getting back to work. We'd both been hitting the phones all day lining up as much of the team as we could. We were aiming at January the 8th to have everybody back and ready to resume. Jen and I would spend the time in between reviewing what we had already and refining the schedule. Even with Barney's investment, we were trimming as much as possible from the budget.

By four o'clock, nobody was answering their phone. I decided it was time to take the hint and prepare to spend the next couple of days with Jen and Charley. I had my overnight bag, and I was all set. The presents were all wrapped.

Since yesterday, I'd been so busy I hadn't had time to think about the rather enormous elephant in the room. What should I do about the job offer? Flic wanted me to start in New York by May. The schedule for the film suggests that we would have everything wrapped by then, and if all went well, we would hand it over to the distributor. In theory, I could fly to New York and begin a new life. A life with a salary and a job I could only have dreamt about. A life without Jen. Could we stay friends if I was three thousand three hundred and forty-eight miles away? Obviously, I'd checked how far. Other people do it - make long distance relationships work. It might even make the lack of a physical relationship easier. There was always FaceTime. Would I be able to smell Jen's hair on FaceTime?

Should I stay? We could achieve anything with a successful film under our belts. Carry on working together. Maybe, given time, Jen would decide I was worth the risk. Maybe.

I arrived at Jen's just after six and walked into excited screeches. Charley, resplendent in a monkey onesie, had worked herself into a pre-Santa frenzy. As much as anything, Jen looked relieved to see me.

"Reinforcements! Great timing."

"I also bring wine and gifts."

"Even better. Would you mind entertaining madame while I grab a quick shower? Great, you're a star."

Before I could think of a decent excuse, she was gone. Charley was great fun to be with. The bonus was that it was always via a bedtime story that I had the sole responsibility. At that point, she was pretty dopey and manageable. This was different. She expected me to take part in the game she was playing in front of the TV. I had to join in the dance steps demonstrated by some noisy pixie on the screen. How hard could it be? Charley appeared to be an expert. I was tentative at first, but soon got the hang of it. My mind flashed back to The Temptations' shuffle incident — not my finest moment.

The steps got quicker and more involved. At least this would burn off the excess energy, and Charley would be quieter. Twenty minutes later, I was a sweaty, bedraggled mess, ready to collapse into the armchair. I was just about to surrender when the music finished.

Charley, the pixie, and I took deep breaths. All three of us clapped. Charley's cry of "again" almost reduced me to tears.

I negotiated a break, and we agreed she would do some colouring. I flopped into the chair just as a refreshed Jen returned.

"It's all right for some, sitting around. Madame's run me ragged all afternoon."

I was too out of breath to argue my defence and could just nod when Jen waved a wine glass. Within minutes, the three of us were watching *The Muppet Christmas Carol*. It had a magical effect on Charley, who returned to tranquillity. In fact, it worked so well that within half an hour, she was fast asleep. With the effortless movements of an expert, Jen picked her up and transferred her to bed. No story necessary. Maybe the dance routine had done the trick, and I'd exhausted her. When Jen returned, she asked me to choose between Muppets and food. The food won.

Over dinner, we talked about Barney's offer and how the film was back on the cards. Jen had protested that she wasn't up to directing by herself, but I was having none of it. She was just as excited as I was that we could complete the project. New York was on my mind, but I bottled it.

I'd eaten my weight in pizza, convincing myself that the small green salad made it healthy. I was about to pour more wine when Jen made a polite coughing noise.

"What have I done?" My default position was that I'd done something. I checked my shirt for spillage, but it was clean.

"Don't worry. You're not in trouble yet. It's just that you said–"

The penny dropped. "The doll's house?"

"I promise I'll open another bottle once it's done. I just can't see you coping with it if you have a glass too many."

"True. How hard can it be? Point me at it and give me ten minutes."

We cleared the table, and Jen pulled the box out of the under-stairs cupboard. I told her to cue the film, and I'd be with her in no time. An hour and a half later, Jen came to rescue me.

"Where did you get this from? Toys-Are-Bastards?"

"I thought you said ten minutes? Can I help?" I considered throwing a strop, but just nodded. Jen picked up the instruction diagram and considered the pile of debris I'd created on the table. "I think this bit might be the wrong way up," she said.

"But it says insert B into that hole there. The hole's in the wrong place."

Jen turned the offending piece the other way up, and B found its home. I slotted the rest of the bits in, and we had a complete doll's house in seconds.

"My hero!" Jen came behind me and kissed the top of my head. It felt nice.

"Are you sniffing my head?" She laughed and clipped me round the ear.

"Charley'll love that. You'll be a proper hero. *Love Actually* awaits. Come on."

When the film finished, *Celebrations* wrappers surrounded us and I felt well and truly festive.

"*Die Hard*?"

Jen looked at her watch.

"It's a bit late."

"Are you saying Rickman gets away with it because it took me so long to put the house together?"

"Not at all. I'm very grateful, and I think we both know Bruce will kick his arse whether or not we watch it tonight."

Die Hard had become a Christmas tradition, but Jen could do no wrong in my eyes.

"How about you pick some music?"

I didn't need to be asked again. In seconds, Jason Isbell's *It Takes A Lifetime* was floating across the room.

I topped up our glasses and settled back into the overstuffed sofa. We sat in silence, side by side, and listened to the music.

"That's a clever line," said Jen. "Man is a product of all the people that he ever loved. And it don't make a difference how it ended up."

"He's a clever man."

"Except it makes a difference, doesn't it? Every experience adds something. Each person you ever get close to affects the person you are and what you'll become."

The song closed with the line, "Our day will come if it takes a lifetime." Jen squeezed my hand.

"Like you said, he's a clever man. I know I'm a pain in the arse." She took a sip of wine and pondered.

"Most of the time, you're not." She laughed and slapped my hand playfully.

"But I am. I know how much you mean to me, and I appreciate the time you spend with Charley and me."

"It's not a hardship. The pizza was lovely." I shut up. Jen wanted to say something.

"Look, I'm trying. Honest, I am."

"I know, and I understand. Sean was everything. He left an enormous gap." Jen nodded and stared into the flickering fire. After a pause, she continued.

"It can't be easy for you. Look, I'll try to explain." Jen put her glass on the table and turned to face me. "It hurts so much when you're a kid and fall off your bike. You put a plaster on your knee. The plaster comes off a few days later, and you're left with a scab. Every kid picked at the scab, always too soon. You pick it off before it's healed, and it hurts even more. It scabs over again, but you can't help picking at it. One day, the scab comes off, and the skin underneath has healed. No pain. Back on the bike, so to speak."

"So you've still got scabby knees?"

"Right."

I held out my right arm, and Jen snuggled under it.

"I can wait."

"Are you going to sniff my head?"

"Probably."

"Fill your boots. Merry Christmas."

38

Exactly a week later, my anxiety levels were through the roof. I'd tried to tell myself it was stupid. My choice was between two excellent outcomes. Should I take the job in New York? I'd have creative control over my own media division, considerable budgets to make things happen, and a spectacular loft overlooking Central Park. Fair enough, I'd made the last bit up. The dream apartment was out of my league even with the salary on offer, for now.

If I stayed, I would start a new project with Jen, and maybe, just maybe, she would be ready for a life partner. We would become a family: me, Jen, and Charley. There was sometimes a dog in that fantasy—a golden Labrador. In other versions, there was no dog. The thought of having to pick up dog poo every day didn't figure high on my bucket list.

Somewhere between these two fantasy worlds was me. The same me that had spent New Year's Eve two years ago, not realising that Cheryl had left me to live with my best mate. The same me had spent weeks not speaking to a soul, drinking a lot and becoming ever so slightly smelly.

Then there was last year. I'd spent Christmas with Jen and Charley but New Year's Eve alone, licking my wounds after my wedding to Robbie had exploded in my face. Another year on, still just uncle Frankie, with the prospect of starting another new year on my own.

I'd turned down plenty of invites. Joe and Rupert were hitting a club in Leeds, while Ambrose and Stella were having a grown-up dinner party. Jen was spending the evening with her parents. Even my Mum and Dad had suggested I go to stay with them. I made different excuses for each of them.

Maybe it was melodramatic, but I hatched a plan in my head. I ordered a pizza. The wine was chilling. I had a fresh bottle of Spanish brandy and I was ready to sit in my back garden to watch the fireworks at midnight. Two draft emails sat in a new folder. One accepts the job, and the other turns it down. I would send one email at 1am. I picked the time based on having a nice extended sit in the garden and getting to bed at a reasonable time. Maybe I was getting old. However, nowhere in the plan did I consider that getting very drunk was not an excellent preparation for making the most significant decision of my life. Then again, I had no other suggestions. I promised myself that if I sent the mail at exactly one o'clock, whatever I picked would be the right decision, and all would be well. If I didn't send it, everything would turn to shit—again.

I opened a bottle of Cloudy Bay Sauvignon Blanc. Important decisions justified expensive wine. As you might expect, I'd prepared a playlist for the evening. It started with *The Rise And Fall Of Ziggy Stardust And The Spiders From Mars*. This playlist meant business.

For the task ahead, I had post-its and different coloured pens. I planned lists of pros and cons for each future. I would apply method and logic.

In the end, I got pissed and fell asleep in the chair.

The fireworks woke me up. I felt like crap, but I had to get the plan back on track. Pulling on my fleece, I grabbed the brandy. I'd always loved other people's fireworks, but I couldn't face spending loads of money on them. As Alan Partridge said, you're just setting fire to your money.

I'd slept through a good hour of my playlist. We were now on to *Around The Sun* by REM. Maybe my subconscious had timed this song for about now. Michael Stipe's words hit me hard. '*It's easier to leave than to be left behind. Leaving was never my something or other. Leaving New York never easy, I saw the light fading out.*' I'd never understood the song, but it all seemed profound and appropriate, given my drunken state.

By five to one, the fireworks had died out. Revellers from The Crown were making their way home. I rose unsteadily to my feet and went back inside. I closed the door and sat in the dark at the kitchen table. My laptop sprang to life. I clicked send, farted loudly, and went to bed.

39

I was at a loose end. After working flat out for months, I was a bit bored today. I'd agreed with myself not to dwell on the email I'd sent in a drunken haze. It was done, decision made and worrying about it would not make a blind bit of difference. I felt guilty that I hadn't discussed everything with Jen. I tried to justify myself by remembering that every time I plucked up the courage to speak to her, something dramatic prevented it. Whatever the future held, making a success of *The Hubberholme Syndrome* was my immediate focus. It was the only thing I could influence for now. At least, I would if everybody wasn't on holiday.

The team was due back at work in a week. Jen was away for a few days with her family, and nobody seemed to be available to keep me entertained on a cold, wet January morning. Whenever this happened, I took solace in the cafe.

"Morning Frankie, Happy New Year!" Ildiko was her usual cheerful self, making me feel guilty for being miserable.

"Happy New Year, Ildiko."

"Coffee and bacon sandwich, as usual?"

I was about to agree but embraced the new year with a new me.

"Actually, no. I'm in the mood to shake things up a bit. I'll have tea and a fried egg sandwich, please."

"Very decisive. Have a seat, and I'll be with you in a minute."

I slumped into a seat in the window and yawned. I could do with a jolt of caffeine and called through to the kitchen.

"Ildiko, scrap the tea. I need coffee - a large one, please."

"Okay, no problem." Before she went back to her task, I made another decision.

"Tell you what, that bacon smells nice. Can I have some in my egg sandwich?"

"Of course, coming up."

I looked around at the cosy cafe and wondered how often I'd been here for breakfast. It must be in the hundreds by now. When I started coming, I would have a full English. But, after several egg-related tee-shirt incidents, I'd migrated to the traditional bacon butty. Today, I was wearing my much-loved Saw Doctors tee-shirt. The thought of getting egg yolk on it was worrying.

"Ildiko. Hold the egg. I don't want to take the risk."

"So, coffee and bacon butty, as usual."

"That would be very nice. Thank you."

Effecting change was all very well, but I know what I like, and I like what I know. Just then, the door opened, and I glimpsed a high vis jacket as it passed me at speed and headed downstairs to the toilets. Its more leisurely partner paused by my table. It was Smirky.

"Morning Frankie, I'm glad we've bumped into you. I could do with a word."

What the hell had I done now?

"Have a seat. I'm all yours."

"Thanks, I'll just order our coffees to go."

Ildiko had spotted him and shouted across the room that she'd be with him in a minute as Smirky pulled out the chair opposite and sat down. He fiddled with the salt cellar but didn't meet my eye.

"You said you needed a word. I can't be a suspect again?"

"No. Nothing like that." Having dropped the salt cellar, he brushed the mess from the table and placed the small glass bottle back upright. "It's DI Cagney."

"Oh, great. How have I upset him this time?"

"No, nothing like that. The inspector's in a bit of bother."

"Good. Well, not good, but he made my life miserable. What's wrong with him?"

"He's getting a lot of stick from the other detectives because of the ransom note. They all think it's hilarious. He doesn't. He's been getting one a day left on his desk."

"Seems quite funny from where I'm sitting."

"It's not just that. The Assistant Chief Constable, DI Cagney's boss, is on the warpath. Between you and me, he's worried that you'll make a complaint. He thinks that the note was such a cock-up you could make things very embarrassing for the force if you wanted."

"That's not a bad idea. I need something to do this week." Smirky shifted in his seat.

"The thing is, the ACC wants to make sure you and the press don't cause him any embarrassment."

"So why is he sending you to speak to me? No offence, but why pass that message via you?"

"He doesn't know I'm here. He'd kill me if he found out. Mum suggested it."

"Your mum suggested it?"

"The Assistant Chief Constable is Uncle Ronnie, my mum's brother."

For once, I was speechless. Smirky continued.

"He's a good person to have on your side. If there is anything you need, he can make things happen."

Ildiko arrived with my breakfast and two takeaway coffees. She asked Smirky how his mum was before returning to the kitchen. I took a sip of hot black coffee and toyed with the idea that had just come to me.

"If he's that worried, maybe there might be something he could help us with. It might distract me from any idea of going to the press."

"Just between us—what would that be?"

"Do you fancy being a film star?"

"How do you mean?" Tinkle arrived and slipped into the seat next to me.

"We still need to film a few scenes featuring a couple of detectives. A police car and smart officers in uniform would come in handy. It would save us a fortune hiring them. If we can use you two, maybe Cagney and Casey, for a few hours, I may just forget all about any complaints. You never know."

"Interesting. I'll have a word with my mum, see what she can do. I've always fancied myself as an actor."

40

With the sun shining, and the adrenaline pumping, I nosed into the car park in Kettlewell. The production bus was already there, making this real. This film was happening—again. I felt like I was in an opening sequence, greeting the production team with handshakes, hugs and cheery waves. It was great to see them again. They all knew what they were doing and were happy doing it. Jason had arrived last night and got everything organised. Jen and I had spent the previous night re-working a couple of scenes ready for shooting today.

Listen to me. Shooting. I sound like I know what I'm talking about. Despite the outer confidence, the nagging voice was still in my head. I was an imposter, and the coming days would expose me. Everything I owned rode on this being a success. I tried my hardest not to dwell on that thought. My achievements so far would mean nothing if this failed. I'd be skint and starting from scratch. Still, at least I'd decided about New York. Now I could concentrate on putting everything into the film.

Jen arrived at the pub, where Jim had laid on pastries and coffee. Behind Jen were two locals who had small parts in today's scenes. Roddy was treating an audience to one of his stories about the sixties. Sitting opposite Roddy and Toni, Phil and Alice were holding hands. It was good that Toni was here. Things were going well.

I thought about what I was a part of. We'd put together this talented team, but I knew from my IT days that it was temporary. The very definition of a project is a temporary organisation put in place to achieve a goal. If we followed the current schedule, filming would be complete in six weeks. Jen and I would work with an editor for a few weeks after that. Then we'd be done. Only time will tell whether it will be good enough, but it will end. The team will disperse and become part of other teams all over the country.

I reached out and took the last pain au chocolat. There were perks to being an investor. Jen took charge of the gathering. She clapped her hands twice, and the room fell silent. She gave the team a great pep talk. Jason said a few words too, and I just took a bow. To be honest, I'd just crammed the last mini croissant in, and any speech was beyond me. Jen led a group round of applause. We all trooped outside, and the filming began.

41

The last time I'd been here, it was only half finished. I was excited to see how it had changed. Tonight was massive for Joe, Rupert, and Ambrose. Joe had sold the evening as a low-key opening for a few friends, but couldn't suppress the theatricality that ran through him. The rain that had threatened all day had held off, and the short strip of red carpet looked pristine. A simple red neon sign proclaimed El Sotano. They had bright lights above the door, and a photographer was snapping away. I felt self-conscious as I walked on the carpet with my brown paper parcel tucked under my arm. Jen had phoned to say she'd meet me there once she'd dealt with a minor insurrection by Charley.

Before I'd reached the door, Joe emerged with arms outstretched.

"Welcome to our humble club." The hug was warm and genuine on both sides.

"Anything but humble. I hadn't expected the red carpet treatment."

"I thought it would be good practice for you. All those glitzy premieres to come." Joe steered me round to face the camera and put his arm around my shoulder. I tried to keep the parcel out of the shot.

"Here. This is for the three of you as a housewarming."

"I would say you shouldn't have, but of course, you should. Thank you. Now, come inside and start on the ridiculous volume of champagne on offer."

Ambrose emerged from the bar with a grin a mile wide.

"This looks fantastic. You must be very proud," I said.

"Most of this is Joe's vision, but I'm so pleased we came up with the idea to knock the wall down. I get to be a club owner and run the best record shop in town."

"Is Rupert around?"

"He's in charge of the sound system. Hang on." Ambrose raised both hands to his mouth and emitted the loudest whistle I'd ever heard. Rupert jogged across the empty club.

"Right," I said. "Now I've got the three of you together. You can open the present."

Joe made quick work of the pathetic wrapping. Dad had done a great job of turning the photographs of Roy Orbison and Miles Davis into pencil drawings. It was uncanny. Joe and Ambrose looked delighted; Rupert just looked confused.

"Sorry, guys. I can see they're excellent, but am I supposed to know who they are?" I was about to respond with abuse when Joe stepped in to save me the trouble.

"My dear boy, you've made me feel ever so old, but thrilled by the opportunity to broaden your education once again."

Stella and Jen arrived and interrupted Joe's lesson. After more hugs, Joe took us to a raised booth in the middle of the back wall.

"Best seats in the house. We have spectacular entertainment lined up for you later. I think you'll enjoy the show." Joe put a tray of champagne glasses on the table and promised to return later.

There were microphones and a keyboard on the stage. Nobody knew about the entertainment. At least, if Stella knew she was doing an excellent job of keeping the secret as more guests arrived. Joe's original plan had been to limit the numbers to around thirty. The purpose was to allow the staff to get familiar with everything. By eight o'clock, I estimated that there were about a hundred inside. Joe just shrugged and explained he'd found it impossible to keep numbers down, and a similar event was now planned for tomorrow. It seemed everybody wanted an invitation to the new club. Alice and Phil had joined us in the booth, and every now and again, Ambrose or Joe would take me off to introduce me to some new arrival.

Ambrose came over to the booth and slid in next to his wife. We all agreed we were having a great time.

"Actually, I hate to be picky," I said.

"Go on. What's wrong?"

"If I have one more glass of fizz, I think I'll explode. Any chance of a beer?"

"Bottles only, but I've got something you might just like."

The staff looked like models, dressed in all black. Ambrose caught the eye of one of them, who he introduced as Dan. Dan was soon back at the table with an evil-looking wheat beer and poured it expertly. I took a sip.

"That will do nicely. I think I may just enjoy myself this evening." Jen looked over her glasses at me.

"Don't forget we've a busy day of filming tomorrow."

"I'll be fine, honest. There's a limit to the damage I can do drinking these. Anyway, speaking of filming, has anybody seen Roddy yet? He should've been here ages ago."

"Speak of the devil," said Jen. "Right on cue."

Roddy and Toni came down the stairs like Hollywood royalty. The photographer snapped away. I suspect Ambrose started the applause, but by the time they were crossing the dance floor, the entire crowd was cheering and clapping. For a split second, Roddy looked unsure of himself. Then the smile kicked in, and he was in star mode, shaking hands, embracing and chatting. He was wearing a smart tuxedo, and Toni was in a theatrical black dress, all shimmer and class.

I gestured for them to join us, but Joe swooped in.

"Can I borrow these two for a minute? You can have them back soon, honest."

With that, he steered them through the staff-only door.

"What was all that about? The poor bugger only just arrived. Is he signing them up as bar staff?" I asked.

"Probably has the press back there. You know what Joe's like," said Jen.

Five minutes later, Joe appeared on the stage. He thanked everybody for coming and got Ambrose and Rupert to bow to loud applause.

"And now, ladies and gentlemen, we have not one, but two big surprises for you." Joe gestured to Rupert to join him on stage. As somebody who was quite shy, he looked like he wanted the ground to swallow him, but did as Joe asked. "Over the last few months, this man has made me happier than I could have dreamed of." There was a raucous cheer and warm applause from the room. "Ten minutes ago, I asked him to make my happiness complete and marry me. He said yes!"

This time, the cheering was wild. Watching Joe and Rupert embrace on stage brought a tear to my eye. Jen was cheering, tears streaming down her face. Joe raised both hands and gestured for us to calm down.

"Now, for my second surprise. Performing together for the first time in, dare I say it, fifty years. Please welcome to the stage Miss Toni Trulove and the man himself, Roddy Lightning."

I looked at Stella and Jen, who both just shrugged. The crowd went crazy, even though half of them, including me, weren't even born the last time they appeared together. Toni stood behind the keyboards and launched into *Can't Take My Eyes Off You*. At first, Roddy's voice was hesitant, but his confidence grew as everybody joined the chorus. By the opening chords of *For Once In My Life*, he was the old Roddy. He removed his jacket for an extraordinary rendition of *You Can Leave Your Hat On*, and it enthralled the crowd. As the applause died down, Joe brought a stool on stage. As Roddy was getting comfortable, Toni spoke for the first time.

"You're very kind, thank you. I can't tell you what it means to us to have reconnected again after so long. Lots of people have made tonight possible, but I'd like to thank two in particular for everything they've done. Frankie and Jen, who believed in Roddy and offered him a part in their upcoming blockbuster, *The Hubberholme Syndrome*." The spotlight lit up our table. Jen tried to hide behind me, but Ambrose ensured we both stood and acknowledged the applause. "This next song is my way of thanking them. We wrote it just this week, and we hope you like it. It's called *One More Indian Summer* and sounds a bit like this."

The song turned out to be a jazzy, smokey duet, all about second chances and late-in-life romance. There was a verse about being never too late to change paths and how risk should find a reward. Toni played the piano refrain before the last verse and I was welling up. I looked at Jen, who was in tears. I reached into my pocket and handed over a fresh handkerchief, leaning close to her.

"This should be over the closing credits of the film."

"I was just thinking the same thing. It's beautiful."

We sat in silence as Roddy and Toni repeated the first verse and finished the final chorus. I reflected on the last few weeks since I'd sent the fateful email to Flic. I'd decided at the time that I had to devote myself to making the film a success. There'd be plenty of time to talk to Jen about the future once we'd finished.

Now the film was looking very real. We were almost at the end of the schedule and would wrap things up next week. One of my jobs was adding a soundtrack to the finished version and negotiating deals to include a few of my favourite songs. Now we had the perfect closer.

The applause was deafening. Roddy and Toni looked stunned. They finished the set with a medley of three of the Thunderbolts' biggest hits. We all got up and danced, but all too soon, it was over. Joe was back on stage, leading the applause, and Rupert took over the music. I danced with Stella to a couple of old Motown hits. Jen was being thrown around by a very enthusiastic Ambrose. I was just about to rescue her when Joe was suddenly back on stage to tell us the buffet was open.

We returned to our seats and ordered more drinks. Rupert sold me a fistful of raffle tickets for the local hospice. Roddy and Toni joined us in the booth.

"You crafty old bugger. How did you keep that quiet?"

"All down to this beautiful young lady." Roddy kissed the back of Jen's hand. She blushed and giggled.

"You were behind this and kept it secret?"

"Toni did most of the work. I was just a facilitator. I like to make things happen!" Jen laughed again and clinked glasses with Toni.

We laughed, drank, talked, ate, and drank for a couple of hours. All too soon, the music had stopped, and the crowd had thinned out. It appeared the evening was coming to a close. Ambrose retrieved coats for Stella, Jen and Alice. We were about to leave for the taxis queued up outside when Joe took us to one side.

"Tell your dad thanks for these and get him to come to see us soon." He pointed to the wall. The two pictures were on display, replacing the ones from earlier. "They look great. I'd love to pay him handsomely for a few more."

"I'll let him know. It'll make his day. Thanks for tonight. This will be an enormous success," I said, shaking Joe's hand.

"So will the film. Things are looking good."

"By the way, congratulations to you and Rupert. Look after the plonker."

"Oh, I intend to, don't worry."

42

After filming on Friday, Toni invited me to have dinner at her house. Jen had taken her mum and Charley for a weekend in London, so it was easy to accept. Toni was a superb cook, and I enjoyed every minute. The plan had been to speak to Roddy to tie up loose ends for his book. However, ten minutes after eating, he was in his armchair, snoring contentedly. Toni eased a small cushion under his head.

"Bless him. He's worn out," she said.

"He's been incredible, really. Only a week to go. In fact, if all goes well, it could be just a couple of days for him. We have a few general outdoor shots, but that's it."

"What happens then?"

"Editing. From what I understand, Jason locks us in a room with a twelve-year-old editor to knock all the scenes into shape."

"Is he really twelve?"

"No. Just seems it. That's unfair. His reputation is great. He just sees me as a bit of a dinosaur."

"I'm sure he doesn't. Experienced, maybe." Toni grinned and started clearing the table. I joined her, ferrying dishes to the kitchen while she loaded the dishwasher.

"If only I had more experience. I'm not kidding. It's my

first film, and I feel like everybody knows more than me what needs to be done. I bought *Filmmaking For Dummies* at the start of all this."

"As producer, you don't need to do it all yourself. You need to make sure it gets done," said Toni with a grin.

"I'll remember that. Good advice."

"Brandy?"

"Why not?"

"Let's take it through to the snug; let Roddy have half an hour in peace."

We made our way to a small room at the back of the cottage. The room lived up to its name, cosy and snug. Against one wall was an impressive-looking electric piano.

"Very nice piece of kit," I said, gazing at the thing of beauty.

"My only indulgence. Do you play?"

"I wish I did. I tried to teach myself a few years ago. Bought the keyboard and had online lessons but ended up drifting away from it. I think it's in the big scary cupboard now."

"You should retrieve it. Playing is the one thing in my life that has brought me genuine joy. Until Roddy, of course."

"Do you play every day?"

"I do. It was because they expected it of me when I was a child. Now it's just part of my life. It's how I relax."

"I loved the song you played at the club the other night. I'm delighted you're okay with including it on the soundtrack."

"You're joking. It's exhilarating, like being twenty again."

"Would you play it for me?"

Toni sat on the stool and flicked a power switch. I was in awe as she played. It seemed effortless. When she sang, everything seemed simple. Her voice was rich and soothing. Toni finished the first chorus, bowed theatrically and picked up the brandy glass from the small table.

"That was wonderful. You make it look so easy." Toni laughed and stood up. She pointed to the seat.

"It *is* easy. It's a straightforward melody. Sit down and I'll show you."

I was about to refuse before realising I would love to do this.

"Can you remember where middle C is?"

I placed my right hand on the keys and looked at her.

"One to the right. That's it. Now. Just copy this." Toni leaned in close and picked out the first few notes. I attempted to copy, but it sounded nothing like. "Just relax. Think of the rhythm and try to copy it. Light touch."

I tried again. This time I recognised it as the tune. Toni was very patient, adding a few notes each time until I could play the chorus unaided. I was thrilled.

"There you go. That's what you've achieved in fifteen minutes. Imagine what you could do if you practised for a couple of hours a day."

"I think my hand would drop off." I rubbed at my aching fingers. "Thanks for that. I think you've inspired me."

We moved across to sit in the armchairs on either side of the fireplace.

"Actually, my job for the next couple of weeks includes coming up with the soundtrack's music. I always assumed I'd be good at that bit, but it's harder than it looks. I've lined up a few songs from the sixties. Jason is handling getting clearance to use them. What I could do with is one or two original pieces. I don't suppose you've got another couple of brilliant songs up your sleeve?"

Toni sat and thought for a minute. I wondered if I'd put her in an awkward position. After what seemed like an age, she spoke.

"I've got a few half-finished songs, instrumental piano

pieces, but quite catchy. My problem is the lyrics."

"But the words to *One More Indian Summer* are perfect."

"If only I'd written them. It's actually a poem that was written by Renata for Roddy. The words seemed to go well with the melody I'd written."

"It's beautiful. I don't suppose Renata wrote other poems we could use?"

"No. I think she wrote it towards the end of her life, a sort of leaving gift for Roddy."

We lapsed into a comfortable silence. I was thinking how much the song must mean to Roddy. It was a perfect song to end our film. We needed more. Could we use Toni's music without lyrics?

"It's a shame," said Toni. "If only we knew writers. People who are good with words and love music. They could write the lyrics. If only."

I took a sip of brandy and thought for a moment, savouring the slight burn of the alcohol.

"You must know people from your showbiz days. Is there anybody you could ask?"

"Jen's right, you know. She said you could be thick." I must've looked hurt, but Toni continued. "Don't look like that. She also said you were an extremely talented writer. Why don't you write the lyrics?"

"But I've never done that before," I protested.

"Have you ever made a film before? Have you ever written a biography before? Had you written a series of children's books before you actually did it? No. So why couldn't you do it? You know the scenes you want the songs for. You know what the songs should say. Just write them."

"Is that how it works?"

"No reason it shouldn't. I'll send you the music. Have a listen and get writing. We can experiment with the tune and rhythm if we need to. Just get it done."

"Okay. You're on." Funny how this kind of thing keeps happening to me. It appeared I was going to be a songwriter.

We chatted for a while about how happy Toni and Roddy were to have met each other again.

"Was there ever anything between you when you were still in the band?"

"You've got to be joking. I was staying well out of it. At first, Roddy was all loved up with Penny. Then he exploded that with Crash. I could see at the time Roddy fancied Renata as well. I knew he was a charmer, but I didn't want him enough to make the dramas worth the effort."

"Is it easier now?"

"It is. The old guy has worked through most of his demons. His health isn't what it could be. You must've noticed his memory."

I nodded.

"Has he seen a doctor about it? I tried to talk to him about getting help, but he dismissed it," I said.

"We saw my GP last week. I noticed that he'd zoned out in the middle of a conversation a few times. It was like somebody had switched him off. He was back within a minute as if nothing had happened."

"What does the doctor think?"

"He wants to refer him to a specialist. Roddy refuses point-blank."

"But isn't it better to know so that if there's something wrong, he can get treatment?"

Toni swirled the brandy around her glass and stared at the fire. She appeared to be deep in thought. Moments later, she continued.

"We had a long talk the other night. Roddy's not daft. He's worked out something is wrong, but he saw what Renata went through for all those years. It didn't end well. I'm afraid his logic is simple. He's loving life now, and we have a great time. He's excited about the film and everything. But, before too much longer, he'll be in his eighties. He's done the calculations and says he'd rather enjoy whatever time he's left, live life to the full. Roddy hates the idea of going through what Renata did and having the last few years of his life being an endless round of hospital beds."

"So he's just going to give up?"

"No. Far from it. Roddy's going to live his life and live it well, whether it's six months or twenty years."

"Surely there's something we can do?"

"There is. Be there for him. Help Roddy live his life. Make a success of the film and the book. Make him happy."

"Is he? Happy?"

"Yes, day to day. He's happy. The one sadness in his life is the broken relationship with Penny. Because of that, he has a daughter who won't speak to him and a grown-up granddaughter he's never met. He's quite pragmatic about it. Sees it as the universe punishing him for the bad choices years ago. If I could fix one thing, it would be that."

We both stared at the fire as the logs spit sparks up the chimney. I suppose I could see Roddy's point about living life to the full. Just then, the door burst open.

"There you are. I thought we were having a drink and a natter about this book. Or were you just here for a free meal? I was thinking you'd both buggered off and left me on my own."

Roddy roared with laughter, and Toni got to her feet.

"You sit down. I'll bring the brandy through and leave you to it."

She kissed him on the cheek and disappeared into the kitchen.

"Wonderful woman, that," he said as Toni left.

"She's definitely a keeper."

"Lovely arse too."

He was living life to the full.

43

I was back in the office early on Monday morning. It was all quite surreal. We'd finished filming on Thursday. From what I remember, we'd had a good night in the pub for the traditional wrap party. Everybody had too much to drink except Alice. She announced she was drinking orange juice all night. Phil explained he would drink for two. I'm delighted at their news. It seems the film was doing a great job of bringing couples together. Roddy and Toni were an item; now Phil and Alice were planning lives together. I was still living in hope, waiting for Jen's scabby knees to heal.

Everything felt strange after the team had disbanded and headed home. The house felt empty and quiet, with Roddy at Toni's. Things got so bad I'd begun sorting out the scary cupboard. I'd rescued my Yamaha keyboard and set it up next to the telly. After a couple of hours of practice, I could just about play *One More Indian Summer*. Impressed by my musicianship, I'd grabbed a beer and settled down to crack on with lyrics to Toni's tunes.

So far, I'd started two sets of lyrics. I took a red pen to most of the first attempt and scrubbed out any line I'd lifted from Smokey Robinson. It left next to nothing, but the second one wasn't half bad. I'd poured my heart out about how I would wait for Jen to be healed enough to want a relationship. I didn't name her, obviously. The song fitted around a scene in the film that saw Phil and Alice's characters getting closer.

Late last night, I'd plucked up the courage to email the attempt to Toni. By the time I'd gone to bed, I'd had another beer, watched *The Vicar Of Dibley*, and felt much better.

At the office, I checked my email as soon as I'd made coffee. Part of me knew Toni wouldn't even have seen it yet, but I was excited to know what she thought. Jen arrived just after nine. We compared notes on the party and agreed it had been a good one. We were due at the editing suite in Leeds at 11 o'clock to meet Ben, our editor. Then we had two weeks to edit the entire film and add the music to the soundtrack.

In the meantime, Jen was working on some notes. In theory, so was I. In reality, I'd been staring at Jen and thinking. I still hadn't been brave enough to have *that* conversation. How hard could it be to unburden myself about how I felt? Mind you, that meant talking about life-changing decisions and events. It was all too scary. It was impossible to know how Jen would react. I knew I should grab the bull by the balls or whatever the phrase was. Just as I took a deep breath, an email pinged into my inbox. It was from Toni.

I scanned the message. She'd changed two lines and suggested some that she thought could stand a bit of work, but overall, she gave me the thumbs up. My heart was pounding. Had I just co-written a song? Then I saw the attachment. Toni had recorded a demo. She apologised for the sound quality, but I didn't care. It was our song.

"Can we listen to this?"

Jen didn't even lift her head.

"Knock yourself out, as long as it's not too shouty."

"I don't think it's going to be shouty."

"Good."

I downloaded the song and fired up the speakers. The

piano intro was very familiar, then Toni's beautiful voice. And she was singing my words! Jen was still bent over her notes. I wanted to tell her to stop what she was doing. This was my song. I tore a page from my notebook, screwed it up, and launched it at Jen's head.

"Oy. You should listen to this." Jen looked up and smiled.

"I am listening. It's beautiful. I take it this is what you've been working on with Toni?" I nodded, and we both listened to the chorus. "It's bloody good. Heartfelt. Sincere. You know what they say. If you can fake sincerity, you've cracked it. Seriously, it's great. And I hear the message."

This was it. Time for the talk. Deep breath.

"Shit," said Jen. "Have you seen the time? We need to be not here. Do you mind if we take both cars? I've got some stuff to pick up later. Come on. I'll see you in Leeds."

With that, she was gone. I sat and stared at the closing door. Now that wasn't my fault. I was all set to have the talk and work intervenes. She was right, though. We were going to be late. I grabbed my laptop and headed for the door. The talk would have to wait. Again.

44

The two weeks in the editing studio with Ben had been intense. In particular, the second week comprised long days, coffee, square eyes, and more coffee. But, late on Friday night, we had it. Ninety-seven minutes. All the work over the last seven months boiled down to just over an hour and a half. But what an hour and a half. We were all delighted with the outcome. It was strange to think that it was just a job to Ben. He would have another film to edit next week. For Jen and me, it was our baby. Jason had joined us for the last day, but he had mixed news about interest from distributors. He'd done a great job presenting the clips and selling the idea. There was a possibility of a limited release, not the mass screenings I'd dreamed of, but a start. Everything would depend now on getting bums on seats in cinemas.

How much I had invested in this was on my mind constantly. There'd been a lot of sleepless nights with the realisation of how serious this could be. I could lose my house if this flopped. I wouldn't even have an OEIC (whatever that was).

However, today I had to forget all that. Today, Joe and Rupert were getting married; that was all I should think about. One of the few traditions they'd stuck with was not seeing each other on the day until the service. In a departure from most weddings I'd been to, both grooms had a best man, hence Rupert snoring with gusto in my spare room. Ambrose was looking after Joe. The latter was ruling the day as if it was a Broadway production. Joe's tailor (obviously Joe had a tailor!) had taken old, grainy footage of Roddy in his heyday and replicated the outfit he wore. We looked a bit like the boy band that had taken a wrong turn, but the suits were immaculate. It had thrilled Roddy to be included in the group fitting and said he would wear his every day after the wedding. It was at that point that Joe unveiled his master plan. We were to become honorary Thunderbolts for the day.

Roddy and Toni had agreed to do a short set at the wedding. Joe hatched an evil plan with Roddy that, as we had the suits, Rupert, Ambrose and yours truly, would join them for a couple of songs. It was okay for Ambrose. He was a decent enough bass player. Rupert had taken drum lessons for six weeks as a teenager. In his book, that meant he could play. Me? The sum total of my musical experience was one lesson on keyboards from Toni. Joe found it a hoot that I was now the lead guitarist for one of the most successful groups of the sixties.

"Don't worry, son. Just look like you're playing. That's what we did on *Top of the Pops*, and no bugger complained," Roddy said, whilst almost choking, he was laughing so much.

So, they did not expect me to play, but I was still nervous. I wanted to look good in the video, but I hadn't even posed in the mirror with a real guitar. Rupert had laughed and said I was a born poser. He'd assured me all would be well on the day. I wasn't convinced.

I switched on the coffee, took both suit carriers from behind the kitchen door and went upstairs to wake the groom, one of them anyway.

"Rise and shine, sunbeam."

There was a groan from under the duvet. I think he'd proposed that he may have time for ten more minutes of sleep, but there were a lot more 'f's in his version.

"Do you think Joe's plan allows for ten more minutes? Arse out of bed now. While you're in the shower, I'll nip across the road and get us two bacon butties from the cafe." There was another muffled groan from deep beneath the duvet. "Yes, you can have Tommy sauce, but only if you shift now."

I hung his suit on the back of the door and went along the corridor to my room. I draped my suit on the bed, grabbed my wallet and keys and made my way to the cafe.

A smiling Ildiko greeted me. She handed over the bag that contained our sandwiches.

"Bless you. How did you know I'd be in?"

"It's on the plan from Joe. Look." She pointed, and sure enough, there it was. He really had thought of everything.

"All set for later?"

"Of course. All the food is ready. Just getting the breakfast rush out of the way, then we'll set up at the club," said Ildiko.

"Brilliant. I'll see you later."

The coffee was ready when I got back to the house. Rupert was singing something vaguely operatic in the shower. I pulled two plates from the cupboard. It occurred to me that maybe I'd grown up at last. I was about to use real crockery, and there were clean plates in the cupboard. To top off the picture of domestic elegance, I placed red and brown sauce bottles in the middle of the table. I was just pouring the coffee when Rupert appeared, clad in boxer shorts and a Ramones tee shirt.

"Very cultured. Couldn't you at least have put some trousers on? I'm very impressionable."

"Didn't wanna risk a sauce incident."

"Wise move, but the least of our dangers today when you

think of the colour of those suits."

"I know. Light grey is not forgiving in the splash department. What time do I have to be ready?"

I looked at the plan, then at my watch.

"You have forty-three minutes to enjoy a leisurely breakfast, then you need to be shaving."

"Already shaved," said Rupert.

"In that case, you have about fifty-two minutes before we need to be suited and booted. Call it an hour. I got Joe to add in half an hour's contingency, which I translated as a pint in The Crown to calm our nerves." Rupert grinned at me.

"You're very good at this."

"The best, hence my title for the day. The car's picking us up from the pub car park. Jen and Charley are meeting us there."

"Has Charley calmed down yet?"

"What do you think? It took her a while to get her head around the title of flower girl. In her head, she's a bridesmaid, even without a bride. Nice touch to get her and Olivia involved. Stella's taking her straight to the registry office." I pointed at Rupert's chest. "Sauce—all down you."

"Great," he said, using his finger to remove the offending blob. "Told you it was a good idea not to get dressed."

"Just another twelve hours to navigate. You'll be fine."

The service had gone well. No major drama, just an awkward moment when I met Rupert's mum. We both knew that, had her daughter and husband not proven to be crooked, she would now be my mother-in-law. We settled on a brief hug and agreed that Rupert looked thrilled.

It still felt strange that Rupert used his real name— Dominic—for the swapping of vows. It caused a stir, with about half of the guests only knowing him as Rupert. Even his mum uses his nickname these days.

Jen and Stella both cried as they watched Charley and Olivia scatter petals down the aisle. Joe had a cleaner on hand to sweep up the mess. A small donation had made the registrar overlook the infringement. Best of all, I didn't lose the ring or get it stuck on my finger.

Now I was free to concentrate on my role as lead guitarist. My pulse quickened as we got to the club, and I saw the stage already set up. I knew this was just a photo stunt to give everybody a laugh, but in my tiny brain, I was the guitarist in The Thunderbolts. It was tempting to pick the guitar up, just to get in the right headspace. Then I felt the tug on the back of my jacket. I looked down at Charley.

"Uncle Frankie, Mum says she's dying of thirst."

She delivered the line deadpan and pointed to the corner table. Jen and Stella waved and clutched their throats to emphasise the message. I retrieved a tray of fizz from the bar and orange juice for the girls. That set the tempo for the rest of the afternoon and evening. We drank, laughed, talked, panicked when we couldn't find our speech, thanked Jen for having it in her bag, drank more and, above all, felt overjoyed to be amongst beautiful friends. Did I mention we had a few drinks? I'd had more than a few. As a result, I made my stage bow, wishing three things.

Wish number one was that I could play the guitar. That would've been cool to play alongside my childhood hero. At least miming, I couldn't mess it up. I also wished that the room would stop tilting from side to side. It was a good thing that I was only miming. My third wish, as usual, was I'd gone to the toilet before we started. Too late now.

There was a massive cheer as Roddy introduced us all on stage. Toni nodded at Rupert, who counted us in, and we were away. Toni did a remarkable job drowning out the amateurs in the rhythm section. Roddy launched into his best John Lennon to deliver, *I Saw Her Standing There*. I grinned like an idiot all the way through and forgot all about miming. I sang badly at the top of my voice. My bow at the end was bordering over-enthusiastic, but somehow, I managed not to go arse over apex. Joe surprised me by jumping on stage before the second song. Still, it was his day.

"Don't worry, I'm not doing another speech. Although I've always had a fantasy about drummers, so, you know…"

Rupert hit the snare and cymbal and drew a loud cheer.

"We are very grateful to Roddy and Toni for agreeing to put the Thunderbolts back together after too long apart. Please give it up for Thunderbolt two, Frankie."

Again, a loud cheer. I waved and grinned sheepishly.

"Thunderbolt three, my husband, Rupert."

Rupert rose for a very theatrical bow.

"Next, Thunderbolt Four, the ace of bass, the hardest working man in the record business, Ambrose." This felt so good. "And, of course, the glamorous and talented fifth Thunderbolt - miss Toni Truelove."

As the applause reached a crescendo, Toni unleashed a dramatic church organ-type solo from her keyboard, complete with thunder crashes.

"Now, ladies and gentlemen. A slight change to the lineup."

As he said this, I felt a tap on my shoulder. I looked around and recognised the face in an instant. It was Penny. She motioned for me to hand over the guitar. In return, she gave me a tambourine. "Roddy, apologies for springing this on you. Please welcome on stage Thunderbolt Two, Miss Penny Peal. On drums, she flew in from her home in Stuttgart an hour ago, the fabulous Connie Crash. And a special guest, Thunderbolt Four, Roddy's daughter Polly Thunderbolt."

The guests erupted as Polly came on stage. She hugged Roddy and said something that none of us could hear in the din. Roddy was helpless with tears and wouldn't let go of

Polly's hand.

Joe raised his hands to get the audience to calm down.

"Now, we realised Roddy might get emotional seeing the Thunderbolts back together with one undeniable and sad exception. So, we thought he might appreciate a helping hand on vocals. Please welcome, to sing with her granddad, Miss Amber Thunderbolt."

This almost finished Roddy off. The granddaughter he'd had no contact with all those years was here and about to sing with him. It took a while for Roddy to regain his composure. I considered making a dash to the Gents, but I didn't want to miss this.

It was then I made eye contact with Maggie. I pointed at her. "Is this your doing?" I mouthed. She nodded, smiled, and pointed at Jen. They must've cooked this up when Jen was in London for the weekend. Before I could think of anything else, Toni and Penny started playing the intro to *In The Middle Of Nowhere*. The Thunderbolts had covered the Dusty Springfield song as a duet between Roddy and Penny. It was an enormous hit just before the band broke up. Fifty years later, Roddy was flawless. The joy on his face as he sang to his granddaughter was special. The band sounded great. It was ridiculous to think they hadn't played together for half a century. Also, if I say so myself, I was brilliant with the tambourine alongside Ambrose on maracas. Rupert and Joe danced as if nobody was watching, the best first dance a wedding had ever seen.

All too soon, the song was over. The DJ took over, the dance floor filled, and in a booth at the back of the club, Roddy, Polly, and Amber talked, laughed, cried and hugged for the rest of the night. I decided I should attempt to sober up by mingling and chatting. The plan backfired when I kept accepting the offer of drinks. Maybe sitting down was a better plan.

A while later, I was concentrating hard while crossing the dance floor coming back from the Gents.

"There you are. Dance with me."

It was Jen. She'd disappeared a while ago to take Charley to her gran's for the night. Olivia was with them for a sleepover. Now she was back and looking fabulous. We danced for ages, me with more enthusiasm than skill, until the DJ played *My Girl*. At that point, we knew our routine from the day practising in the office. Ambrose and Stella joined us, and everybody formed a circle and clapped. We lasted the whole song because I got the turns right this time. I was relieved it was only two and a half minutes. I looked at Ambrose at the end. He was exhausted, shirt untucked, tie askew. I laughed because I knew I looked a complete mess too. Jen and Stella still looked immaculate. How was that possible? The DJ took pity on us and followed it with a slower song. I was heading for the safety of my seat when Jen took my hand.

"Where do you think you're going?"

We danced. The Lettermen's version of *The Way You Look Tonight* was perfect. The rest of the guests seemed to fade from view. All I was aware of was Jen. We looked into each other's eyes and smiled for what seemed like forever. She rested her head on my chest and didn't even take exception when I sniffed her hair. My evening was perfect by the time Roberta Flack and Peabo Bryson had done their thing. Dancing with Jen felt right. Everything worked. As the romantic song ended, Jen whispered in my ear. I couldn't be certain, but I'm pretty sure it was something about scabby knees.

45

We were in the pub in Kettlewell.

"Come here, let me fix that," said Jen with a smirk. She set about fixing my pathetic attempt at a bow tie. I'd been practising all week, but the latest farce looked set to collapse in a gentle breeze.

"What time is the car due to pick us up?"

"Still six o'clock."

"And what time is it now?"

"It's exactly five minutes since you last asked at ten to six." I must've looked puzzled. "Five to six. It's five to six. Now, will you relax? The work is done. We're supposed to enjoy tonight. You don't often get to attend the premiere of your own film."

"But what if..."

"Nothing is going to go wrong. Thirty people will be there if it does. It's mainly family and friends with a handful of house-trained journalists." She pulled the tie slightly tighter than needed and patted my chest. "There, all done. And don't fiddle with it. How come you were late coming down, anyway?"

Should I admit I'd been taking selfies in the mirror, emulating James Bond with the hairdryer as a gun?

"I needed to look my best."

The front door opened, and an extremely sophisticated-looking Jason came in.

"The car's here," he said.

I waved Jen and Jason closer for a group hug. I felt like I needed to mark the occasion with a short, dignified speech. All I could manage was, "I need a wee."

When I returned, the moment had gone, and the other two were already in the back of the limo. Phil and Alice were in the back of the second car. I climbed in beside Jen, and we pulled away.

Bernard had done us proud, and his tiny cinema was enjoying its own Hollywood moment. Thanks to Joe, we had a red carpet. It was from the club and installed on the garden path leading to the cottage. We'd arranged a couple of press photographers and bright flashes greeted us. A large group of villagers had gathered. Rupert's social media campaign had built an interest in *The Hubberholme Syndrome*. We had a deal for showings in a few independent cinemas from May 4th. Bernard was also playing a blinder. Not only was he hosting our premiere tonight, but he had sold out a two-week run just from locals.

Word was spreading further afield. The local news covered tonight's event, and Jen was first on the red carpet to be interviewed. Phil and Alice were busy signing autographs for the crowd of people lining the street. This suddenly felt very exciting. Maybe it wasn't the Odeon in Leicester Square, but crossing Bernard's hall and walking down the stairs to his cellar was a genuine thrill. There was a bustle as people were taking their seats. It was strange being in a place like this and knowing almost every face. I spotted Barney and his wife chatting to Jason.

"Hello, partner," he boomed as he shook my hand.

"You look elegant."

"You too. Not bad for a couple of scruffy little, snotty-nosed kids from Bradford."

"Let's hope this is a success. Then we can feel smug." Jason apologised to Barney as he whisked me away to meet a handful of journalists. Posing for more photographs followed. I even greeted DI Cagney like a long-time friend. Casey hovered behind Cagney, just like he had in the film. I thanked Smirky for his part in arranging the cameo appearances just as Tinkle dashed upstairs.

As director, Jen had agreed to make a brief speech to welcome the audience to the premiere. I could see she was pretty emotional, but held it together. Then, just like that, we were in our seats, and the lights dimmed. As the screen came to life, the audience clapped loudly. That should've calmed my nerves, but all I could think about was that I should've gone to the toilet.

I was fidgeting, wishing we were at the back, where I'd be able to see the crowd's reaction. I risked a look over my shoulder. All eyes were fixed on the screen. Jen took my hand and whispered, "Relax. It's going well."

She was right. People seemed to like it. Then again, I knew it was good, even though we'd seen it in the editing suite a hundred times. This could work. Then again, it had to. I'd invested everything I owned in this film. I liked to tell myself that failure was not an option. Who was I kidding? Failure was the case for most movies, especially for tiny independent ones like ours. Then there was the immediate future. Had I made the right decision about New York? We'd know in the next few weeks.

The biggest thrill in the entire film was hearing my words sung beautifully by Toni. Then it was over, and the credits were rolling with *One More Indian Summer* playing. Now it was my turn to make a speech.

The applause lifted me to another level. As it died down, I

nervously pulled the two sheets of paper from my jacket. My hands were shaking so much that I had trouble seeing the words. I started.

"Ladies and gentlemen." I stumbled over the following sentence and gave up. I screwed up the papers and threw the ball over my shoulder.

"You know what? I don't need that." This got a laugh, and I relaxed a bit. "Hearing your applause and seeing so many familiar faces tonight makes me happier than you can imagine. Jen and I had the idea almost a year ago, sitting at her kitchen table with a glass of wine, and now we have a proper film. It just blows my mind. I know it's cliched to talk of being on a journey. But that's what it has been. A journey where we've learnt so much and made so many new friends. Such an experience. But also sad that not all of us made it."

I tried unsuccessfully to blink back the tears. Each time I tried to speak again, the sobs convulsed me. Jen came to my rescue and hugged me, whispering, "It's okay, it's okay."

I looked at Toni, who was also sobbing. The framed charcoal drawing of Roddy was on the seat beside her. His cheeky smile beaming back at me. The applause was spontaneous, heartfelt, and still ringing in my ears as we returned to the limo.

46

As I enter the airport terminal, I think back to that first hour of this year. I'd been drunk at the time and worried about whether I'd made the right decision. Almost six months later, so much has happened.

Rupert's social media campaign has been a tremendous success. Enquiries from cinemas are flooding in. Jason is confident of landing one of the big chains with almost guaranteed success if he can. *One More Indian Summer* has made it to the Radio 2 playlist, and Toni is due on Graham Norton's show. Phil and Alice have announced they're getting married at the end of the summer. They both have offers of film roles with major studios.

The news is spreading further afield. We didn't meet the criteria for official screening at the Cannes Film Festival. Still, they invited us to attend thanks to Jason's connections and the surge of interest in the film. We have a private screening and Jason has set up meetings with the great and the good. Jen has already flown out, taking the opportunity for a family holiday by the beach.

Roddy's biography is all set to be released at the end of the week, and the publishers are confident it will top the bestseller lists on orders alone. Vince Taylor has another enormous success. I am so proud.

I push through the terminal, navigate security and find my way to the business class lounge. Helping myself to a coffee, I glance at the departure board above my head. It's a weird coincidence. Two flights that had meant opposite outcomes for my future. The flight to New York leaves in just over an hour. The flight to Nice is seven minutes later.

I try to concentrate on the crossword in the paper, but it's no good. Staring into space seems like a good option for the next twenty minutes.

The departures screen shows both flights are boarding. I finish my coffee, pick up my bag and make for the gate.

The Author

Roy Burgess was once an IT manager. This involved sitting in a cubicle and making stuff up. Having retired from this high octane lifestyle, he now sits in his home office and makes stuff up.

The Fifth Thunderbolt is his second book in a trilogy. There may be more than three. Who knows?

The first book in The Fifth Trilogy is called The Fifth Tweet and is available now from Amazon in paperback and Kindle formats.

West Yorkshire born and bred, Roy spends a lot of time staring out of the window at the Leeds - Liverpool canal. Music is a constant companion to his writing. If he's not writing he listens to more music and presents two shows on OverTheBridgeRadio.com A playlist of songs and artists mentioned in the book is on Spotify - just search for The Fifth Thunderbolt. Roy is also the proud owner of an OEIC (whatever that is).

Keep in touch with Roy by signing up for the mailing list at royburgess.com.

* * *

Twitter — @royburgess40
Facebook — @royburgess40
Instagram — royburgess40

Also by Roy M. Burgess

The Fifth Tweet - The Fifth Trilogy Book 1

Would you trust the first five tweets in your timeline to rebuild your life? Frankie did. It worked. Right up to where it didn't.

Frankie's girlfriend has walked out and taken with her an original copy of Ziggy Stardust, two grand from their savings account, the charger for his electric toothbrush, and his best mate and business partner.

Because of the Twitter challenge, things improve.

A fictional character based on his new girlfriend points the way to fame and fortune, but is The Woman In The Yellow Raincoat too good to be true? Is real-life mirroring fiction? How will our hero cope with a toothbrush on borrowed time?

Available now from Amazon in paperback and Kindle.

* * *

Reviews on Amazon:

"This is one of those 'I couldn't put it down' kind of books!" - JKF ☆☆☆☆☆

"I'm in the USA, and quite a few things I didn't understand... for instance, what in the world is a "bacon butty?" - Susan VW ☆☆☆☆

"Really enjoyed this book. The writing style was easy and flowed well." - Paul ☆☆☆☆☆

Also by Roy M. Burgess

The Fifth Man - The Fifth Trilogy Book 3

Frankie's screwed up again — big time.

A stroke of luck, most often reserved for other people, offers a lifeline. Writing a TV script based on a true story could be his way out. Trouble is, he only knows half the facts behind a series of daring robberies that ended in murder. Turning detective, he teams up with a lapsed arsonist and sets out to reveal the truth. With his search threatening to put his loved ones in danger, he must uncover the mysterious Fifth Man.

But the clock is ticking, and the killer is ready to strike again.

The Fifth Man is book three in The Fifth Trilogy

Printed in Great Britain
by Amazon